THE CATHAYS FILES 25

Haydn Thomas

RESARTON BOOKS

Published by Resarton Books

132 Great Ancoats Street,
Manchester,
M4 6DE,
Britain.

www.resartonbooks.com

Copies of the book have been sent to the
relevant legal deposit libraries

Contents

Preface

This book is an abridged version, with some revisions, of "The Cathays Files", 9th edition, plus additional material. The chapters 2014 to 2021 are all "additional material".

The book contains details of one of the most disgraceful british government cover ups that's ever taken place. It looks like the Prime Minister at the time, Margaret Thatcher, authorised or directed it. The Queen, who was named in university regulations as the adjudicator for disputes in the two universities involved, could also have known about what was going on.

I start the book by telling you about criminal acts that were carried out by staff in Swansea university in 1975. The acts were using forged documents (altered examination question papers) and forgery (making false documents to defraud). The forged documents were given to me in an end of academic year examination (the other candidates were given the correct question papers). My course of study was stopped because I 'failed' the examination (I passed the other subjects). At the time I didn't know about the forgery because I was deceived, I was led to believe that a mistake had been made. Nevertheless Cardiff university allowed me to continue my study. They gave me fraudulent/false end of academic year examination 'fail' results in 1976, i.e. my course of study was again stopped.

It was a person outside the universities, an ex-policemen, who was at this time working in a high level government position (in the security services), that arranged these occurrences at the two universities. I have in the past referred to him as Group X member number one, I will call him Gx1 from here on. He used covert activities together with open requests to get me stopped. He also had a part completed plan to murder my father. And, in 1967/68, he twice made arrangements to murder me, by accident. And in 1977 he again attempted to have me 'accidentally' killed.

I tried to get what happened in the universities cleared up and this led to my starting civil court proceedings in 1981. However, this was cancelled at an early stage by the court.

I looked more closely at what had happened in 1975. And made enquiries. It was not a mistake at Swansea university, it was the criminal acts of forgery and using forged documents.

In 1983 I gave the police details of the forgery and expected a prosecution to start. They investigated and were given the 1975 cover up story by Swansea university staff ('it was a mistake').

However in 1987 the police confirmed they had forged documents, i.e. the question papers I had been given in an end of academic year examination at Swansea university in 1975 were forged (altered). Within three months instead of a prosecution being started the situation was blacked out, censored by the government (with no explanation). It was evident that Margaret Thatcher was involved.

Because, in 1990, I couldn't break the censorship, meaning I couldn't get the media to publish anything on it, and neither could I get the authorities to proceed in accordance with standard procedure (start a prosecution), I decided to give up trying to get the situation straightened out and at sometime in the future write a book about it. And I'd leave it to the book to get the answers to the numerous unanswered questions, hoping of course that by the time it was written the censorship would be removed.

I wrote the book in the second half of the nineties. It became apparent to me in November 1998 that the government was continuing to censor the affair. Regardless of the censorship the book was manufactured in small numbers in hardback in November 2000 under the title, "Minus One is Forgery".

New chapters were added to the book and in 2006 it was published in hardback under the title, "The Cathays Files". It was censored.

Some details had only became apparent to me in 1994. This is when I realised that occurrences that had taken place in 1979/80 were government hits. In October 1980 government officials planted false evidence into my dispute with Cardiff university to ensure I lost it. This meant that the fraudulent examination results stayed under wraps, and this kept the forgery at Swansea and the Gx1 part completed murder plan covered up. I added these details to the book and in 2011 produced a 6th edition of The Cathays Files. Toward the end of 2013 I produced a 9th edition. The censorship stayed in place.

In 2014 "Manor Bier" came into being, it was an abridgement of The Cathays Files, 9th edition. It stayed censored.

New editions of Manor Bier, each containing more information, were produced. All were censored.

Most of the details that have gone into the books since 2006 are on the corrupt/criminal activities of Gx1. He had been covertly carrying out these activities for years before he arranged the forgery and the fraud in 1975/76. It was the fraud at Cardiff university in 1976 that caught him out. But he was not brought into the open (apprehended) because the 1980 false evidence plant stopped Cardiff university verifying that I was right about having been given false fail results.

In June 2021 I produced "The Cathays Files 25". It contained all of what was in Manor Bier, which reached a 15th edition, together with some additions and revisions.

I produced new editions when revisions were necessary and in August 2023 I produced this book, the sixth edition of The Cathays Files 25.

Notes

I use the word "hit" to mean any act that a person does deliberately and covertly that is intended to adversely affect someone. Examples of "adversely affect" are to put someone out of a job, or to get him physically hit.

In the main body of the text I use two typefaces, one is lighter and slightly smaller than the other. The purpose of this is to try to make it easier for you to distinguish between what I know now (the lighter typeface, this one), and what I knew at the time I'm talking about (**the heavier typeface, 1975, etc**).

In this book I use single inverted commas to indicate possible or likely quotes and also to indicate words that are not used in a literally exact way. Double inverted commas are used to indicate exact quotes.

In some places I refer to "TCF", it's an abbreviation for, "The Cathays Files". TCF6 means the 6th edition and TCF9 the 9th edition.

1974

It was at the end of my first academic year of full time study in a university that I first realised that some influential people outside the university were fixing things in my life. I refer to them as "Group X". One of them was closely related to my family.

When I started writing a book about all this, in 1998, I decided to begin it in September 1974, when I entered Swansea university, by detailing the events at the university that caused me to become aware of Group X's activities.

I shall usually refer to Swansea university as UCS (it was known as University College Swansea at the time).

1975

The end of academic year examinations started toward the end of May. All of them were college examinations, i.e. the lecturers who taught the subjects set the question papers and marked the answer papers. Three subjects, each divided into two parts meant six three hour examinations. I had to pass all three subjects to be able to continue to the next year. The result in each subject being the average mark for the two answer papers. There was a very unusual occurrence in the pure mathematics examination, the following describes what happened.

SF was one of the lecturers for the subject and what he had taught was to be examined in "Pure Mathematics Paper I", SJ was the other lecturer and what he had taught was to be examined in "Pure Mathematics Paper II". The two examinations were scheduled a few days apart. On the day of the first examination, Pure Mathematics Paper I, I took a seat at a desk in the examination hall along with all the other students who had done the subject and waited in silence for the examination question papers to be brought around. There were about thirty of us. SJ was on his own at the front of the hall, he was the invigilator.

Many of you reading this may not remember much about sitting examinations so I will remind you of a few of the procedures and rules that applied to all end of academic year examinations in colleges at this time. Silence was the general rule upon entering an examination room/hall and this certainly applied once an examination had started. If a student wanted to say something to an invigilator, a request for more paper for example, he had to put his hand up, the invigilator came to him and then he quietly told him what he wanted. Students were usually seated at their own small desk, these desks were spaced about six feet apart. The distance between desks was of course designed to ensure that if one student looked across at another student's papers he couldn't read what the other student had written. The number of invigilators depended on the number of students taking the examination, one or two invigilators would usually be present for this number of students (30). The majority of courses had a single three hour examination in

12

each subject at the end of the academic year and it was normal practice for a lecturer who taught the subject being examined not to invigilate it. Although SJ had taught the subject he had not taught the topics that were on this question paper, so you could say that this fitted in with normal practice.

When everyone was seated SJ walked round handing out the question papers, he probably put them face down on the desk, to be turned over when he said. When I looked through the question paper I became more and more astonished, the questions were not on SF's topics, they were on his topics. It wasn't the wrong question paper because the heading on the paper was Pure Mathematics Paper I, which was correct, it was the right question paper with the wrong questions on it. I looked around at the other students, a few of them seemed to be uneasy but that was about it, they were starting to get on with it. For me the situation was disastrous.

The most important part of my revision procedure had always been the couple of days, nights and hours before an examination. This, the final revision, was the time when the years work was concentrated into perhaps ten hours of study, probably less when I was working as well (day release education) and maybe a bit more when in full time education, but in both cases the amount of time available for the final revision could be reduced to a few hours if the examinations followed each other in quick succession. I was making a thorough job of my revision for all my subjects and as far as I was concerned I was going to pass them.

Pure mathematics was my weakest of the three subjects. When I knew that I was weak in a subject the final revision for it became more important than ever. My final revision had of course been done on SF's work because the first examination, Paper I, was his examination. Now I found myself in a position where the revision I'd just done was almost useless and I had not done my final revision for the questions that were in front of me. What could I do? What was the point of objecting about the paper when it had the right heading on it? Anything I could have said to SJ about the paper having the wrong questions on it was being answered there and then by the fact that the other students were getting on with it. If they were getting on with it I had to get on with it.

Perhaps a few of them were very good at the subject and so the unexpected questions didn't concern them so much, but I couldn't understand why most of them didn't look as astonished as I was. I sat there in disbelief for about fifteen minutes doing nothing and then I started to answer the questions, there was no hurry for me to start because there was only one or two of them that I could give a complete and hopefully correct answer to.

With almost all the examinations I had done before this I had worked through to the end of the three hour period, on only a few occasions had I left an examination before the time was up and even then it was no more than ten minutes from the end. But in this one after two hours I had done all I could, about half an hour from the end I got up and walked out. Never before had I sat an examination that had been anything like it. It had been an awful experience.

On leaving the examination I walked back to my accommodation which was about half a mile from the college. I was the only person in the house who was studying at the college.

With lectures finished it was only the examinations that brought the students on my course together. When we met for the next examination, in one of the other subjects, I might have said a few words to a couple of them about the pure mathematics examination but no more than that was said because thoughts were concentrated on the examination that we were only minutes away from.

It was obvious that with the Pure Mathematics Paper I question paper having had SJ's questions on it that the Pure Mathematics Paper II question paper had to have SF's questions on it. So in the day or so before the second pure mathematics examination I again revised my notes on SF's work.

In the Pure Mathematics Paper II examination SF seemed to give me a long look whilst he was still about three students away from me as he was giving out the question papers, but I thought nothing of it. The question paper had his questions on it. He was invigilating the examination on his own and he was not conforming with the normal practice of not invigilating what he'd taught, SJ had also ignored it, but I wasn't concerned about this minor irregularity. I used all of the three hours to complete my answer paper.

The examination results were published on a notice board in the college toward the end of June. I went into the college to look at them. There were not many students around at this time because most of them had gone home to all parts of the country but I intended to stay in Swansea through the summer. Pure mathematics was the only subject I'd failed. I was already unhappy with the pure mathematics examination, now I was a bit annoyed to see that SF and SJ had failed some students who'd sat it when SJ had ruined the examination in the first place. I thought that any student who'd made a decent effort should, under the circumstances, have been given a pass. I'd certainly made a decent effort and apparently all the others had as well (I was the first one to leave the first examination).

I immediately went to see SJ. I told him that I was very unhappy about what had happened in the examination and the result I had been given. He said he had added on a percentage to everyone's mark to make up for it. [I think he said ten percent.] Apparently a mistake had been made in the preparation of the question papers. He also said that the results stood. I still didn't like it but anyway I left his room and didn't do any more about it. It meant that I had a pure mathematics re-sit examination to do in September.

During the year I had spent a good bit of time in the college library. Quite often I had read books or magazines that were not connected with my course, perhaps it was from these that I got ideas on getting on to the economics degree course in September, instead of the electronics or computer technology course that I was due to start.

A couple of days after I'd met SJ I went to see an economics lecturer who was responsible for course entrants and I told him that I wanted to start an economics degree course in September. He would not give me an acceptance to it there and then, he said that I should return to see him in September after I'd sat the pure mathematics examination. He recommended that I read an economics book by Lipsey in the summer. Economics contained very little pure mathematics, if any, which suited me, because I certainly didn't want to do any more of that subject the following year.

It was about the end of June when someone where I lived told me that there might be a job going with the council. The result was that I got a job as a labourer with Swansea Town Council's Highways Department, they were happy to take me on for a couple of months.

Early September, the time for the re-sit examination, arrived. I had made a thorough job of my revision for the May/June examinations (apart from my disrupted pure mathematics revision that is) because I had the time to do it, but the situation for this re-sit examination was very different. The labouring job I was in was low paid, so to keep my finances straight I had to work to within a couple of days of the examination.

The economics lecturer's book recommendation when I met him in June seemed to be nearly an acceptance onto the course and it made me think, knowing that pure mathematics had almost no relevance to economics, that it wasn't really necessary for me to pass the examination. Then of course the May/June pure mathematics examination experience had not exactly helped my appreciation of the subject. I still intended to pass the re-sit examination but all this meant that I didn't do a lot of revision for it.

This time the examination question papers were correct, Pure Mathematics Paper I contained questions that were based on SF's lectures and Pure Mathematics Paper II contained questions that

15

were based on SJ's lectures. The first examination, Paper I, was invigilated by SJ and the second examination, Paper II, by SF.

The result came out about a week later. I was failed. I was not very concerned about it because I thought I'd still be able to get onto the economics course.

I went to see the economics lecturer I had seen in June. He asked me the result of the re-sit, I told him and asked him if it was okay for me to get onto the economics course regardless of the result. He told me to come back the following day when he'd give me an answer.

I went to see the lecturer again the next day, he said that because I had not passed in pure mathematics he could not let me enter the economics course. I was stunned. He said that I could go to see the college careers officer if I wanted to.

As I left the building I was convinced that some people who lived in the Cardiff area had used their influence to get me stopped. I felt sure that the economics lecturer had been subjected to this outside influence, but I thought there was no way I could get him to say anything to me about it. I thought that left to himself he would have accepted me onto the course. It also occurred to me that what had happened in the May/June pure mathematics examination could have been caused by these Cardiff people, having been told I was weak in the subject they perhaps thought that it would trip me up ('give them all the wrong questions in the first examination, that'll give them something to think about' and, 'the ones who are weak in the subject will be hardest hit,' being typical remarks). But again I thought that even if I was right there was no way I could get SF or SJ to admit that it had been planned in advance in response to outside influence.

I was fairly sure that I would have passed pure mathematics in the summer if the examination had been conducted properly, there was no doubt at all that it was my best chance of passing the subject.

I had left a good job with International Computers Limited to get a degree, I had not left the job for one year of full time study that ended in 'failed'. It was a disaster for me.

My grant situation was such that I could not get a grant for a repeat year so a repeat year was not even mentioned by me or the economics lecturer (presumably he knew it). I had to pass and continue to the next year for the grant to be payable. It was a local council grant (South Glamorgan).

I went to see the careers officer and he told me that there was a full time one year course at Glamorgan Polytechnic that I could go and see about, it was in management or something like that. I moved out of my accommodation and returned to Cardiff to stay at my parents house.

I went to Glamorgan Polytechnic (which was about ten miles north of Cardiff) and met the lecturer responsible for the course that the UCS careers officer had told me about. We briefly talked about the course and I mentioned my grant situation, saying that I couldn't get a local council grant for it (I assumed the fail/no grant stipulation meant no grant for any full time course after a fail). He had some details on a Manpower Services Commission grant that he thought I'd be able to get. Before we could say yes or no to my starting the course, though he seemed quite happy to say yes, I had to find out if I could get the grant. We left it at that for the time being.

I went to see someone in the MSC office in Cardiff. They either said I could have a grant or I would probably get one and they'd let me know for sure in a few days.

I was still very unhappy about what I'd lost or more accurately been done out of at UCS, my year there with all my honest endeavours had only placed a black mark on my record. I would have been far better off if I had stayed in my ICL job. As for the course at Glamorgan Polytechnic, well, I'd studied there before (part-time) and that had been okay but I had no wish to return there for something that seemed pointless.

As a last chance of continuing at university I went to Cardiff University [I shall usually refer to it as UCC, it was known as University College Cardiff at the time.] and saw CN [C means a UCC member of staff, the second letter denotes the individual.], an economics lecturer, he admitted me to the first year of a three year degree course in economics. He said that my pure mathematics fail result at UCS was not a problem as far as he was concerned. I was therefore continuing onto the next year of study (from the Intermediate year at UCS), which meant that my local council grant was payable.

I had to choose seven subjects from about thirteen, there was to be one examination in each subject at the end of the academic year.

About two weeks after starting the course CN told me that there was a problem over my entry to the college, someone or some people had objected to it and it was possible that I'd have to leave the course. I assumed that it was Group X, or someone in UCS who had been involved in stopping me there and didn't like the idea of me continuing at UCC. A week or so later he told me that everything was okay.

Since starting at UCC I hadn't been concerned about Group X, yes I was sure they had got me stopped at UCS and it followed that they'd like to do the same at UCC, but UCS was an Intermediate year, now that I was on the first year proper of a degree course I thought they wouldn't be able to interfere with my progress, tell the UCC staff what to do in other words, meaning that even if they did tell them to stop me I thought that they wouldn't co-operate with them. But nevertheless for a few days here I wasn't sure what was going to happen. Then when I was told that the problem had been dealt with I continued to think that Group X wouldn't be able to interfere at UCC.

One night in November one of the people in Group X showed extreme animosity toward me. I hadn't seen him since perhaps March earlier in the year and then our relations were normal. I hadn't told anyone in Group X that I thought he/they had got me stopped at UCS, and I hadn't told anyone else about it either. There was no point in accusing any of them of it, they'd obviously deny it, I had nothing to prove it and they knew it. So I was amazed at what he had done, and I was annoyed about it. But anyway I intended to have nothing to do with him. [This was the last time I saw him for some years. When I met him, it was about 1979, nothing was said about what happened on this night in November.]

1976

In February/March I was given a poisoned drink. The result was that I was ill in bed for about a week. I was sure that Group X arranged it.

The end of academic year examinations started toward the end of May. They were college examinations (set and marked by the lecturers). It was one three hour examination for each of the seven subjects. They were all as expected and properly conducted.

The examination results came out toward the end of June, I went into the college to look at them on a notice board. I had passed four and failed three. I was astonished at the results. One of the examinations I had failed had been my best subject, I had done all the necessary work for it and therefore found the examination easy. The other two subjects I had been failed in had also been straightforward and I'd had no difficulty with their examination papers. Course work marks I obtained for essays I did during the year in these three subjects were as follows: (i) 55%, 65%; (ii) B, C+, B; (iii) C+, B. These were all good or very good marks, they indicated that I should have passed the examinations with ease.

I simply did not believe the results, I just thought that for some reason some college staff wanted me to take re-sits in September and so I left it at that for the time being.

In September I sat the three examinations again. A few days later the results were published in the college, I went in to have a look at them. I was still failed, my June results, which were unbelievable, had been repeated. I was stunned, I didn't mind failing examinations when I hadn't done the work but this was definitely not one of those occasions. As far as I was concerned I had passed them in May/June, I didn't say anything about it then because all it meant at the time was that I had to take re-sits a couple of months later. Now it was different, the results meant that I couldn't continue at the college and I had to stay on the unemployment register. I immediately went to see some members of staff in their rooms to express my disbelief at the results I had obtained.

I felt cheated, I knew that Group X had got at me again. I had thought that they wouldn't be able to get me stopped at UCC but somehow they had managed it. I didn't tell any of the lecturers that I thought that Group X had got me stopped because I had nothing to prove it. I left it at that. After two years of full time study all I could add to my work/education record was 'one year at UCS and one year at UCC - failed'.

1977

The end of May arrived. I had done some part-time work since the September 1976 re-sit examinations but nothing more than that. I had applied to UCC to re-sit the end of academic year examinations again (all seven), this time as an external candidate, knowing that if I passed them I could continue with my course at the college in September. I started to sit the examinations but I was unhappy about doing so because I had simply lost faith in the marking procedure and I could not check my marked answer papers. How was I to know that the same thing, false fail results arranged by Group X, wouldn't happen again?

I did not sit all seven examinations, I decided that university was not for me, in doing so I was giving up the chance of improving my qualifications, I didn't like doing that, but I did not intend to put any more time and effort into something in which the end product could be fixed.

The examination results came out a few weeks later but they were of no interest to me, as far as I was concerned I had made my position clear by not sitting them all. I was disgusted with the events of recent years, I knew I'd been hit, a few times, by Group X, but I didn't think I could do anything about any of it.

I use "hit" to describe any act that was intended to adversely affect someone, therefore, for example, arranging to stop me at UCS was a hit. There are occasions of course when someone deserves to be hit but that didn't come into it. The reasons Group X had for stopping me did not justify their arranging to get me stopped and anyway they had no right, in my opinion, to get me stopped. The fact that they had succeeded at two university colleges made it all the more ridiculous. How did I know that it was Group X that stopped me? It was obvious from what was happening in my social life outside of the colleges.

More Odd Occurrences
Explained

Near the end of 1977 it started to become apparent to me that some odd occurrences that had taken place before I went to Swansea university had also been caused by Group X. In this chapter I summarize the "odd occurrences", that I realised, in the years 1977 to say 1982, were Group X hits.

It was 1979/80 when I realised, found out, that it was the Group X member that I refer to as Gx1 that thought up and arranged the hits.

In the 1960s Gx1 stopped my relationship with two very good females (the AEI tracer and Miss C).

In 1968 Gx1 used a meeting to issue covert signs that said he was going to 'butcher' my rugby and the plans that some people had to send me on a full time university degree course.

Later in 1968 Gx1 used the 'accident' method (a planned accident) to hit me, the purpose being to stop my rugby because I was getting too successful for his liking. At the time I was captain of a college rugby team (Llandaff Tech) and staff at the college had me on route for playing for Cardiff rugby club. After the 'accident' he had a false diagnosis of a hairline fracture of an ankle ready for my arrival at the Cardiff Royal Infirmary (plaster and crutches for two months).

In the 1969/72 years Gx1, using more covert methods, again stopped me going to Cardiff rugby club, and he ensured that I did not play for the Wasps first team. And he stopped me playing for the Penarth first team. These "covert methods" included poisoning me prior to a trial game I had with Cardiff, to make me incapable of playing the game.

In 1971/72, when I was working in a London hospital, Gx1 stopped my relationship with two more very good females (Miss L and the Bart's nurse).

And Gx1 stopped me getting a first class job with an electronics company in 1972.

The motives Gx1 had for carrying out, arranging, the above hits was the knowledge that he planned to ship me to Australia (one way). Obviously my not being attached to a female, or in a good job, or playing first team rugby with Cardiff/Wasps/Penarth, would ensure that when the time came for shipping me out (1972) I'd be easier to shift.

By the time 1979 arrived I had formed the belief that Group X, in 1973, were out to murder my father. The hospital diagnosis of cancer, which I considered to be odd at the time, was false. They had arranged to have the false diagnosis given to him as a way of murdering him quietly, i.e. poison would be used to kill him, when the time was right, with no one suspecting any foul act.

And before the end of 1982 I knew that Group X, in the form of Gx1, had attempted to murder me in 1977, using poison that was given to me by a hit man.

In the years following 1982 I became aware of many more dirt activities carried out by Gx1, I detail these later in the book.

1978

In 1977 and 1978 I got some work but it was obvious that what had occurred in university had actually damaged my career prospects. It was going to be very difficult to get into an electronics job comparable to the one I had been in before going to UCS, never mind improve on it. My being away from the industry for two and a half years or more with no gain in qualifications was a problem. And at UCC I had done an economics course which made prospective employers believe that I didn't really want to work in electronics. And because I didn't get a qualification in economics I had nothing to use to get a job in that direction.

In August 1978 I wrote to UCC about what had happened in the end of academic year examinations I had sat in 1976. I received a reply saying that the results would stay as they were.

I wrote to two people who were part of UCC's governing structure.

1979

I received no satisfaction from the two letters I had recently written and so I began to think in terms of starting court proceedings (a claim for damages).

During this year I went to two firms of solicitors, they wouldn't start proceedings.

I wrote to my MP. He made some enquiries at UCC but then he wouldn't do any more.

I had been put in contact with a university professor in London. He told me that he could write out a document for sending to the visitor of the University of Wales that summarised what had happened at UCC (UCC being a part of the UW). The visitor of a university is a person who is expected to resolve any disputes that occur in that university. The visitor for the UW was the Queen.

1980

The London professor sent me the document that was addressed to the Visitor. He said I should post it to the Clerk of the Privy Council, which is what I did.

After a while the clerk told me that the Visitor would not, or could not, adjudicate the dispute. I considered this to be odd.

I returned to trying to make progress by using court proceedings. And this time I was going to include the examination irregularity that had taken place at UCS in 1975, as well as what had happened at UCC in 1976.

I wrote to UCS to see what they had to say about the 1975 examination irregularity.

1981

UCS replied to my letter, in which I asked for an explanation for what had occurred in the 1975 examination, by saying that there was no irregularity. At about this time they changed their library's records for the 1975 examination. It was obvious to me that some strange activities were taking place at UCS as a result of what I'd told them had happened in 1975.

I met Michael Roberts in the Welsh Office in Cardiff. He was a Parliamentary Under-Secretary of State. Basically he wouldn't say anything. I was quite sure he knew some very odd things had been going on.

In September I started a claim for damages from the UW over the events at UCS in 1975 (negligence) and UCC in 1976 (breach of contract – false results). I prepared, filed in the court offices and sent out the documents myself because I couldn't find a solicitor who would do it for me.

1982

In April my claim against the UW was struck out (cancelled) at a pre-trial hearing.

Soon after I gave the police details of what had happened in 1975/76. These included the dinner-dance assault of November 1975 and the poisoning of 1976 as well as the false results at UCC and the negligence at UCS. The assault and the poisoning had not been reported to the police in 1975/76.

The police investigated. But they wouldn't say anything about the results of their investigation.

I appealed against the decision to stop my UW claim. Neither a hearing in Cardiff nor the London Appeal Court would change the decision.

I wrote to the press, perhaps they could throw some light on what was happening. I got nothing from them.

1983

It had been obvious for some time now that strange things had been going on at UCS after I'd written to them in 1980 about the 1975 examination. And so, as they seemed to deny that anything out of the ordinary had occurred in 1975 (in their March '81 letter), I continued, in 1981/82, to make enquiries about what had happened at the examination by trying to contact people who had sat it. I wanted evidence to support my version of events in other words.

In January of this year I fully realised, after having suspected it for some time, that I'd been the only one to have been given fixed/ altered question papers in the 1975 UCS examination. I updated the police with this information and they told me they would investigate this if I gave them copies of the correct question papers and copies of the fixed question papers. I had the fixed papers I'd been given but I was having difficulty obtaining copies of the correct question papers, partly because UCS had, in 1981, taken the correct question papers out of their library's records and replaced them with facsimiles of the fixed papers I had been given (to give the impression that everyone had received the same as me - the cover up story).

By July I had formed the opinion that it was correct for me to call the fixed papers I'd been given in 1975 at UCS forged documents. [In this chapter in TCF6 and TCF9 I give a full explanation of this.]

In September I sent the police copies of the forged papers I was given at UCS in 1975 and facsimiles of the correct question papers (I had been unable to get copies of the correct question papers).

A week or so later the police wrote to me saying they had investigated my allegation of forgery at UCS and they gave me the results of their investigation. They had it seemed been given the 1975/81 cover up story by staff at UCS, 'it was a mistake'.

I sent the police evidence in the form of statements from other people who sat the disputed examination that supported my allegation of forgery.

1984

In May I wrote to the police enclosing two affidavits. One was mine, giving details of the forged documents I was given at UCS in 1975, the other, that supported what I said, was from a person who had sat the disputed UCS examination. There was now, on the basis of what I'd given to the police, no doubt that a prosecution should take place.

On 12th July my claim for damages from UCC was struck out (cancelled) at a pre-trial hearing in Cardiff. I had started this claim in 1983 because my claim against the UW had been brought to an early conclusion by the court leaving me with the impression that it was the wrong corporation to sue, which presumably meant that UCC was the correct corporation to claim against for what had happened at the college.

I was astonished that the district registrar had struck out the claim. One of his jobs in pre-trial proceedings was to help to get the evidence together and he hadn't done that, the interrogatories, questions that would decide the issue one way or the other, were to remain unanswered as far as he was concerned.

On 26th July I received a letter from the police in which they said they wouldn't do any more.

I again went to the press to see if they could say anything about a situation that was obviously out of order. I got nothing from them.

1985-90

The chapters 1985 to 1990 were all shortened/edited for the seventh edition of The Cathays Files (and later editions) and placed into one chapter, "1885-90". So if you want complete information on what happened in these years you will have to look at the sixth edition of TCF.

In February 1985 I delivered the forged (altered) examination question papers I had been given at Swansea university (UCS) in 1975 to the police headquarters in Bridgend. I had kept all my UCS and UCC papers (lecture notes, essays etc and examination question papers). [The Cathays Files, a title I first used in 2006 for a book on this affair, refers to these papers that I had at my parents house in Cathays, Cardiff.]

As far as I was concerned the civil proceedings I was pursuing, claims for damages (money), were postponed, to be continued after a prosecution of the individuals involved in carrying out the criminal acts of making and using forged documents at UCS, and fraud at UCC. This was standard procedure in law, i.e. when an act incurs criminal and civil liability the criminal liability is dealt with first.

Later in 1985 I made my case, that I had given the police evidence that substantiated my accusation of forgery at UCS and that contrary to standard procedure a prosecution had not been started, to the media, two firms of solicitors and some MPs. I didn't make progress with any of them, until, that is, an MP, after I'd asked him to, said he'd write to the Attorney General about it.

I had the impression that Michael Havers, the Attorney General, was on my side, in other words that he wanted to see the situation properly dealt with. I formed this opinion when I stayed in his south London constituency for a few weeks in 1983 (I never met him).

Mr Havers, was however, away from work for a period of time, so he didn't answer the letter, it was forwarded to the Solicitor General, Patrick Mayhew, then on to the Chief Constable of the South Wales Police. And he just repeated the results of their 1983 investigation (the UCS cover up story).

Was Mr Havers being kept out of the situation by people who wanted nothing done about it, or had he decided to stay out of it, or was his being away from work a coincidence?

I asked J. Rooker MP to write to the Prime Minister, Mrs Thatcher, about it. He did and in February 1986 he sent me a reply he had received from her. She quoted the results of the 1983 police investigation and said, "there is no evidence" to show that a criminal offence was committed. She said nothing about the point I was making, that I'd given the police evidence that substantiated my accusation of forgery at UCS after their investigation. So I replied to her letter enclosing copies of the evidence I was talking about and said, "in 1984" I gave the police evidence that proved they had been given a cover up version of events. I received a reply from her office saying she would not do any more.

I again went to the media, thinking they would clear up the situation. I mean all a newspaper had to do was put the obviously unacceptable situation into print and the police and the Prime Minister would then have to produce sensible explanations. The press/media however would not publish a word on it.

In October 1986 I gave the police a 175 page manuscript I had written on what had been going on in the seventies.

In September 1987 the police acknowledged in writing that documents I'd given to them, the examination question papers I'd been given at UCS in 1975, were forged documents. I assumed a prosecution would start. But this did not happen. And so I contacted solicitors, MPs and government officials, saying that a prosecution should be started because the police had said they had forged documents and they knew who used them, and almost certainly knew who made them. I received no sensible explanation from anyone as to why a prosecution had not been commenced. Once again I went to the media, they wouldn't publish a word on it.

I continued till 1990 trying to get the authorities to start the prosecution and at the same time I tried to get the press to publish something on the situation. But I got nowhere. Censorship was obviously the order of the day, every day. And in 1990 I gave up trying to get the situation properly resolved and decided to write a book about it and I'd leave it to the book to get my questions answered.

Conclusion (1)

This chapter is a brief summary of the most relevant parts of the situation as I knew it in 1990. In the years following 1990 I became aware of more details and these are given to you later on in the book.

In October 1974 I started a full time degree course at Swansea university (UCS). Gx1 (in a high level government position) knew about it and he told UCS staff to make sure I was out in one year. UCS staff said, 'yes sir, no sir'.

In September 1975 I was out of UCS 'failed'. I had 'failed' an examination in which I was given altered/forged question papers, as arranged, it seems, by Gx1. But in 1975, having been deceived by staff at UCS, I didn't realise I'd been given forged papers.

Within days I went to Cardiff university (UCC) and was allowed to continue my university study. Gx1 was shocked. He tried to get me stopped immediately. But UCC would not stop me. I continued on my course and made good progress.

Gx1 knowing he could not get UCC staff to do what he wanted, arranged a number of covert hits, all aimed at getting me off the course. The hits involved smearing/dirtying me and feeding the dirt into UCC. This way of stopping me worked. In September 1976 UCC told me I could not continue at the college (failed, false results). My university study ceased.

My employment prospects were abysmal as a result of what had happened in university and in 1978 I wrote to UCC to see if I could get the situation resolved in some way.

In 1981 I started civil court proceedings. Not long after this, via private investigation, I found out more about what had happened at UCS in 1975, it was forgery (fixed/altered question papers). I gave the police details. They investigated but didn't confirm the forgery, they were given cover up statements by UCS staff.

I then gave the police evidence that substantiated my accusation of forgery and I expected a prosecution to start. However a prosecution wasn't started and so I asked the authorities to explain why they hadn't started a prosecution.

For a while I received no satisfactory response. Then in

September 1987 the police confirmed they were holding forged documents (the question papers I was given at UCS in 1975). They undoubtedly knew who used them (gave them to me), and they presumably knew who made them. I therefore again expected a prosecution to start.

I asked the police what they'd found out about my other accusations, i.e. the false results at UCC (fraud) and that Group X (Gx1) had hit my father in 1973 (part of a conspiracy to murder him). They would not tell me anything. A prosecution wasn't started and the situation was blacked out, censored by the government, in December 1987 (giving no explanation).

The Government Planted False Evidence in 1980

It was 1994 when I first had enough information/knowledge to fully realise that two "odd occurrences" that had taken place in 1979/80 were government hits.

In late 1979 and 1980 I didn't know I'd been hit, which explains why I've not mentioned these hits in the "1979" and "1980" chapters earlier in this book, I was aware of odd occurrences but I didn't realise what was going on.

In one of these hits the government planted false evidence into my dispute with UCC, to ensure that I lost the dispute. The hit took the form of a covert electron 'bullet' fired at me by a government hit man during a seated public meeting when I was expected to say something. It made me collapse. I was made to look stupid in other words, with the result that I lost the backing of UCC (who knew I was correct about what I had said), i.e. without their support I had lost the dispute.

Why did the government want me to lose the dispute? Because UCC would say that I was correct and that Gx1 (who was in MI5) had deceived them, pressurised them, into stopping me by giving me false fail results. And the government did not want the activities of an MI5 man to be made public. Especially when some of his other activities could also get out. His "other activities" included the forged documents at UCS in 1975 and the false diagnosis at the UHW in 1973.

Who thought up and arranged these 1979/80 hits? Near the end of this chapter and in the next chapter I talk about the people who are the suspects.

I will now give you the details on the hits. I will proceed by assuming that Gx1 was involved in making the hit arrangements, i.e. that Mrs Thatcher, who was apparently told about the dispute in 1979, had given him the go ahead to continue using his MI5 position.

Let's start by recalling part of the situation that existed in 1977. Gx1 was pleased that his efforts had stopped my university study, he'd ruined my job prospects.

In 1978 I wrote to the registrar of UCC referring to what had happened when I was with them. I followed this up by writing to and seeing some other people about what had happened and in one of my letters I also mentioned the procedural irregularity that had occurred in an examination in 1975 at UCS. As a result of all this it would have got through to Gx1 that the events of 1975/76 concerning me at the two universities were being looked at. I had not talked to anyone in Group X about what had happened at the two universities so he didn't find out about it from me.

I knew that some of the lecturers at UCC and two decent people outside of UCC wanted to improve the position I was in. Perhaps the lecturers were contemplating bringing the false results into the open. [And it could be they were also thinking about uncovering the forgery (maybe one or two of them had found out about what had happened at UCS). Gx1, obviously, wanted nothing done about the false results, he was concerned about keeping all of what he'd done under wraps.]

In early 1979 I was unemployed. The Jobcentre put me on to a temporary clerical job with the Welsh Office, which lasted a few months, then a temporary job with the Inland Revenue. In September 1979 I started work for an insurance broker located in north London. I continued to live in Cardiff, travelling to the broker's office about once a fortnight. I was to sell their life insurance policies to students in South Wales. My wages were on a commission only basis. I was successful in the job and in April 1980 stopped working for them and joined the Cardiff office of a company that sold financial plans. This job however never got going and I left them some months later.

The point I want to bring out here is that the insurance broker's office was in Mrs Thatcher's constituency. I was aware of this at the time but thought nothing much of it. She had become Prime Minister in May 1979, taking over the job from James Callaghan, a Cardiff politician.

If I'd been wrong about my being given false results at UCC in 1976 no one would have raised an eyebrow, 'he's wrong and it's as simple as that', it was because I was right and that some people wanted to get something done about it (UCC lecturers amongst them) that was causing a problem (it seems) for people in higher positions, meaning the UCC principal, the Welsh Office and the Prime Minister. 'How can we resolve it', they presumably said to each other, and in 1979 they got me into three jobs (as stated two paragraphs back). These jobs were to act as 'signs' and tests. My performance in the jobs was perfectly satisfactory and the people who were on my side therefore expected to have things put right for me. At this point I was hit.

The first hit was carried out on 31st December 1979, it was meant to finish the next day with me dead. It wasn't a direct attempt to kill me but it certainly appears that whoever arranged it hoped I'd be dead at the end of it. I came through it unscathed.

The second hit, in October 1980, was 'necessary' because the first hit hadn't succeeded, I was still alive and on course for resolving the dispute in my favour. The plan was to secretly smear/dirty me and get news of the dirt to the people who were on my side who would then have to say they'd lost their case. The plan worked, which meant the UCC false results and the UCS forgery would stay under wraps.

I'll now give you the details on these two hits.

My job with the insurance broker was, as I've said, going well, I was selling quite a few life insurance policies to students. This meant that I was earning good money and I decided to take a holiday on my own in Spain for two weeks over the Christmas and New Year period.

I was staying in a hotel in southern Spain. In the early evening of New Year's eve I became ill. I thought it was probably caused by a meal I'd had earlier in the day. I had a bad stomach but it wasn't just that, I soon had flu like symptoms as well, and I became somewhat delirious. I confined myself to bed in my room. [I was poisoned. In early editions of "The Cathays Files" I said this happened on 30th December, but having given it more thought I think it was 31st December.]

I was in no shape to take part in any New Year's eve celebrations. I recall leaving my room at about 11pm to see what was happening in the hotel. There was a party going on in one of it's large rooms, I looked at it for a few seconds and returned to my room and got into bed.

The next day I received a phone call asking me to meet someone on the top floor of the hotel. I was still ill in bed but able to get out of bed and walk round when I wanted to. I said okay, I'd be there in a few minutes. I took the lift to the top floor. I don't remember the time but it was during the day, let's say about 1pm. I didn't know the person I was expecting to meet but he seemed to know me so I got out of the lift and looked round. I was in a casino, a few people, perhaps four, were at a roulette table, but apart from that the place was empty.

There were open doors near to the lift, I stepped outside them and found myself on the hotel's flat roof. No one was out there, it was just a large empty area (no tables, chairs, etc). I walked to the railings at the edge of the roof and looked down. The hotel was about eight stories high. After a minute or so I went back into the casino and took the lift down to my room and thought no more of it. Nobody had come up to me.

I went to a chemist and got some medicine for a bad stomach and flu. My condition improved. I obviously wasn't enjoying the trip. I went to the airport to see if I could get on a flight home straightaway. But no, I was told I had to wait for the flight I was booked on two days later, which is what I did.

[Let's move on to what happened in October 1980.] I haven't mentioned it before but in 1979, after I'd written to the National Council for Civil Liberties in London about the false examination results at UCC, I got involved with their activities in Cardiff. This, ostensibly, had nothing to do with the letter I'd written to them which they'd forwarded to the London professor mentioned earlier. I met other members of NCCL in Cardiff and we formed a Cardiff committee. As a venue for our meetings we sometimes used rooms in UCC.

In October 1980 a public meeting was to be held at Swansea Town Hall. [It was also known as the Guildhall. Swansea became a city a few years on from here.] I can't remember what the subject of the meeting was (it had nothing to do with my dispute with UCC). Anyway NCCL was interested in it and I said I'd go to it as a representative of the Cardiff NCCL committee. When I arrived there early one evening I joined a couple of hundred people in the seated audience. About six people were sat on the stage, a few of them said what they had to say and then the chairman said people in the audience could ask them questions.

After one or two questions I quite happily stood up to ask a question. I asked it then the chairman, instead of asking one of the people on the stage to answer it, asked me to say a bit more about it.

At this point a loud deafening noise appeared in my ears, it stunned me. It continued for about thirty seconds. I didn't say a word and collapsed onto the seat I was next to.

In TCF6 I called it a headache, but I knew that it wasn't, in ordinary terms, a headache. It was a loud continuous high frequency tone that blocked out all other sound.

When the noise in my ears ceased my head immediately cleared and I heard the chairman ask me if I was satisfied with the answer. I was in a stunned condition, I just said yes.

Apparently the chairman, when I gave no response to his request for more details, had kept the meeting running by asking one of the people on the stage to answer my question. I'd heard none of this, for thirty seconds I'd been deafened by the high frequency sound. The meeting continued with someone in the audience asking another question.

In 1980 what happened at this meeting didn't make any sense to me. How had I heard the thirty second noise, which was deafening, when the other people in the hall obviously hadn't heard it? All I knew was that something very odd had happened at the meeting.

The Cardiff committee of NCCL fell apart soon after through lack of interest amongst those involved.

I'll continue now as if it's 1994. By this time I had become fully aware that these two 1979/80 occurrences were government hits that were designed to keep the false results at UCC and the forgery at UCS quiet. Keeping the false results and the forgery quiet would ensure other Gx1 hits would be kept quiet. And so, in 1994, I was in a position where I could add the following details to what I've said above.

It seems that the Prime Minister (who, in 1979, had apparently been made aware of my dispute with UCC) had said that Gx1 could continue to use his high level government position to 'arrange' things. At this point she was presumably not aware of many of his dirt activities of earlier years. Not aware that he was totally corrupt in other words.

Gx1 knew that one way of achieving the cover up of his past activities would be a dead H. Thomas, me. He did not however go for the direct act of murder, perhaps because it was a bit too difficult to get passed, and another thing, if he'd arranged to have me murdered a police investigation could have pointed the finger at him. But being in a top position would anything have come of it? Anyway to play safe he went for the suicide route, Spain being the scene of the action. He said to himself:

'make him ill, using poison, which will ruin his New Years eve, then get him onto the roof of a high building and depression will do the rest, he'll climb over the railings and fall to his death. At least I hope he will. If he does it'll be my problem solved, it'll look like a run of the mill suicide because of his university failure and I can tell UCC that he was an unstable individual (saying nothing about the poison of course).'

But it didn't happen. Well most of it did but the last bit, me dead, didn't come off. It didn't happen because he had some things wrong. Hoping I'd kill myself as a result of depression was way out. I wasn't depressed, I was angry. I'd been angry since 1975 when I was sure Group X had covertly arranged to have me stopped at UCS. When they did the same at UCC a year later I was even more annoyed. That they could get away with what they'd been doing to me seemed ridiculous. The trouble was I had nothing to prove they'd got me stopped at the two universities. I was working on it though. I was trying to get the UCC false results into the open, which would, I hoped, drag Gx1 out from undercover.

At this point you see, 1979/80, I'd told precisely no one that I knew it was Group X that had got me stopped at both the universities. It wasn't until sometime later, when I started my civil court claim against the UW in 1981, that the authorities found this out by reading the documents I filed with the court. So Gx1 didn't know I was angry about being stopped at two universities. Presumably he thought I was mystified as to the cause of the UCC false results, disappointed, and depressed. But there again how he could think I was depressed when I was selling a lot of insurance policies I don't know. Perhaps he had his doubts about the 'depression' angle but decided to give the suicide plan a go anyway, if it didn't work he'd have to find another way of making sure the UCC false results and the rest didn't get out.

My return from Spain meant that the Gx1 method of keeping the false results and the forgery quiet had failed, his plan hadn't produced what he'd hoped for. The people who wanted things put right for me were still pushing to get something done about it, i.e. the false results and perhaps the forgery into the open. Gx1 wasn't going to let this happen and he proceeded to watch for his next chance to get at me.

I was involved with NCCL activities in Cardiff, here perhaps was a way in for him. 'I'll use these activities to destroy his case', he apparently said to himself. Here enters the Swansea Town Hall meeting. He arranged the meeting for the express purpose of using it to hit me, using it to smear/dirty me. Being one of the leading members of the NCCL Cardiff committee it was fairly easy to get me to go to it. It seems he done this by getting one or two people on our committee to say I should go to the meeting. I had no objections and said okay I'd go.

Gx1 had an audience participation meeting lined up, members of the audience putting questions to 'experts' on the stage. He told some of the people who were pushing for positive action for me to have their representatives at the meeting to watch my performance. He told them, deceitfully, that if I done well at the meeting the false results and perhaps the forgery would be let out (he knew I would not do well at the meeting).

There was no guarantee that I'd stand up to ask a question but it was very likely that I would (as I say NCCL had a particular interest in the meeting and I was the only committee man present). If I did ask a question that would be the time the government hit man would strike, he'd make sure I failed the test. If I didn't ask a question he would have postponed the test to another time when he'd have put the same sort of plan into effect.

The meeting arrived and in a confident manner I stood up to ask a question. The chairman asked me to say a bit more about it and at this point I was hit. A government hit man in the row of seats behind me fired a device at my head, he had it covered up in his coat or in a bag so no one saw it (or it could have been housed in a small camera laying unused but pointed at me on his lap).

In 1994 I believed the device to be something that emitted an electrical beam of some sort (an electron/laser gun). The beam (it was probably a diverging beam, from a small source to say twenty inches wide at my head, which means it didn't have to be precisely aimed) was kept pointed at my head for the thirty seconds, the amount of time I had the loud continuous high frequency tone in my ears. When the device was turned off the sound ceased and my normal hearing and thought process returned. My not saying a word during the thirty seconds is not surprising, I was incapable of speaking with such a noise in my head.

Gx1 then said to the people who were pushing for the false results and perhaps the forgery to be brought out, 'there, you've seen for yourself, when it matters he breaks down, collapses. So it was right to stop his study'. The people who were on my side, knowing nothing about the covert hit, were no doubt very surprised at what they'd seen but they had to agree and they stopped making efforts to correct things for me.

In other words the government's hit, the false evidence plant, was successful (they had made me look stupid). UCC were taken in by it, deceived, and they stopped supporting me (stopped saying that I was correct). As far as the government were concerned I had lost the dispute about being given false results at UCC.

The way I was hit at the town hall public meeting reinforces my saying that it was carried out by people in the government's covert area (MI5 or MI6 or police personnel working covertly) because only official people could obtain the sort of device I've described. There's a possible exception here, some university research staff could also have such devices, but they can be ruled out of the decision to hit me process because they weren't running things. And what happened to me in Spain also tells us that it was MI5 or MI6 or other covert officials that were responsible for that to. Why do I say this? There's a number of reasons, they'll become apparent as I continue.

How did Gx1 find out about my proposed trip to Spain? Well about a week into December I booked the holiday over the phone. Presumably he was told about it by the police or MI5 who were monitoring my mail and the phone in the house where I lived. My mail and phone were monitored because Gx1 was concerned that some lecturers at UCC might try to get some evidence to me that verified I'd been given false results. Recall for a moment my meeting with Michael Roberts in the Welsh Office in 1981. I told him that I believed my mail was being intercepted/monitored. He did not say I was wrong. Assuming I was right about the mail it follows that the phone was also being monitored.

When my flight to Spain arrived in the country a couple of days before Christmas I got out of my seat and queued in the aisle of the aircraft waiting to disembark. For some reason there was a hold up, the stewardesses wouldn't let the passengers off the plane, it lasted a couple of minutes. Whilst I was standing there someone gave me a black horse rider's helmet to pass along the queue to someone who was a few places in front of me. [This was a group x type 'sign' saying, 'you could do with one of these because you might be taking a fall soon'. A

41

sign in it's own right you could say that foretold the events of the next week or two, but there's more on this one.]

The name of the hotel I was staying at when the poisoning, the lead up to the fall, took place was the Cervantes hotel. Cervantes, as you may or may not know, is the author of a tale in Spanish fiction that's well known in English literature. It's about the experiences of Don Quixote who travelled around Spain on a horse. So put the horse riders helmet with the horse at the Cervantes hotel and you have me falling from the roof of the hotel.

This 'pass the horse rider's helmet' occurrence tells us that perhaps two people travelled on the same flight as me who knew me, recognised me that is. These two were presumably british officials sent over to get the poisoning and suicide arranged. One of them must have told the stewardesses on the plane to delay opening the exit doors till they gave the okay, using the delay to get the helmet passed to me. An official's identity card in the form of a policeman's id gets stewardesses, and people in many jobs, to respond with, 'of course, anything to help you do your job'. If they were MI5/6 personnel they would have had police id cards ready for use in such circumstances because the word 'police' is far more generally accepted than 'MI5/6'.

[And here's another Gx1 'sign' for you.] A week or so before I left Cardiff to travel to Spain someone came up to me to try to sell me a watch. I bought it from him simply because he only wanted £5 or something like that and it looked quite impressive. It was the sort of watch used by underwater swimmers. [It was a diver's watch. And that was what Gx1 had lined up for me, I was, he hoped, soon going to take a dive from the roof of a high building.]

I can say more about the diver's watch. Some of you may pick this connection up anyway from what I say later in the book where I tell you about the 1968 Gx1 BD hit, but I'll place these words in here because it ties in with the last paragraph and it will ensure everyone knows about this point. The BD hit, which took place in Jersey, is where Gx1 tried to kill me using drowning as the cause of death. He ensured that my air supply ran out when I was alone on an underwater dive. This means that this diver's watch, which I was wearing when I went to Spain, was, as well as indicating a dive from a high roof, also a reference to the Jersey underwater dive, i.e. the same person, Gx1, was involved in arranging both these 'dive' activities.

Gx1 was 'saying', 'it's more of the same', i.e. he tried to kill me in the Jersey dive and he was now trying to kill me in a dive in Spain.

I have said that I booked the holiday over the phone. In more detail what I did was book the flight, to Malaga, out and return, on the phone. It was my intention to hire a car on my arrival at the airport in Spain for about five days and use it to have a look at places on the coast near Malaga. And I'd find my own accommodation. Then at the end of the five days I'd return the car to the airport and find a hotel in Torremolinos, which is the closest resort to Malaga airport (about 5 miles away), ready for my return flight. [So anyone listening in to my phone call knew I was going to Malaga for two weeks but not much more than that. So how did the Cervantes hotel come into this? Well Gx1 came up with it, not me. He picked on a high rise hotel in Torremolinos and said to himself, 'I'll get him into it'. And how did he get me into it? Read on.]

On my last day with the hire car I booked into a hotel in Torremolinos, it was an ordinary looking hotel two or three stories high. I then returned the car to the hire place at the airport and got the bus back to the hotel. The next day, during the day, when I was in the hotel having a sit down in the bar, a british bloke aged about forty, who I'd never seen before, came over to talk to me. We had a few friendly words and he went on to say that the hotel we were in wasn't up to much, and I had to agree with him, it was okay but nothing special (he wasn't staying there, he was just having a drink in the bar). He recommended another hotel in Torremolinos, saying it wasn't far away and it was the best hotel in the town. And it was doing special accommodation prices. Soon after our conversation had finished I walked to the hotel he was talking about, the Cervantes hotel, to have a look at it. It looked very good, far better than the one I was at, and yes I could have a reduced price. I booked into the place, returned to the hotel my case was at, booked out, and got a taxi to the Cervantes hotel. [A day or two later I was poisoned.]

I can tell you something else here. The man who told me about the Cervantes hotel seemed nervous when he was talking to me, but I couldn't understand why and thought nothing of it. [Yes, I'd now say he was an official who'd travelled over with me and he had a very good idea why he was telling me about the Cervantes hotel. Or there again it's possible he was a british tourist who had been put up to it by 'my' officials and he was uncomfortable in his role.]

The poison, I believe it was given to me when I had the meal I've mentioned at a cafe in the middle of the day. The meal stood out in my mind because I'd had it only a couple of hours before I became ill. The cafe was just about empty when I went in, I told a male employee what I wanted and received the food a few minutes later. I give you the following as a possible train of events. A Spanish official was following me, knowing I'd be getting food or drink somewhere. When I went into the cafe he entered it just behind me and watched and listened to what was going on. Then, after I'd given my order and sat down, he went behind the counter to talk to the employee at the same time showing him his official id. He then distracted whoever was preparing my meal and when no one was looking sprinkled a poisonous substance (a colourless liquid perhaps) on the meal. This example of how I could have been poisoned uses an official who was presumably working for the Spanish equivalent of MI5/6. The british officials who'd travelled with me to Spain having previously arranged with Spanish officials to get one of their people to follow me and put poison into my food/drink.

Why did Gx1 and these british officials give 'signs' that foretold their 'dive' in Spain plans? Perhaps it's standard practice for officials who work in this area, covert policing, to place signs into their arrangements/plans. Maybe they feel it boosts their self esteem, 'we give covert signs, isn't that good?' But whether or not giving covert signs is standard practice, and why they give them, doesn't really concern me right now, what I am saying here is that Gx1 in these Spain activities definitely gave covert signs that indicated what he was going to do.

Now I get to the list of suspects, who arranged these 1979/80 hits? One of the first questions often asked in investigating the cause of an occurrence that was a deliberate act is 'who had a motive for doing it?' And the answer here is the people who would find themselves in trouble if the fraud, the forgery or the part completed plan to murder my father got out, all of them had a reason/motive for arranging the 1979/80 hits. Yes, but a number of them, the staff at UCC and UCS have to be ruled out because they were not running things, in other words they were not able to tell "MI5/6 or other officials" what to do. And it's quite obvious that "MI5/6 or other officials" were instructed to carry out the hits.

Gx1 was certainly able to get his hits carried out by "MI5/6 or other officials". I've already, earlier in this book, told you about a number of his sixties and seventies hits that were put into effect by "MI5/6 or other officials", and later on I tell you about more of them. I've previously told you that the authorities did, in about 1982, realise that he was corrupt and stopped him using his position to arrange things, but at this 1979/80 time he was still accepted by the authorities as being a credible official.

And then we get to the staff in the Welsh Office, could they tell "MI5/6 or other officials" what to do? MI5/6 doubtful. Other officials, perhaps. If we call these other officials police the answer is probably yes in some areas.

Mrs Thatcher is the next on the list. I'll assume she was told about the situation in 1979. Well the assumption anyone would make is that she, being above the Welsh Office, took over responsibility for it. Were the 1979/80 hit plans thought up by Gx1 and forwarded to her, and she said, 'yes go ahead', authorised the hits in other words? Or was the situation made known to her and she then told "MI5/6 or other officials" to hit me, to ensure that it was all kept quiet?

Then we get to the Queen. In 1979 the London professor told me she was the adjudicator for UW disputes. Then, in 1980, via the Clerk of the Privy Council, I sent her details of what had happened at UCC. The clerk replied saying that she would not adjudicate the dispute. Not long after this I was hit at the town hall meeting. Did she tell MI5/6 to stop my progress, hit me, at the town hall? Or did she just leave it to Gx1 to do what he wanted?

"The 1979 Boundary Change" and "The Welsh Office Job in 1979" sections later in the book give you more details on what happened in 1979/80.

Questions to be Answered (1)

These questions are all about what happened in the years 1983 to 1990. This was the time when I was expecting a prosecution to start (for the forgery etc). I couldn't understand why the authorities hadn't started one. And so I wrote to numerous people and the media in an attempt to get a prosecution started.

In 1994, as detailed in the last chapter, I found out that in 1980 the government had planted false evidence into the dispute. This explained why censorship was applied to this affair in the 1980s. It was because the government prosecutor, DPP/CPS, decided not to start a prosecution that would be a corrupt prosecution, "corrupt" because it would use the October 1980 false evidence as genuine evidence. And censorship was the answer to the problem because it would ensure that the media did not present some awkward questions, such as, 'why no prosecution when there is evidence of forgery that can start a prosecution?'.

The DPP could have started a prosecution in the 1980's and at the outset said that the October 1980 town hall evidence was false and that the government had planted it, created it, but evidently the people who run this country would not let him do this.

So all the questions in this chapter could be answered with words like, 'the government was censoring us, telling us not to do anything', or, 'we didn't do what we would normally do because we did not want a corrupted prosecution to start'.

So if I know what the answers to these questions are why have I got them in this book? Well they serve as a concise record of what was going on in the 1980s. And besides some of them might get answered if the book gets out.

This book, being an abridgement of TCF9, does not give details of the correspondence/documents referred to in these questions. To see the details you will have to look in TCF6 (for all the details) or TCF9 if the details you are interested in are before 1985 (in TCF9 the years 1985 to 1990 were edited into one short chapter).

Questions 1 to 26 are about my accusations of forgery and using forged documents (altered end of academic year examination question papers) made against staff at Swansea university (UCS).

1. To the South Wales Police. Soon after your investigation at Swansea university in September 1983 I supplied you with statements from three people who'd sat the examination (witnesses) that verified what I'd told you had happened and proved that the results of your investigation were wrong. Why didn't you correct the results of your investigation and use the evidence to start a prosecution?

The above question and questions 2, 3, 5, 11, 15, 30 and 31 should also be put to K. Lee (Deputy Chief Constable in 1982/83), Mr Chapple (Acting DCC in 1983), David East (Chief Constable from 1983 to 1988) and A. Vickers (DCC from 1983 to 1989), they might have something to add to the answers from the people who presently head the SWP.

2. To the South Wales Police. In November or December 1983 you carried out a second investigation at Swansea university and produced the same results as your first investigation. How could you produce the same results when you had evidence that proved that the results of your first investigation were wrong?

3. To the South Wales Police. In May 1984 I supplied you with more evidence, in the form of a detailed affidavit from a witness, that supported my accusation of forgery at Swansea university and proved that the results of your investigations at the college were wrong. Why didn't you correct the results of your investigations and use the evidence to start a prosecution?

4. To Lord Mayhew. [He is now deceased.] In October 1985 Robin Corbett MP wrote to the Attorney General (Sir Michael Havers) about my accusation of forgery at Swansea University. It appears that he enclosed some of my correspondence in which I said I'd given sworn evidence to the police that substantiated my accusation and contrary to the usual procedure they hadn't started a prosecution. The Attorney General was expected to be away from his job for sometime so R. Corbett's letter was passed to you for a reply. Presumably you knew that the police are supposed to start a prosecution when they have evidence that supports an accusation. Why didn't you question them about the situation instead of just forwarding his letter to them?

5. To the South Wales Police. In November 1985 your Chief Constable wrote a letter to R. Corbett MP, in it he said all the people that sat the disputed examination at Swansea university received the same question papers. Would you please explain how he could say this when I had told you that all the people that sat the examination had not received the same question papers and I had supplied you with two statements and an

affidavit from three people who sat the examination that verified what I said?

6.   To the Prime Minister, Rishi Sunak. Perhaps you can answer this question and questions 7, 24 and 26 by referring to government records. Jeff Rooker MP wrote to Margaret Thatcher, the Prime Minister, on 9th January 1986 about my accusation of forgery at Swansea university. In her 4th February 1986 reply she said, "there is no evidence of the commission of any criminal offence as alleged by Mr Thomas." How could she say this when I had given evidence that supported my accusation of forgery at the university to the police?

7.   To the Prime Minister. On 22nd April 1986 I wrote to M. Thatcher, referred to her 4th February 1986 letter to J. Rooker, and said she was wrong to say "there is no evidence ...". I enclosed copies of two affidavits. One was mine, in it I gave details of my accusation of forgery at Swansea university, the other was from a witness, he verified what I said had happened, his affidavit also proved that the results of the police investigation were wrong. In her 23rd April 1986 reply she said she wouldn't do any more. Why didn't she admit she was wrong to say "there is no evidence ..."? And why didn't she tell the police to correct the results of their investigation?

8.   This question applies to the period 30th April 1986 to 11th June 1987. It should be addressed to a number of newspapers and magazines, Central TV, the BBC, Keith Lewis and Masons (as referred to in the sixth and earlier editions of TCF). I sent you (or gave you, or both, depending on who the question is addressed to) copies of:
       (i)   The Prime Minister's 4th February 1986 letter, in which she said "there is no evidence" to show that a criminal offence had been committed at Swansea university.
       (ii)   My 22nd April 1986 letter to the Prime Minister in which I referred to her 4th February 1986 letter and said she was wrong "to say there is no evidence ...", and I verified this by enclosing copies of some of the evidence.
       (iii)   The 23rd April 1986 reply from the Prime Minister's office in which she said she wasn't going to do any more. Which meant she either hadn't realised that the witness's affidavit supported my accusation, or she was refusing to correct her error.
       (iv)   Two affidavits.
Why did you do nothing about it?

9.   To Lord Rooker (an MP in 1986). On 14th June 1986 I sent you copies of:

48

(i)   My 22nd April 1986 letter to the Prime Minister in which I referred to her 4th February 1986 letter and said she was wrong to say "there is no evidence ..." and I verified this by enclosing copies of some of the evidence.

(ii)   The 23rd April 1986 reply from the Prime Minister's office in which she said she wasn't going to do any more. Which meant she either hadn't realised that the witness's affidavit supported my accusation, or she was refusing to correct her error.

(iii)   Two affidavits.

You did not reply. Why didn't you reply? I think you should have told her she was wrong to say "there is no evidence ..." because the witness's affidavit supported my accusation and proved that the results of the police investigation were wrong.

10.   To Lord Owen (an MP in 1987). On 3rd February 1987 I sent you copies of:

(i)   The Prime Minister's 4th February 1986 letter, in which she said "there is no evidence" to show that a criminal offence had been committed at Swansea university.

(ii)   My 22nd April 1986 letter to the Prime Minister in which I referred to her 4th February 1986 letter and said she was wrong to say "there is no evidence ...", and I verified this by enclosing copies of some of the evidence. The witness's affidavit supported my accusation and proved that the results of the police investigation were wrong.

(iii)   The 23rd April 1986 reply from the Prime Minister's office in which she said she wasn't going to do any more. Which meant she either hadn't realised that the witness's affidavit supported my accusation, or she was refusing to correct her error.

(iv)   Two affidavits.

Why didn't you write to the Prime Minister pointing out that she was wrong to say "there is no evidence ..."?

11.   To the South Wales Police. On 16th September 1987 you sent me a letter in which you confirmed you had forged documents (altered end of academic year examination question papers that were given to me at Swansea university in 1975). You knew who used them, two people, and you most probably knew who made them. Why didn't you start a prosecution? Or, why didn't you give me an explanation for why a prosecution wouldn't be started that took into account the fact that you had forged documents?

The above question should also be put to Assistant Chief Constable Evans, he signed the letter.

12.   To Lord Owen. You told me, in a letter dated 29th October 1987,

that the police had told you they had no evidence to start a prosecution. On 30th October 1987 I showed you the letter from the police in which they confirmed they had forged documents. There was obviously something wrong here somewhere, the police had given either me or you incorrect information. Why did you tell me you wouldn't do anything about it?

13. To Lord Rooker. In November 1987 I sent you and in February 1988 gave you copies of the letter from the police in which they said they had forged documents. This letter proved in it's own right (quite apart from the evidence I'd given to the police) that what the Prime Minister had said in her letter to you dated 4th February 1986 was wrong. You wouldn't do anything, why?

14. This question applies to the period from 8th December 1987 to 31st December 1988. It should be addressed to a number of newspapers and magazines, Central TV, the BBC, K. Lewis and a number of firms (or ex-firms) of solicitors in Birmingham and London (as referred to in the sixth and earlier editions of TCF). I sent you (or gave you, or both) a copy of a letter from the police in which they said they had forged documents and copies of other letters, including (in most cases) the Prime Minister's February 1986 letter (in which she said there was no evidence to show that a criminal offence had been committed). You could see that:

(i)   The Prime Minister's error stood uncorrected.
(ii)   A prosecution had not been started.
(iii) The authorities hadn't given me any sort of explanation as to why a prosecution hadn't been started.

Why did you do nothing about it? There are a couple of exceptions to this question, two newspaper reporters apparently made enquiries with the South Wales Police, but nothing was published in their papers.

15. To the South Wales Police. On 27th July 1988 you sent me a letter in which you said you had no evidence to support my accusations, please explain this letter, bearing in mind I had given you evidence that supported my accusation of forgery and that in your 16th September 1987 letter you said you had forged documents.

16. To Mr Oliver (a stipendiary magistrate in 1988). On 3rd August 1988 you said the police had not confirmed, in their 16th September 1987 letter, that they had forged documents? Your saying this was contrary to a proper understanding of the English language. Presumably you said this, knowing you were wrong, because you didn't want to start a prosecution. Why didn't you want to start a prosecution?

17. To the Crown Prosecution Service in Birmingham. I sent you a letter dated 21st September 1988 letter concerning my accusation of forgery at Swansea university. Apparently you asked the SWP about it and they told you they had written to me in 1983 saying there was no evidence that showed that a criminal offence had been committed. And you wouldn't do any more. But in the correspondence I'd sent you (the letter and copies of letters) it was stated that the SWP had confirmed in writing in September 1987 that they had forged documents (that were made at Swansea university). Didn't you realise this or did someone tell you to ignore the fact that the police had updated their 1983 letter?

The above question should also be put to two people who were with you at the time, T. McGowran (crown prosecutor) and I. Manson (Chief Crown Prosecutor).

18. This question applies to the period 9th January 1989 to 9th March 1990. It should be addressed to a number of newspapers and a magazine), some firms of solicitors in Bridgend, the BBC, HTV, the Mid Glamorgan Press Agency and the person/people that ran the Cambrian News Agency (as referred to in the sixth and earlier editions of this book). I sent you (or gave you, or both) a copy of a letter from the police in which they said they had forged documents and/or copies of other letters that showed that a prosecution had not been started and that the authorities hadn't given me any sort of sensible explanation for the situation. Why did you do nothing about it?

19. To the people that ran Randalls (the firm is not now in business). On 23rd January 1989 I gave you a copy of a letter from the police in which they confirmed they had forged documents. On 25th January I asked you to send a copy of it together with copies of other letters to the Director of Public Prosecutions. You said you'd do it, but you didn't. Why? The question should also be put to N. Osborne (one of their solicitors).

20. To the Director of Public Prosecutions, Max Hill. Perhaps you can answer this question and question 25 by referring to government records. On 17th February 1989 and 2nd December 1989 I sent copies of the 16th September 1987 letter from the police, in which they confirmed they had forged documents, to the DPP (Allan Green). Why didn't he, or the staff in his office, start a prosecution and give me an explanation for why it hadn't been started before? Or, why didn't he, or the staff in his office, give me an explanation for why a prosecution wouldn't be started that took into account the aforementioned letter from the police?

The above question could also be put to Sir A. Green, E. Williams and J. Coussey (the last two sent replies to my 17th February and 2nd December 1989 letters).

21. To the Crown Prosecution Service in Cardiff. Your Chief Crown Prosecutor in 1989 (H. Wallace) said, in a letter dated 20th March 1989, that the police had not said, in their 16th September 1987 letter (a copy of which I'd sent to him), that they had forged documents? His saying this was contrary to a proper understanding of the English language. Presumably he said this, knowing he was wrong, because he didn't want to start a prosecution. Why didn't he want to start a prosecution?

The above question should also be put to H. Wallace.

22. To David Prosser & Co. On 4th July 1989 I gave you a copy of a letter from the police in which they said they had forged documents. I asked you to write to the DPP telling him that the police had stated, in writing, that they had forged documents and ask him why a prosecution hadn't been started. You wouldn't do it. Why?

23. To Win Griffiths (an MP in 1989). On 4th August 1989 I wrote a letter to you and handed it in at your Bridgend office. The letter contained copies of nine letters, one of the copies was a letter from the police that confirmed they had forged documents, some of the other letters referred to this letter stating that it was confirmation from the police that they had forged documents. Did you or did you not read these letters and realise that the police had said they had forged documents? Assuming you did why didn't you make this point to the police or Director of Public Prosecutions and find out why a prosecution hadn't been started?

24. To the Prime Minister. On 9th March 1990 I sent a copy of the letter from the police, in which they said they had forged documents, to the Prime Minister (Margaret Thatcher). I received a reply dated 21st March 1990 that said my letter had been forwarded to a government department. I heard no more on it. Why didn't she make sure that a prosecution was started and that I was given an explanation for why it hadn't been started before? Or, why didn't she make sure that I was given an explanation for why a prosecution wouldn't be started that took into account the aforementioned letter from the police?

25. To the Director of Public Prosecutions. On 10th August 1990 I wrote to the DPP. I said, "in your letter of 2nd February 1990 you acknowledged that you have received a copy of a letter signed by an Assistant Chief Constable in which he confirmed that he had forged examination question papers in his possession", and I asked him to tell me when a prosecution was going to start. He didn't reply. Why didn't he reply?

The above question should also be put to Sir A. Green.

26. To the Prime Minister. Amongst other things this affair includes the following:

(i)   In 1987 the police confirmed they had forged documents that were made at Swansea university, they know who used them and they probably know who made them.

(ii)   Neither the police nor the CPS started a prosecution.

(iii)   No one in the police or CPS (or anyone else in the government) gave me an explanation for why a prosecution hadn't been started that took into account the fact the police had confirmed they had forged documents.

The media and other people could have made sure I got sense from the authorities but all these people were blocked, censored. It looks as if the censorship was applied from 1984 on, censorship was definitely applied in the years 1987 to 1990. Why did the government censor this affair in these years?

The following questions, 27 to 30, relate to my claim for damages from Cardiff university (UCC) for breach of contract, fraud.

27. To the people that ran Morgan, Bruce & Nicholas (the firm is not now in business). Why in 1984 did you apply to the court for an order to strike out my claim against Cardiff university?

The above question should also be put to G. Jones (one of their solicitors).

28. To H. Jones (a district registrar in 1984). On 12th July 1984 you presided over a pre-trial hearing in Cardiff that concerned my claim for damages from Cardiff university. In line with standard pre-trial procedure I expected you to state that the university had lost the claim on default because they had not filed a necessary affidavit (as required by the rules of the court) or give them ten days to file it. Instead of proceeding as expected you struck out the claim. Why did you do this?

29. To the Secretary of State for Justice, Dominic Raab. You are responsible for ensuring that rules of court are applied correctly. Perhaps government/court records will help you to answer this question. Question 28 refers to the actions of District Registrar H. Jones at a civil court claim for damages pre-trial hearing in July 1984. [Details of this hearing are given in TCF9 pages 95 to 97, and TCF6 pages 91 to 93.]

In my opinion the district registrar disregarded the court's rules as follows:

(i)   The defendant, Cardiff university, had not complied with the rules and he did not penalise them by stating that they had lost the claim on default, or, he did not state that they had ten days to comply with the rules.

(ii)   Instead of (i) he struck out the claim, i.e. he cancelled the claim, saying it was an abuse of the court and/or frivolous. It was neither or these things, it was a claim for damages that had been correctly detailed and filed.

I should make it plain that District Registrar Jones made no attempt to obtain some important evidence before cancelling the claim (answers to interrogatories).

In January 1987 the Lord Chancellor (Lord Hailsham) was questioned about the district registrar's actions by J. Rooker MP. He answered him in a letter dated 18th February 1987, in it he said that the claim had been properly looked at by the court. Will you please explain the Lord Chancellor's remark?

30.   To the South Wales Police. In a letter dated 23rd November 1987 I asked you if your enquiries had confirmed that fraudulent end of academic year examination results were given to me at Cardiff university in 1976. In your reply, in a letter dated 27th November 1987, you made no attempt to answer my question. Would you now like to answer my 23rd November 1987 question?

The following question relates to what Gx1 arranged to have done to my father.

31.   To the South Wales Police. In a letter dated 18th November 1987 I asked you if your enquiries had confirmed that the accusation I had made in my letter to you of 1st July 1985 (that Group X, Gx1, had hit my father) was correct. In your reply, in a letter dated 24th November 1987, you had nothing to say. Would you now like to answer my 18th November 1987 question?

In September 2021 I sent a copy of the first edition of "The Cathays Files 25" to Boris Johnson, the Prime Minister at the time. The book contained the questions that are stated above. I said that the affair, the book, had been censored by the government up to the time of my sending the book to him. And I asked him to remove the censorship. I received a reply from his office saying that he wouldn't do anything, i.e. my questions to him, as stated in the book, were unanswered. The book stayed censored.

In July 2022 I sent a copy of the second edition of "The Cathays Files 25" to Mr Johnson (the PM). I did not receive a reply. The book stayed censored.

In December 2022 I sent a copy of the third edition of "The Cathays Files 25" to Rishi Sunak, the PM. In the letter I enclosed with it I said that the book was being censored by the government and I asked him to remove the censorship. I did not receive a reply. The book stayed censored.

Details on the government's 1979/80 activities are to be found in the chapter "The Government Planted False Evidence in 1980", and the sections, "1977 to the 1980 Town Hall Electron 'Bullet'", "More on Spain in 1979/80", "The 1979 Boundary Change" and "The Welsh Office Job in 1979". Also see "Conclusion (2)".

Replies to any of the questions I ask in this book can be sent to me at Resarton Books.

Questions to be Answered (2)

Most of the questions in this chapter are directed at finding out who arranged the 1979/80 hits (detailed in the chapter "The Government Planted False Evidence in 1980"). Since I initially put the questions some people have died, I leave the questions in here as a matter of record. And anyway other people might have something to say about the questions. When I say "the situation" I mean at least one of the following:

    (i)   What happened to me at UCS in 1974/75.

    (ii)   What happened to me at UCC in 1975/76.

    (iii)   What happened to my father in 1973.

32. In the 9th edition of TCF I put this question to Lord Crickhowell (Nicholas Edwards, the Secretary of State for Wales from May 1979 to 1987). But he died in 2018. The question is as follows. "In 1979 were you aware of the situation and did you forward details of it to Mrs Thatcher?"

I also put question 33 (ii) to him

In September 2021 I sent a copy of the first edition of "The Cathays Files 25" to the Queen. University regulations brought her into the dispute (see the 1979 chapter). In the letter I enclosed with the book I said that the government was censoring the book. In July 2022 I sent her a copy of the second edition of the book (with a letter). I did not receive a reply to either of the letters, i.e. my question to her, as stated in the books, was unanswered. And the book stayed censored. In September 2022 the Queen died. The question (in two parts) is as follows.

33. (i)   In 1979 a professor in London told me that you were the adjudicator for disputes in welsh universities. I sent details of my dispute with Cardiff university to the Clerk of the Privy Council for forwarding to you. I received a reply saying you would not adjudicate the dispute because students were not covered by the dispute system. Very odd. What are your comments on this?

    (ii)   In December/January 1979/80 government officials got me poisoned (made ill) and directed to a high roof. In October 1980 they covertly planted false evidence to ensure I lost my dispute with Cardiff university. What do you know about these occurrences?

In May 1979 Mr Callaghan's Labour government was put out of it's job and Mrs Thatcher's Conservative government took over. It seems that the situation was made known to Mr Callaghan before May 1979, when he was the PM. [See "The 1979 Boundary Change" and "The Welsh Office Job in 1979" sections later in this book.] But since Mr Callaghan is not alive today no questions can be put to him. However the Secretary of State for Wales under Mr Callaghan, John Morris, now Lord Morris, is still with us, perhaps he can answer the next question and question 33 (ii).

34. To Lord Morris. In 1978/79 were you aware of the situation and did you forward details of it to Mr Callaghan?

I would also like question 33 (ii) to be answered by the people who were in charge of MI5 and MI6 in 1979/80. And by the present heads of these two organisations (presumably they can check their records on what they've done in the past).

In the 6th edition of TCF I put a question regarding what happened in 1979/80 to Sir J. Woodcock (Chief Constable of the South Wales Police from 1979-83), but he died in 2012. So I will here put question 33 (ii) to K. Lee (Deputy Chief Constable of the SWP in 1983) and J. Vaughan (the present Chief Constable of the SWP).

The next question relates to my meeting at the Welsh Office in 1981 with Michael Roberts, a Parliamentary Under-Secretary of State. He died in February 1983 aged fifty five, a natural death apparently. I was very surprised when I read about it in a newspaper, when I'd seen him he looked perfectly healthy.

35. Does anyone, in particular the people that are related to or knew Mr Roberts, consider his death to be an odd occurrence, i.e. think his death may not have been from natural causes?

Was Mr Roberts unwilling to go along with the Prime Minister? Had he, in 1983, found out more about what had been going on (including the 1980 government false evidence plant) and he wanted to, or was about to, get it all into the open?

1982 and 1983 were notable years for people in some top jobs at the South Wales Police and Swansea university (UCS). Chief Constable J. Woodcock and Deputy Chief Constable K. Lee both left their jobs in 1983. And three members of staff in the UCS administration offices that I'd been in contact with in 1981/82 about what had happened to me when I was at the college also left their jobs in 1982/83, as follows, the academic registrar left in February 1982, the registrar in September 1982 and the principal left in April 1983. Let me remind you that in 1983 I uncovered the forgery at UCS and sent evidence of it to the SWP. The evidence not only verified my accusation of forgery it also in effect established that some UCS administration staff had, in 1981/82, conspired in a cover up of the forgery. I leave it to you to form your own opinion as to why all these people left their jobs in a short space of time.

Editorial Note

From the start of this book, up to here, the chapter headings that are given in years, contain details of what happened in those years.

From this point on in the book the chapter headings, all in years (apart from the Conclusion), indicate when I wrote the chapter.

2006

1972-1979, More Details

This chapter in TCF6 and TCF9 is reduced in size from fifteen pages to two pages in this abridgement.

Yes I'd returned from Australia in 1972, Gx1 had failed in his efforts to place me there permanently, did that mean he had now lost interest in me? No, he continued to covertly hit me, fix my life.

I started a relationship with a female in October 1973, I refer to her as Miss D. She was a Gx1 selection. He knew she was trouble, and that's what he wanted me to have.

He used Miss D in early 1974 to issue what was in his mind a very clear 'sign'. It 'said' he was planning to kill my father and me (the piano song).

In September 1974 I left a job and started a full time course at Swansea university. It would I thought help to finish my relationship with Miss D.

Some months after starting there was the 'acid laces' incident (in TCF6 and 9), a Gx1 'sign' that said, 'your rugby is going nowhere'.

At the end of my academic year at the university Gx1, who of course wanted me stopped, arranged for staff at the university to give me fixed question papers as part of his 'stop him' activities. I quote two paragraphs from the 9th edition of The Cathays Files:

"Where did the idea to switch the headings on the two Pure Mathematics examination question papers come from? Who first thought it up in other words and then got the idea put into practice? It is possible that it was someone in UCS, SX or SV for example. But, as I've said in earlier editions, I believe the idea was thought up by one of the people in Group X. I'll tell you why.

The two lecturers, SJ and SF, in handing out fixed examination question papers to me, both committed the act of using forged documents to defraud. This criminal offence is specified in section 6 of the 1913 Forgery Act (which was in force at the time). In other words both of the lecturers committed section 6 offences. Two sixes were very relevant figures in the minds of Group X. They had me on route for Miss D, yes, you know all about that. Well Miss D lived at number 66. Was all this just a coincidence? My answer is no. Two of the people in Group X were ex-policemen and one was a policeman. They all had some knowledge of the Forgery Act. For the one that thought this up it was a clear indication, in his covert way of going about things (a 'sign'), that I was going to end up back in Cardiff soon with Miss D, and Swansea university was at an end for me."

In the quote I refer to "one of the people in Group X" as having arranged to have the headings switched. I meant, to be exact, Gx1.

In September 1975 my university study was stopped, by Gx1. Note that this is 'again', because in 1968 he made sure I didn't start at a university.

Nevertheless I managed to continue my university study at Cardiff university. This infuriated him.

During my year at this second university he covertly hit me a number of times, all were aimed at making sure my university study was stopped. He succeeded, my study was stopped at this second university in 1976.

In 1977 he arranged to have me murdered. I'd caused him a lot of problems. And I could cause him more. The murder however didn't come off, I came through it without suspecting that I'd been deliberately poisoned (the cross country walk). Before the year was up he tried again to kill me, by 'accident'.

He formed new plans to ship me to Australia.

In 1979 I started work for an insurance broker, selling policies to students. This job led to my being poisoned and a high roof.

Gx1's Miss D

The main points in this chapter in TCF6 and 9 are as follows.

(i)   Miss D's pure church going girl disguise.

(ii)   When Miss D froze as soon as I asked her about her "Brotherly Love" book. At the time I did not know that for her the book meant, 'I am in a secret sexual relationship with my brother'.

(iii)   My unexpected arrival one evening when Miss D and her brother were having sex.

(iv)   The night Miss D's mother was covertly viewing my preparations for sex with Miss D.

(v)   Miss D's mother's 'tips', to have sex with her daughter backwards.

(vi)   The dinner-dance assault carried out by the Group X member who was close to Miss D's family (her godfather).

(vii)   The turn round request, yes, Miss D was definitely in a secret sexual relationship with her brother, and it was backwards with him.

(viii)   My finishing with Miss D. I had said nothing to her about her sex with her brother, it would cause serious problems if I did. In other words she did not know that I knew about it. She thought I had finished with her because I had said 'we don't get on with each other', which was in it's own right quite correct.

(ix)   Another Group X covert sign. This one was on the number plate of the car Miss D drove, NOJ. The covert sign was, 'my brother backwards' (her brother's name backwards), sex being the obvious connection.

(x)   Miss D's close relationship with her godfather.

(xi)   Gx1 planned to have sex with Miss D.

2009/10

Gx1 Puts a 'Bullet' in My Head in 1968

Let me tell you about a joke that Gx1 thought up in 1968. It was about a greyhound that was very fast and it's owner/trainer had ran it in greyhound races. One day the owner was talking to a friend of his about the dog, he said the dog could make him a lot of money, but there was a problem, it was so fast it couldn't go round bends. At the first bend on the track it always ran into the outside fence and took no further part in the race. His friend said to him, 'I've got the answer, weigh him down on one side with a piece of lead, that'll get him round the bends'. 'That's a good idea,' said the owner. His friend continued, 'put the lead in his ear using a gun'.

Why do I tell you about this Gx1 joke? Because it was put together for my benefit. I was the greyhound, i.e. I was fast and it looked like a successful rugby career was in front of me. And in Gx1's warped mind that, as I've previously told you, was potentially a big problem for him. Too much success playing rugby could halt the plans he had for me and my father. Which were, I'll remind you, 'transport him to Australia ... one way', me that is, and for my father it was death. In the 1967/68 rugby season, when he thought up this joke, I was aged nineteen/twenty and I was playing rugby on the wing for Llandaff Technical College, at the end of the season I was elected captain for the next season.

Gx1 used the following to assemble the joke. My brother's name is Col T, the T being Thomas of course. What does Col T make you think of? Put Col T like this, Colt. Well there are a couple of answers, the one that Gx1 had in mind is the gun known as a Colt, a make of gun that became well known in nineteenth century America. He was going to use, 'he's going to Australia, permanently, to join his brother, I say so, he doesn't know it', as a reason for 'killing'/stopping my rugby, by putting lead, a 'bullet', in my head.

So, as the joke says, to stop my rugby he was going to weigh me down on one side. And that's exactly what he did at the beginning of the 1968/69 season. The planned accident he arranged (preceded by the 'butcher' meeting) resulted in my having the lower half of my left leg encased in plaster for two months. I was weighed down on one side. He hit me to put me on crutches to stop my rugby. I'll give you more details on what he did here at some other time. Just bear in mind that Gx1 was an official bright boy, top quality dirt.

I can tell you where Gx1 got the idea for this greyhound joke from. Greyhounds connected, in these nineteen sixties years, very closely to Cardiff RFC. The perimeter of the Arms Park, Cardiff's ground, was used for greyhound racing, the meetings took place regularly (once or twice a week). So the fact that Gx1 thought up this joke tells us, is evidence if you like, that some people/lecturers (having seen me play at Llandaff Tech) had me lined up for Cardiff RFC. Word of this got to Gx1 and in his warped way of thinking he had to block it somehow, stop it happening, hence his greyhound joke and the 'accident' that put me on crutches in September 1968.

'Your Boots are in a Funeral Home' in 1969

In the next season, the 1969/70 season, I decided a month or so before the season began that I'd go to Cardiff rugby club and train with them. And when training started in early August I joined them for training twice a week.

[This is when Gx1's Autocar visit to our house took place, the 'u to Australia' visit that I've told you about in TCF6 and 9. Here's more on it.] When he was leaving he asked me if he could have a look at my new car. In the previous month or two my parents and I had reorganised the car situation. My father took over the one I'd had since I was seventeen and we bought a new one for me to use. I mean by that a new second hand car, which we bought from a car dealer. As was the case with my first car my parents were again involved in helping me financially here. [I probably put what I could toward it and paid for the insurance monthly or something like that.] Back to where I was, I walked out of our house with Gx1 and to my new car which was parked outside. He walked to the back of the car looked at the number plate and said to me, 'you understand number plates don't you?' I said, 'yes'. I assumed he meant that from a number plate you could tell where a car was first registered, the car was first registered in London. He then left.

Now let me tell you what was in the mind of Gx1, what he was thinking during this number plate part of his visit. The number plate, he knew, was a 'sign' (yes another Gx1 sign) that 'said' that my rugby was dead, and he was, in highlighting the number plate 'letting me know it'. Letting me know it is in single inverted commas because of course he wasn't literally telling me that my rugby was dead, he was highlighting a covert 'sign'. How did this number plate 'say' that my rugby was dead? I'll tell you. The name of a funeral home about two hundred and fifty yards from where I bought the car was Pidgeons. The number plate was PGN 321E. PGN reads as, or is certainly a close approximation to, pidgeon. Gx1 referred to the number plate on the back of the car, on the boot in other words. Boot is closely connected to rugby. He was 'saying' my boot, or boots, were at a funeral home, they were 'dead'. My rugby was 'dead'.

Gx1 got the car placed at the car dealers, the closest car place to the funeral home, by using his influential position, then he got me directed to it. With the price making it into a good buy I selected it and we bought it.

Soon after this visit from Gx1 he arranged to have me poisoned prior to the start of season trial game I played in at Cardiff, to make sure I didn't continue there. I went to Penarth where Gx1 then made sure I didn't play in the first team after having had a very good game in the one first team game I did play in. In the space of twelve months Gx1 'killed' my rugby three times. At Llandaff Technical College in 1968 and, in 1969, at Cardiff and then Penarth.

1966/67, Miss C

It was in the years 1965 to 1967 that Gx1 stopped my relationship with two important females. Had he not done this I would have married either of them. I must tell you more about Miss C, the girl I went with for six months in 1966/67.

I met Miss C at a dance in Cardiff. She was with a girl who did clerical work where I was working. I thought she was very good indeed, attractive and well dressed. And she seemed to be happy with me. The thing is she knew about me and liked what she knew. Her girlfriend had obviously told her about me, I was in a good draughtsman's job wasn't I. I took her home in my car and from saying goodnight it was easy to see we were both very keen on each other.

I took her out in my car once or twice a week (two evenings a week I was in college remember). We usually went to one of two country pubs a few miles out of Cardiff. Quite often we drank coffee with cream on it. And somehow we were always engrossed in conversation. She seemed to have been at a better school than I went to in that they had taught French (there were no foreign languages at my school). She had a girlfriend in France who she wrote to in French. I asked her if she'd say a few words to me in French, she said no. I think modesty stopped her here (she could certainly have said something in French even though she apparently had only been taught written French). That was a characteristic she definitely had, she was too modest to try to impress me.

On Christmas eve we went for a meal at one of the country pubs we usually went to, a friend of mine with his girlfriend were with us (they later married). At the end of the night Miss C told me she wanted me to take her to a midnight church service, so that's where we went.

It was a Saturday during the day when for some reason I took her back to my house for the first time. It has to have been a Saturday because my father was there on his own (he worked the rest of the week, my mother was out, she worked Saturdays). I would be a while in my bedroom (I must have had some gear to sort out or something like that) and I left Miss C in the living room to talk to my father. Perhaps eight minutes later I returned to them and was surprised to see them playing chess. Anyway Miss C and I left to go wherever we were going, they didn't finish the chess game. I was surprised because I didn't know Miss C could play chess. During our conversations I had undoubtedly told her I played chess and that I sometimes played the game with my father, she did not however respond by saying she also played chess. [Getting the chess out was probably my father's idea, thinking that it would be a good way to spend ten minutes with her and if she didn't play the game he'd teach her the basics.]

Gx1, when he stopped my relationship with Miss C, blocked a great route that I was proceeding along in my life. And he did this, destroyed a good route I was taking, many times. He was bent, and, worse still, he was a bent official. Why do I say that bent officials are the worst? A bent individual can only get his close acquaintances to do what he wants done, a bent official can get numerous 'yes sir, no sir' people to do what he wants done.

My Parents

[Let me tell you a bit about my father, the man Gx1 was planning to kill.] It must already be apparent that my father was important in my life, he was my inspiration for rugby at the beginning and for many years rugby was a big part of my life. As soon as I was old enough to drive, seventeen, I did. I had a car within weeks of my seventeenth birthday and soon passed my test. My father hadn't had a car up to this point, well his job had never been a big payer. He and my mother earnt enough to pay the bills and that was it. We soon realised that the thing to do on weekends, particularly a Saturday morning was building jobs. My father, being a tradesman in the building industry, often got asked to do small building jobs (outside of his regular job). Well with the car that we now had we could do them. My father was a plasterer by trade but having spent his life on the building he could work in other areas of it. We often found ourselves repairing slate roofs for example. And any small alteration work, like installing a new window, was okay. My father was very good to work with, we had a great understanding. And do you know what, you might not believe this but it's perfectly true, whenever we got paid for a job it was always half for me (after materials money had been deducted). But I was only the helper, the labourer, never mind that, it was half for me. These years have to be the best years of my life.

And let me give you some words on my mother here. In the months before my father married her he was told by her mother/father (I'm not sure which), 'if you marry her you'll never go hungry'. My mother was outstanding in the kitchen, she was a great cook. I could detail a lot here but for now I'll just tell you that every Sunday it was a roast dinner with her also making tarts, trifles, cakes, etc on the same day. She did the lot, and it was all superb.

Thinking about it know I consider it to be amazing, all the recipes came out of her memory, she got it all from her mother. She once said, in about 1970, that the only thing newly married girls/women could do in the kitchen 'these days' was use a tin opener, and she ought to know, she worked with women. And along with her cooking was her cleanliness. Every Sunday afternoon you'd find her on her knees in front of the oven cleaning it out. The inside of the oven always looked like new. And washing clothes got just as much attention, and it was completed with ironing and airing.

What I've said in the last paragraph, I have to come back down to earth here, is no doubt part of the reason Gx1 wanted to kill my father. He knew my mother was exceptional in the home. She was also smart and attractive. Her work, in ladies fashion (shops and a department store) tells you this. She, with a paid for house, with my father dead, would be quite a gain for some man. As I've said elsewhere I don't know what Gx1 had in mind after he killed my father, I don't think he had my mother lined up for himself because he had a wife and there weren't any break up problems there that I know of, but who knows, perhaps he had quick departure plans for her when the time came.

The Civic Buildings and the Move to Nottingham

I mentioned in the third edition of The Cathays Files that Gx1 was employed in the city hall in Cardiff. He worked for the local council in other words. Which means his wages were paid by the people of Cardiff (a form of taxation now called council tax, then it was rates from houseowners and rent from council tenants, etc). Did he spend all or just some of his time arranging covert activities ('signs', hits)? In the sixties/seventies I never knew exactly what his job was in the city hall, all I knew was that he did office work. I also knew that he used to be a policeman. It seems to me that when he moved to the city hall 'clerical job' he became an undercover policeman, perhaps he worked for MI5, even if I'm wrong on both counts there is no doubt that he continued to use his police contacts.

The Cardiff City Hall. Would you believe that a man who was involved in covertly hitting us (me and my family) was employed there. My father and his father worked on the museum (now the National Museum of Wales) when it was built around 1932 next to the city hall. And it's more than likely that my grandfather took part in building the city hall, it was put up in about 1903 by a Cardiff company. Both of these fine civic buildings were built in Portland stone. It's a shame that those who ran Cardiff in the fifties to early eighties period couldn't find decent people to do the paperwork in the city hall. Yes but hang on a moment, "those who ran Cardiff", Gx1 was one of them.

My father and mother moved from Cardiff to Nottingham in 1934/5. This move was probably a result of the building of Nottingham Council House in 1929. The museum and the council house have similarities, i.e. they are both built in Portland stone, have large columns at the front and a dome in the roof. The people who built the council house were perhaps looking for building tradesmen for some more work in the city and they'd heard about the new, similar, Cardiff museum that had recently been built, and they told my father's employer to offer him a job in Nottingham. Presumably more money was attached to it to give him a reason for moving to Nottingham. He told me in the '60s that when he was working in Nottingham he had a number of men working on his instructions.

After a few years however my father's progress in Nottingham was interrupted by the war. In 1939 he and his wife moved back to Cardiff. My mother, with a three year old son to look after, was safer close to her parents (who were in Cardiff). My father knew he would probably have to join the army soon (which he did).

One of the things my mother was pleased to say to me (in about 1970) was that my father, ever since she'd known him, had never been out of work. The reason being of course is that he was one of the finest building tradesmen in the country.

In 1923 my father, straight from school, went to work with his father who was a plasterer, to learn the trade from him. My father had three brothers (and two sisters). The fact that my father was the only son to join his father in the building trade shows that they had a special relationship with each other.

[Let me tell you a bit more here that is an illustration of what I've said in

68

this section.] One of the weekend jobs I did with my father (in about 1967) was a small roof repair job on quite a big expensive house (built around 1910). The owner of the house ran a bakery business. When we were doing the job the owner asked me to have a look at some work my father had done recently in one of the front downstairs rooms. My father had been working in the house as part of his normal Monday to Friday job (he worked for a builder who had his yard next to our house) The owner pointed to the cornice in the room saying that my father had done it. Apparently a large part of the original cornice had cracked and broken away and my father had replaced it by running in a new section, making it match perfectly. The cornice had a sophisticated pattern to it. The owner was very impressed by the work my father had done.

If you want a better understanding of what I've just said (most of you reading this won't know much about cornices) read through this paragraph, if not proceed now to the next section. Where a wall joins the ceiling a cornice is sometimes put in place, it can be anything from four inches to a foot wide running along the join. In about 1980 cornices became popular for small houses when a four inch wide ready made polystyrene cornice appeared on the market (in five foot lengths). It was a plain design (with one curve in and two steps) and it was glued into position. But before 1980 things were different, cornices were run in situ by plasterers (and they still are today if required). Meaning that just mixed, flowing but stiff, plaster was applied to the join and it was formed, using shaping tools (a trowel etc) into it's final form as it hardened (plaster can be worked on until it goes hard about an hour after mixing). Plain four inch plaster cornices were around in pre-1980 days but in the case of big houses and buildings (such as the baker's house and the museum) cornices were perhaps a foot wide with patterns in them (a number of curves and steps), and producing them was a work of art.

Rugby's Early Years

I got my interest in rugby from my father (and he got his interest from his father). In the 1930s and around 1950 my father used to go to Cardiff rugby club games and internationals (his father did the same in earlier years). From around the age of about nine, 1957, I used to watch the international games on tv with my father. The school I was going to at the time didn't play rugby. It was however played at the school I went to from the age of eleven and of course it was the sport I took up there, playing for the school's rugby teams, the 11 to 13 team then the 13 to 15 team. I was never out of the team, never dropped and injury never stopped me playing. I took a few knocks playing the game of course but not once did I hold a game up through injury.

My brother's 11 to 16 school rugby, 1947/52, saw him being selected to play for Cardiff Boys. My father went to these games. My brother often went to watch Cardiff rugby club and we used to have an autograph book that he used on these trips. I didn't know much about rugby at this time because I was only in my first few years of life. By the time I got to nine in 1957 (when I started to watch internationals on tv) my brother was away from home and had been since 1953 when he was conscripted into the armed forces, when he left the forces in 1958 he settled down (married) in Australia, where he continued to play rugby. So it was mainly my father that got me interested in rugby.

My brother sent me a rugby ball when I was about fourteen and I used it a lot at a nearby park with my best friend when I was fifteen/sixteen. But I didn't play for a team after the school team until I got to age nineteen (then it was Llandaff Technical College). In my sixteen to nineteen years I maintained my interest in rugby by going to watch Cardiff rugby club (with the friend I just mentioned).

It's through rugby that I've obtained a lot of evidence that has helped me point the finger at Gx1. Direct evidence for example in the form of his fixing up the Bart's stupid on call job to ensure I stayed out of the Wasps first team, and covert evidence such as the PGN number plate. If rugby hadn't come into it, if I'd been no good at the game, there would have been no need for Gx1 to hit my rugby activities, I would in other words have no rugby derived evidence. So rugby has been important to me in more ways than one.

It looks like Gx1 first became concerned about my rugby ability soon after I started playing rugby, which was in school at the age of eleven. This was the 1959/60 season. Read through the next five paragraphs and then I will continue on this line.

In my first year at my 11-15 school I met our physical education teacher, I soon considered him to be very good. My father had created my interest in rugby then this teacher done his bit to encourage me. It was in my first year that the following happened.

It was a Wednesday afternoon game of rugby played between two 11-13 teams, both of which were made up of players from our school. Our physical education teacher was the referee. It was part way through the season and by this time I was established as the school's 11-13 team full back. The school had just the one 11-13 team in a Saturday morning league but there was enough interest in the game in the school to make up two 11-13 teams for the sports

70

afternoon on a Wednesday. There was a line out near the halfway line and a forward from the other side got the ball and started to run through our players. This forward was exceptional. Most of the players on the field were the average height for 11 to 13 year olds, about five foot I suppose, and I was one of them, well this forward was about six foot. He had sprouted up well ahead of his time, he was in his second year so he would have been about 13. Anyway he went through all our side's players that were in front of him and not one of our side was bothering to chase him. I was stood, being the full back, around the twenty five yard line, it was obvious that if I didn't stop him it was a try. He went slightly to one side of me and I tackled him round the legs. He came down and the ball went loose. I got up picked the ball up and went off up the field, I put a kick for touch in as I approached some opposing players.

It was at this point that the physical education teacher stopped the game and called everyone to where the tackle had taken place. He told us that we had just seen the perfect tackle. It was an example for everyone, the way to bring down a player who is coming at you, especially when the player is bigger than you, is to tackle him round the legs. This has to be one of the reasons why the physical education teacher wrote in my end of academic year report that in rugby I was "outstanding".

A cynical person reading this might say, 'I bet what you've told us about in the last paragraph was the only time you managed to nail him and he got past you other times'. Well Mr Cynic you would be wrong, he never got past me. But I should add that he was only rarely in a side I was playing against. At this time of my life I was known for my exceptional tackling and the ability to field/catch the ball and put in a good kick for touch. [My running speed was good but it wasn't till a few years on from here that it increased to a very good pace. Hence my moving from full back to wing when I was nineteen.]

Perhaps nine months or a year after this Wednesday afternoon rugby game the physical education teacher left the school. I was very disappointed to see him go, as I've said I thought he was really good. He took up a post in a high school in Cardiff, our school was called Allensbank secondary modern school, not a high school.

Now taken on it's own this leaving the school move by the physical education teacher would mean nothing at all to us. But, without any doubt, it looks like yet another piece in the jigsaw puzzle that illustrates Gx1 and his warped activities, because it fits in. The teacher probably had big rugby plans for me, and that meant at some stage in the next few years, playing for Cardiff Boys. Gx1, as we know all to well from events in later years, didn't want me to have any significant success playing rugby. So it follows that he got the teacher moved on to where he wouldn't cause him any problems. What's one way of getting someone out of a job? Promoting him is the answer, offering him more money elsewhere, in going from our school to a high school he most probably got a pay increase. Arranging for the high school job to become available and pushing our teacher into it would have been routine stuff for Gx1, he was working in the local council and the council ran the local education system.

My Brother is Poisoned Before a Welsh Boys Trial in 1951

I know that the Gx1 plan to murder my father existed in 1966, when did he first think up the plan? See later in the book, what I will say now is that he (or Group X type people) was having a go at us, hitting us, in the 1950s.

In 1951/52 my brother, aged 15/16, was playing rugby for Cardiff Boys. I remember my father telling me once (in the 1960s) that my brother was selected to play in the trial game for the Welsh Boys team but because he was ill he didn't take part. [I have no doubt what was going on here. For guidance just look at what was done to my rugby in the 1960s/70s. My brother was poisoned by Gx1 to make sure he didn't get into the Welsh Boys team.]

As I have said my brother, via conscription, settled down in Australia in 1958. [It appears to me that it was Gx1 that shipped him to Australia using his surreptitious methods. I'll here give you a 'sign' he gave out in the sixties that not only indicates that my brother was shipped out it also indicates the Gx1 state of mind, the reason for shipping him out.]

On the Geographers street map of Cardiff I noticed, in about 1965, that a clinic was shown as being next door to our house. A house stood there originally but in the war a bomb dropped and hit the house and it was now an open yard that was being used by a company that made gravestones. So the map, showing a clinic there, was wrong, there wasn't and never had been a clinic there. [Let's look at this through Group X 'sign' language. Clinic gives, is very close to, Colin, my brother's name. The 'sign' says that Gx1 had put my brother in a grave, the gravestones, and he did this by shipping him, one way, to Australia. In other words his state of mind, his reason for shipping him to Australia, was to, metaphorically speaking, kill him, as far as this country was concerned he would be 'dead', i.e. he would no longer be here.]

Now where on earth did Gx1 get the idea to poison and 'kill' my brother from?

The Way the People That Ran this Country in the Early 1950s Thought

I'll start to answer the question I asked at the end of the last section by taking you to the USA in 1945. At this time the people who ran the USA were again starting to use government employees to make big public noises about 'dirty commies'. I say "again" because the US government first done this sort of thing in the 1919/20 period when they arrested perhaps as many as 10,000 US citizens and recent immigrants, saying that they were radicals and could destroy the US government. This was because of what had happened in Russia in 1917/18, where russian people had taken over the government in two stages. First, in February 1917 the monarch abdicated, and then in October 1917 they used the force of arms to place the people they wanted at the top. And then in 1918 the ex-monarch and his family were killed by the government.

These events took place because Russia was suffering heavy losses in the ongoing World War One (the main protagonists being France, Britain and Russia v Germany, Austria and Hungary) and many russian people wanted to pull out of the war. But the pre-Feb 1917 monarch would not pull out. Hence he was forced to abdicate. The leaders who replaced him would still not pull out of the war. So in Oct 1917 the russian people, using armed force this time, placed the people they wanted into the leadership of the government. This new russian government managed to agree a peace treaty with Germany in March 1918.

There were however russians that wanted to re-instate the ex-monarch and a civil war started. This led to the russian government killing the ex-monarch and his family in July 1918. Thinking that it could put an end to the civil war (but it went on for a few years).

In the USA at this time the government became worried that the same thing, a takeover of the US government by US people, could happen there, hence in 1919/20 they imprisoned thousands of US people who they thought might support radical ideas.

In about 1922 the russian government started to use the term communism to describe their method of government. The US government then began to equate the word radical with communism. So 'dirty radicals' became 'dirty commies'.

That's enough said about the 1920 area for now because I here want to concentrate on the years after 1945.

Soon after World War Two finished in 1945 the UK and US governments started up with, 'we are against the russians/commies'. The second world war had actually seen the russians fighting as allies of the UK/US, or if not as allies exactly they were all fighting the same enemy, Germany. But then soon after the end of the war, with Germany defeated, the UK/US governments and the russian government somehow became enemies in rhetoric (they didn't start fighting), and this became known as the Cold War, with 'dirty commies' rolled into it.

Some of you reading this will know about the McCarthy years in the USA. These years, 1950/53, were the high point of the US government's big post WW2 public noise period (which ran from 1945 to 1956) against commies in the USA. In these years they labelled numerous people living in the USA commies or commie supporters and vilified them in public. Many of those picked on lost their jobs, some were placed in jail for six/twelve months, and some died by suicide or heart attack. In 1956 the US government stopped doing this, stopped dragging some of it's people into a 'dirty commie' public arena, they continued however with their 'anti-Russia /commie' rhetoric on the world diplomatic stage.

Meanwhile back over here the british government, in this 1945/56 period, didn't follow the US example, i.e. did not drag british people into a dirty commie public arena. Well they didn't have to (they presumably thought), because they could and did achieve the same result, big anti-commie news, by simply having the media tell us all about the events in the USA. The british government was throughout this period and on into the 1990s giving out 'anti-Russia/commie' rhetoric.

So we now have an idea of the 'in public' anti-commie policies of the UK/US governments from 1922 to say 2000. What do you think the UK government was doing about it in private? I hope you're not naive enough to say 'nothing', or 'they don't do things in private'. Well whatever else they were doing the following certainly had to be kept quiet because it would never be accepted by the mass of the british public. I believe that the people who ran the country gave out covert directives saying:

  (I) That 'all workers/commies in Britain should be kept down', meaning not allowed to proceed into important positions, particularly in the political area.

  (ii) That 'all bright sons of workers should be kept down'. Daughters were presumably also included in this but for ease of reference I shall just say "sons".

And they added to their directives, 'or shipped out of the country'. "Kept down" in (ii) also meant that the sons were to be stopped from getting the necessary educational qualifications for the best jobs.

Ordinary sons of workers were not included in this 'keep them down' process because ordinary sons stuck to applying for ordinary jobs, i.e. they didn't try for the best jobs.

I'll say something about the US government's 'publicly persecute people if they are commies' 1945/56 policy, and their 'persecute people if they are radicals' 1919/20 policy. The whole point of democracy, and the US government says it's democratic, is that it's a system of government in which people can form whatever party they want and good luck to them for getting votes. i.e. if some people form the Alaska supporters party or the poor people advocates party or the keep fit party or the we want a commie style government here party, 'so what', democracy says, and 'there's nothing wrong with that'. So the US government, in publicly persecuting people they considered to be commie/radical supporters in the 1945/56 and 1918/20 years were acting against democracy, acting improperly in other words. It seems that many people in the USA said exactly this, which is why the US government stopped doing the 'public persecution' stuff in 1956. But regardless of this it no doubt continued covertly, in the same way as the british government was, to get at, keep down, workers/commies. And that included keeping down any bright son of a worker whose only interest was in working hard and getting on in life.

The Ship Out Scheme in 1945

Let's look at the "shipped out of the country" part of the british government's covert directive. Now what came into existence in Britain in 1945, the year the US government re-started it's in public dirty commies stuff, the year the Cold War (UK/US versus Russia) was getting going? It was the 'find £10 and we'll pay the rest to ship you to Australia' scheme. Emigration for the british public. A coincidence that the scheme began at the same time as the 'dirty commies/workers' rhetoric was starting up again? No chance. The £10 scheme originated from the people who ran Britain, the people who wanted to keep down or ship out commies/workers and their bright sons. And knowing they couldn't go public on it they had it made out as, given to the media as, 'it's simply Australia wanting to increase it's population'.

The scheme was one way of course. Built into it was 'if you want to come back you have to find the full return fare yourself' and 'if you return within two years of going you will also have to pay the full outgoing fare to us'. Someone says, in response to what I said at page 142 in The Cathays Files 9th edition, 'but it was the australian government that was paying the outgoing fare (minus £10)' not the british government, yes that does seem to be the case, but that in no way changes what I've said. The people who ran Britain presumably easily got their australian counterparts to come up with the money, well in the long term the australian government would get the money back from tax paid by the immigrants wouldn't they.

It could be that the initial reaction of the australian government to the british emigration scheme idea was to say, 'well there won't be many people who'll take up the offer because we have no easy life to offer them in Australia, so why bother to set it up?' With the response from the people

75

who ran Britain being 'just go along with us, we'll make sure you get large numbers of immigrants out of it', knowing they would be using their Group X type people to get members of the british public, many of whom were in the 'keep them down' category, onto the scheme.

So the answer I give you to the question I put at the end of the last but one section is that my brother was shipped out, metaphorically killed, to satisfy the people that ran this country. They wanted the bright sons of workers kept down or shipped out and he was a bright son of a worker. The answer is as simple as that.

I will give you some details here on my brother's life in the years around 1950, these are the years prior to his being shipped out, i.e. these details show why he was rated as 'bright' by the Group X type people.

My brother was, as you know, a good rugby player. My father's father takes the family's rugby participation/interest date back to the 1890s (I have no information before then). And with both our parents being very fit, my father in particular was in a physically demanding and healthy job, it follows that rugby and the ability to play the game was bred into us.

I was a good athlete in school yes but my brother had an astonishing record. In his last year at school he won (on the same day) the 100 yards, 220 yards, 440 yards and the 880 yards races. I'll give you my reasoning on this. He was brought up in the 1939/45 war years, and food rationing was present for most of these years. Children in other words got only basic food. My mother however would somehow have made sure that my brother got a good supply of the best food, her cooking (with her own recipes) could not have been any better, Result, when in school in 1951 aged fifteen, he was physically in a far better shape than the other children who were average or below par. So he won the races. When I competed in school, in 1963, the other children were in better condition, so I only won one of the track events (second in another).

And academically my brother was also very good. At age eleven he went to a "high school" (many workers children went to a "secondary" school). To sum up he was a brilliant individual, so it's obvious that he was a prime candidate for the attention of Group X type people, i.e. it looked like he'd really go places, and that meant, because he was the son of a worker (a dirty commie in their distorted minds), he was to be kept down or shipped out.

The Ship In Scheme in 1950

It was around 1950 when the government went in for immigration in a big way. People from a number of countries, such as India, Pakistan and countries in Africa and the Caribbean were brought in, allowed in, to live permanently in Britain. And this continued through the fifties and sixties easing off after that (some restrictions were applied).

The immigrants were housed in the cheapest housing areas of cities and some large towns. In so doing tight knit british worker communities were broken up, diluted. Which is exactly what the people that ran this country wanted, it put into action their 'keep down workers because they are commies' thinking. "Keep down" being much the same thing as break up/dilute.

People living in the areas that were having immigrants inserted into them started to realise that their way of life, their heritage, was being curtailed/altered by these new 'foreigners'. And they wanted the immigration process stopped. So the people that ran this country got parliament in 1965 to bring in a law that protected the immigrants. The law said it was an offence to discriminate against them. This meant that british workers who objected to having their way of life altered had to stay silent. Either that or, if they did voice their objections, they knew they could be easily dirtied. i.e. 'you're breaking the law saying you don't want immigrants fed into your community, that's discrimination'.

Immigration numbers were reduced from the seventies on because by then the immigrants had done their job, diluted, broke up, the inner city/town worker communities. Their large families (many had five or more children) was an ongoing positive factor in the dilution job. It's of interest to note that british workers usually had large families up to say 1930 then they stopped having them and two children became the normal sort of figure (I wonder why that happened?).

The 'Stopped You Going to University' McCarthy Evidence in 1968

Let's go to the 1960s now and I'll show you another piece of evidence that verifies what I said two sections back.

Near the end of June 1968 there were thoughts in my mind of starting a university degree course in September 1968. This came about because my draughtsman job had recently finished, the company I worked for had closed it's Cardiff office, I was out of a job in other words. I had also just sat the ONC (Ordinary National Certificate) examinations at Llandaff Technical College and an ONC was known to be an entrance qualification for a university course (it was equivalent to A level standard). Since starting with AEI (Associated Electrical Industries) in 1964 as a trainee draughtsman I had been studying one day a week and evenings at Llandaff on stages that led up to the ONC examination (AEI management being good enough to give me a day a week off to go to Llandaff).

At the end of June 1968 I went for an interview at Cardiff university. Three months later however, in September, I found myself not enrolling on a university course but instead taking up a

77

new job at the Cardiff Royal Infirmary. And someone started at the same time as me who was about a year older than me, his name was J. McCarthy. We joined a small electronics department that had two people in it when we arrived.

Gx1, when he covertly fixed/arranged things, as you know, often attached a 'sign' to the events. Well here, near the end of September 1968, he gave a 'sign' and I've mentioned it, did you notice it? What was the name of the man who was at the high point of the US government's dirty commies publicity stuff in the 1945/56 period? Answer, McCarthy, Senator J. McCarthy to be more exact. And what do we see at the infirmary in September 1968? A person by the name of J. McCarthy starting at the same time as me. Let's hope no one is silly enough to say 'a coincidence'. Quite obviously this was a Gx1 'sign', and it said, 'I have stopped your progress in this society, stopped you going to university, because you are a commie'. Standard Senator McCarthy stuff. This piece of evidence tells you, without any doubt, that what I said two sections back is true, the people that ran this country, using their covert Group X type people, were stopping bright sons of workers from getting the best jobs. A university course, with a degree at the end of it, meant one of the "best jobs", so they made sure I didn't go to university.

What Gx1 did to me at Swansea and Cardiff universities in 1974/76 was presumably, as far as he was concerned, a continuation of the government's covert 'no degrees for commies' policy, coupled to his plan to murder my father (part completed) which I was getting in the way of.

The Commie Label

Gx1 labelled me a commie. What a load of rubbish. My saying this shouldn't surprise you one bit because you must have realised way back that Gx1, the labeller, was himself rubbish. At this stage in my life I had never even contemplated doing anything political, and exactly the same applied to my brother and to my 'worker' father and mother. In my life I have only ever voted once, and that was a few years on from this 1968 point, I voted to see what the process entailed, no other reason. And as far as I know my father and mother only voted once in their life, that was when one of my father's sisters was standing for the local council (as a ratepayer, a small party), they voted for her of course.

So it's obvious that Group X type people were keeping bright sons of workers down, labelling them commies, simply because they were the bright sons of workers. That's about as vile a government policy as you can get (which is why it was a covert directive).

My parents always stuck to earning an honest living and they were busy enough doing that thank you, they, like me, left the running of the society to those who were paid to run it. The assumption I made, and my parents would go along with this, was that whatever political party those who were running the society belonged to they would at least try to do their job properly and if they didn't they'd get thrown out. And the most important part of doing their job properly was to make sure that people competed fairly in life, i.e. no stealing/fraud for example in the race to get ahead.

As I've said my parents and I almost never voted at elections. More than half of the british population do not usually vote so our not voting can hardly be said to be negative or wrong. When it comes to a general election you might have, for example, one of the two main parties saying they'll have to increase income tax revenue by two per cent, and the other party saying they'll have to increase income tax revenue by four per cent. So what's the big deal? In just these few words do you get my line of thought? It's that whichever of the two main parties wins a general election the society continues in much the same way as it did before the election. In other words as there's very little difference between the main parties in the way they run or would run the country voting for one or the other is neither here nor there, which means that for me, and my parents, voting was unimportant/ unnecessary. The parties pick their candidates for an election so presumably all the candidates have an adequate ability to be an MP/councillor, and the people that do vote decide which candidates get the jobs, and that was/is okay with me.

More Anti-Commie Covert Directives

In 1965 I first had a car and I started to do my own car maintenance. Which means I had a particular interest in cars and I often read motoring articles in the press (I usually read a Sunday paper). I couldn't help but notice, looking at prices of new cars in their manufacturers adverts, that a russian car company by the name of Lada had new cars for sale that cost a lot less than any other new car on the market. I was perfectly happy with the british made car I had and had no ideas at all of buying a new car (brand new) so my noticing this was purely from an objective viewpoint of reading up on the motoring scene. Why weren't these astonishingly cheap new cars outselling their rivals by four to one? The answer could be seen in the write ups the Lada cars were getting in our press. Words like 'they are junk' were applied to them in all the write ups. But how could a brand new car that, like any other new car, had a guarantee and got you from A to B be "junk"? I considered the press write ups to be excessively critical of a make of car that quite obviously done the basics as well as any car. None of the motoring journalists made anything of the fact that new Ladas were close to half the price of any other new car on the market.

This junking of Lada cars by british journalists, completely ignoring the car's very big sales winner, it's price, they were about £500, the cheapest new car from any other manufacturer was £900, was, without doubt, a result of the government's 'dirty anything commie' covert directive. The government did not want any russian products doing well here. The policy was so effective that Lada stopped selling cars in this country years ago, probably in the seventies, because they couldn't sell any.

'How did the people that ran this country do this?' you say. Well no they didn't pay journalists money to rubbish new russian cars, that would be too obvious, too public, and when they want to do things they shouldn't really do (free trade and all that) they don't use the public route, they take up covert methods. Well actually one method used to get russian cars 'blacked' wasn't covert, it's just something that doesn't get talked about, as follows. All our mainline newspapers are owned by people who, whether they admit it or not, are government supporters, none of the newspapers are owned by anti-Britain owners are they? No of course not, the government wouldn't have it. Well every newspaper owner employs management staff who he knows will do the job the way he wants it done. The management then employ journalists who they know will write in a way they like, a way that fits company policy. So what we see in our newspapers is reports/articles that reflect their owners outlook on life. And the owners outlook on life in the sixties for example with regard to anything russian was (in line with government pr output) distinctly anti-Russia, 'dirty commies', hence we got russian cars written about as if they were dirty/junk.

Here's some more on the government's 'dirty commie' pr output, given out without question by the compliant media. In the sixties/seventies/eighties (and presumably the fifties) every newspaper report/article on Russia was full of the 'dirty secret police' and the 'dirty KGB'. Secret police and KGB (the russian security service) were always used as dirty words because of course doing so backed up the 'dirty commies' stuff. The terms have not though been seen in our press since the early 1990s, why? Well part of the answer is that in 1990 the russian government stopped using the term KGB and made it into two separate departments, the FSB and the SVR. Another part of the answer is that Russia, for their part, ended, or certainly downgraded, the Cold War in 1990/91 when they withdrew their armed forces from Eastern Europe. The british government offered no thanks for this but as I say they did it seems reduce the blatant anti-Russia pr in the british media (the terms FSB and SVR are rarely seen).

In 1945 a Communist political party in this country (it started up in

1920) had two members of parliament. However by 1950 they had no members of parliament and the party closed down in 1991. The party never made it in this country because the government was continually giving out dirty workers/commie pr stuff. And of course the Group X type people were doing their covert bit, ensuring that workers/commies got nowhere.

Because of the government's non-stop dirty commie pr output in these years (1945 to 1990s, but presumably it was also pushed out in the 1920s/30s) all british workers (I remind you that I mean manual workers) found themselves labelled as dirty commies even though most of them had no particular interest in politics. The term 'cowboy builders' (meaning rubbish builders) got regular usage in the press, presumably thought up or at least encouraged by the governments 'dirty commie' pr people, to 'tell' the public that building workers (along with all manual workers) were dirty.

My mother said to me (probably in the late 1960s), 'if anyone asks you what your father does don't say he's a plasterer or a building worker, say he's a builder'. I didn't really go along with what she said but I fully understood why she said it. She knew very well that plasterers and building workers had been placed into the dirty category (by the government's pr people). A builder was at least at the top in the building trade.

Fine old buildings have always been admired as such by many members of the public (civic buildings etc). Yet because of the government's dirty workers pr output through most of the 1900s the people who put these buildings up (or those that followed in their footsteps), building workers, got regarded by the public as if they were dirty. This in itself shows the idiocy of the government's dirty workers/ commies pr policy. Buildings, particularly the great natural stone buildings in this country, were put up by fine craftsmen, people who learnt their trade from their predecessors.

A few words here about the chinese. They have some sort of commie system of government in place, yes but the UK government (and US govt) never seemed to be bothered too much about dirtying chinese commies, which is not very surprising when you consider the fact that there are thousands of chinese restaurants and take aways in this country and they started up here over a hundred years ago. What, many of our people enjoy eating their food and we call them 'dirty'? No, the 'dirty commie' stuff has always been (beginning with the US government in 1919) aimed at the russian commies. There used to be no russian restaurants in this country by the way (as far as I know), which is what you'd expect with all the anti-Russia government pr that's been put out for decades. At the present time (2010) there are it seems one or two in London.

Who Issued the 'Keep Down the Bright Sons of Workers' Covert Directive?

I have used the phrase, "the people that ran this country" a number of times. I prefer to use this phrase instead of 'the government' when I'm talking about a nationally applied covert directive, as I am ('keep bright sons of workers down' etc), because it's more accurate. Covert directives are not the way the public face of government, MPs in parliament, run the country. Covert directives come from a source that is outside parliament.

Who are "the people that ran this country"? Well there is no doubt in the minds of the people who are in the armed forces and the police. It's the reigning monarch. All these people swear an oath of allegiance to the monarch when they start their jobs. And an oath of allegiance to someone is equivalent to saying, 'I will do as you say'.

And for now that will do. The monarch, with his/her advisors, runs the country, has the final say. You could perhaps say the advisors run the country most of the time. I say this because they probably make decisions on new policies or problems themselves and only forward details of a new policy or problem to the monarch when it's considered to be a major change in policy or a big problem. So the covert directive, 'keep down the bright sons of workers' was issued by these people. It was probably first issued in about 1919 and re-issued in 1945 and perhaps renewed every few years.

Two Gx1 Attempts to Murder Me in 1967/68

Four sections back I told you about some important evidence that Gx1 came out with in September 1968, the McCarthy/commie 'sign'. Let's now examine more closely, in this section and the following four sections, some events that led up to September 1968. These events are pieces in the jigsaw that I've known all along went into a particular area of it but until now, 2009, I'd been unable to fit them in. I have now fitted them in, as follows.

In 1967 my job with AEI was going fine. The record drawings I produced for them were good and I liked the days on site (one or two every three weeks), mostly in the west of England and the Midlands, and the occasional overnight stay in a hotel or guest house. For perhaps nine/twelve months after starting the job in 1964 our chief draughtsman had instructed us, me and the other two trainees that is, but then he gave us our own contracts to work on. This meant that I was given a location where our company was laying high voltage cable, I travelled there, usually on my own, to take measurements, then, back at the office, I produced the drawings that recorded where the cable was laid. So the record drawings I produced were very much my own work.

In June/August 1967 an odd occurrence took place at Llandaff Technical College. In June I sat the examinations for an ONC in electrical and electronic engineering (my previous one day a week years at the college had been stages building up to this). In August the result came out, I was failed, which meant I'd have to repeat the year. I was surprised, I thought I was okay, anyway I accepted it thinking I'd gone wrong in some calculations. I repeated the year, sat the examinations again in June 1968, and this time I passed.

I now know that in 1967 AEI management (our area manager) and some staff at Llandaff Tech wanted me to go to university to get a degree. They knew however that I wouldn't leave my job to go on a full time university course (in those days a degree could only be obtained by full time study) because it was obvious that me and the job were getting on very well indeed, I liked the job. So, believe it or not, but this definitely looks to be the case (I'll give you the evidence), they arranged between themselves to get me to apply for a university place, and this meant that AEI said they'd put me out of the job by closing their Cardiff office, and they'd do this at about the same time as I sat and passed the ONC examination. Out of a job with an ONC meant my applying for university would be on. In about April/May 1967, when AEI and Llandaff Tech decided on these things, there wasn't enough time for AEI to arrange for the closing of it's Cardiff office by September 1967, university enrolment time, but they could do it in the first few months of 1968. So the gaining of the ONC was postponed by Llandaff Tech to coincide with the office closure. The ONC postponement meant failing me in 1967 and passing me in 1968, it appears therefore that Llandaff Tech falsely failed me in 1967, but they did so with the best possible motive in mind.

[I'll give you more on my situation with AEI. When I was doing the AEI job I just got on with it, I mean I liked the work and thought no more of it, it's only now, looking at those years more closely, that it's quite easy to see things that appear to support my statement that AEI management wanted me to go to university (something I've only fully realised in the past year or so). As follows.] As I've previously told you, soon after my seventeenth birthday I passed my driving test, and not long after this our chief draughtsman told me I could use a Morris Traveller (that our company had as a sort of spare vehicle) to travel to sites. I used the car when I went to sites in the Midlands. Neither of the other two trainee draughtsmen, nor another trainee that joined us in 1965, could drive. This, my being the only trainee able to drive, is a small point but it illustrates that I was especially useful to our chief draughtsman. And I'll tell you about the engineer who worked for the

CEGB (Central Electricity Generating Board), he was in charge of a contract I worked on for some time near Bristol. In the course of my work I didn't have anything to do with CEGB engineers, the site engineers I liaised with were our company's site engineers, but this CEGB engineer seemed for some reason to think something of me. One day when I was leaving the site, walking from it (I used the train through the Severn estuary tunnel and then the bus to get here, there was no Severn road bridge at the time), he stopped in his car and gave me a lift to where I could get the bus into Bristol. And then a few months later at our company's annual dinner-dance in November 1966 he had a talk with me.

Now why would this 'high up' CEGB engineer concern himself with me, an eighteen year old trainee draughtsman? Well perhaps he'd seen some of my record drawings and had said something about them when in a meeting with our area manager. And words like, 'where is his career going', passed between them. And, 'university', got mentioned. These words figure because eight months on from the 1966 dinner-dance the first part of the AEI/Llandaff plan to get me into university in 1968 took place (the 'ONC delay by a year result').

In 1967 Gx1 was in on (had been told about) the university plan that AEI/Llandaff had for me, and he didn't like it one bit. Me get a degree? As far as he was concerned that wasn't going to happen. His plans, which he'd made some years earlier, were, as you know, 'ship him out of the country, one way, in a few years time', me that is, and for my father it was, 'he'll be dead in a few years time', murder. He however had to appear as if he accepted the AEI/Llandaff plan (as decent people would). He of course couldn't say anything to AEI/Llandaff about the plan to murder my father or the 'no top jobs, no degrees, for workers/commies' policy that he'd apparently been covertly implementing for years.

How then was Gx1 going to stop the AEI/Llandaff plan, how was he going to ensure his plans took precedence? In September 1967 he tried to kill me (I'll refer to this as the LK hit), yes murder me if you prefer to call it that, for that's what intentional killing is. Quite simply if I was dead I wouldn't go to university and he could get on with the plan to murder my father. Why haven't I told you this before? Well in 1967 I didn't know anyone was trying to kill me, it's only in recent weeks that I've become quite sure that Gx1 was out to kill me here. Had he succeeded in this September 1967 hit my death would have been classified as an accident. This LK hit was in other words another one of his planned accidents.

I've told you before that the last thing Gx1 would do is take part personally in his hit plans, he always got other people to 'act as instructed', the Mafia routine remember. But killing me by direct means (poisoning for example) in September 1967 was too difficult for him to arrange, he knew he couldn't get it authorised/passed (he used covert official channels to get

84

things done). Which is why he could only go for one of the planned accident hits and hope for the best, hope that the result of the 'accident' was me dead. But it didn't come off, I lived through it without knowing that anyone was trying to kill me. So he found himself still stuck with the problem of stopping the AEI/Llandaff plan.

In the fourth edition of TCF I said Group X placed a 'sign' in 1967 that indicated a death, my death, was imminent. I was a bit out on my date of their placing the 'sign'. The 'sign' was Mr Summers, a new draughtsman they arranged to start alongside me in our office. In the fourth edition I said he started in October/November 1967 but I now believe that to be wrong, he started in June/July 1967. I say this because I recall that on one occasion our chief draughtsman sent me (on my own as usual) to take some measurements at a contract/site he, Mr Summers, had been given to cover, it was in Bath. And on this day it was sunny and warm, so it was probably August, and this would fit in with his being away from work, holiday time. Mr Summers was placed into the job by Gx1 as one of his 'signs' because Summers was the name of a Cardiff funeral home and his presence 'said' that soon I'd be dead. Someone might say, 'just a coincidence that Mr Summers started in your office two/three months before Gx1 tried to kill you'. Let me answer that by saying in 1969 Gx1 used another Cardiff funeral home to 'indicate' what he was going to do (PGN). One funeral home name, perhaps a coincidence, two funeral home names, no coincidence, it was the way he did things, he often placed secret signs into his activities. And besides when the September 1967 planned accident didn't result in my death he used Mr Summers again in April 1968, to 'say' that I'd soon be in a funeral home in Jersey. I will now tell you about what happened in Jersey and the Summers connection.

By February 1968 Gx1 had formed new plans for stopping the AEI/Llandaff university plan. This time he was going to do two things, one of these was, as I've said, another planned accident that was meant to result in me dead, the other was the smear/dirty routine. He added the second because he knew my death by the planned accident was not a certainty, it could fail again, so the smear/dirty routine was put in place to be used if necessary. This new planned accident, the BD hit, was another failure, it did not kill me and so he used the smear/dirt to get my September 1968 university entrance stopped.

[The BD hit took place in August 1968. I was on holiday in Jersey, let's just say Gx1 knew about this because he arranged it, got me to go on it.] I was with a friend of mine from Cardiff, he'd played in the Llandaff Tech rugby team. I was given some information on a place in one of the bays where it was possible to try underwater swimming with an aqualung. We went there and in a wooden shack met someone who was on his own, he was only a couple of years older than us (I was

85

twenty). Yes he could take us on a dive. We changed, picked up the gear and walked to the water. There was almost no one on the beach, it was the end of August and it was a grey cloudy morning. We each put on an aqualung, weight belt, mask and flippers. And went into the sea. I thought it was easy, I was gliding through the water ten/twenty feet below the surface and quite enjoying the new experience. It got deeper as I swam away from the beach. I carried on like this for a minute or so and then looked around for the other two. I didn't see either of them. Well no matter, I was doing fine, and I carried on.

After a few more minutes, I was about twenty feet below the surface, I began to have difficulty drawing air from the aqualung and within seconds I couldn't get any air from it. I immediately headed up and found that as I ascended I could get some air, a small amount, from the aqualung, which means I took no water in, when I reached the surface I removed the mouthpiece and got air from above the water. But I was having trouble keeping my head above the water, the gear I was wearing was pulling me down.

I was now heading back toward the beach, making strenuous efforts, kicking strongly, to stay at the surface, if I stopped kicking I'd sink. I knew I was in serious difficulty but I didn't panic. When I got into my depth I was safe. As I looked at the beach I could see the other two near the shack, they were walking back to it. 'But how about me?' I thought. I joined them at the shack, neither of them seemed at all concerned about what had happened. I just left it at that, well I was okay.

The person who took us on the dive was useless. Gx1 made sure he was running the dive business on his own when we got there. And he presumably got him fed with, 'just look after the tall one, don't bother about the other one'. My friend was about six foot, I'm five foot ten. When we put the gear on no instructions at all were given to us, such as, 'if you get into difficulty you can unbuckle the weight belt and drop it'. Presumably he'd asked us if we'd dived before, we would have said no. We were in fact totally inept when it came to knowing about the equipment and how to use it. When I got into difficulty it didn't even occur to me to unbuckle the weight belt and drop it, as far as I was concerned I had to take all the gear back with me. I could also have taken the air cylinder off my back and dumped that but again this did not occur to me. An air cylinder is buoyant when containing air (hence the necessity for a weight belt), but when there's no air left in it it sinks.

The average single air tank holds enough air for about a half hours dive. Well my air supply stopped after no more than say eight minutes. Had Gx1 made sure the cylinders, or at least the one I was given, were only partly filled? Presumably he thought that when my air ran out I'd panic, stay where I was and take water in, death in a couple of minutes. Or that if I did reach the surface I wouldn't be able to stay there with the weights pulling me down and that my efforts to stay up would exhaust me and I'd eventually start taking water in and die in minutes. Either way it would have been a successful planned accident for him, 'death by accident due to inexperience'.

A bit of explanation here. There is a small device between the aqualung and the mouthpiece that, whilst maintaining the air in the cylinder at high pressure outputs air to the mouthpiece, when the diver draws air, at a pressure that equates to the pressure around him. At a depth of twenty feet the device couldn't give me more air because the pressure of the air that was left in the cylinder was not enough to match the pressure surrounding me. As I ascended the pressure surrounding me decreased and the device could therefore give out the last of the air that was in the cylinder.

[Back to Gx1 and his Summers 'sign'.] **In the days before our Cardiff office closed our chief draughtsman said something that surprised me. There might be or there was a draughtsman's job with AEI going in Jersey and our Mr Summers would get it. It surprised me because Mr Summers had only joined us within the past year. If there was a job going somewhere surely it should first have been offered to one of us in the drawing office who had been with the company a lot longer than he had. But I said nothing.** [This was Gx1 'saying' the funeral he had planned would be in Jersey, i.e. the death, my death, would be in Jersey.]

There is more that connects Gx1 and Jersey. Have a guess where he went on holiday every year? Answer, Jersey.

Two Years Prior to Sept 1968 (1)

Let me now return to the first of the two 1967/68 attempts to kill me, the LK hit. When I thought about the LK hit in the eighties (when I was looking closely at what had happened in earlier years) I couldn't place an exact date on it, did it take place in September 1966, '67, '68, or '69? I wasn't sure (except that I knew it was in September), it was an odd occurrence yes but did Gx1 arrange it hoping I'd end up dead? Perhaps, perhaps not. It's only this year, 2009, that I've been able to put a date on it and form an explanation for why it happened, fit it into the jigsaw. And yes it was a Gx1 attempt to kill me, and the reason he arranged it has been given to you above, it was to stop the AEI/Llandaff university plan and to make sure that his plans stayed intact, at least keep the plan to murder my father intact, I wouldn't be around to transport to Australia but he wasn't too bothered about that, stopping me get a degree and murdering my father were more important than shipping me to Australia.

A few small points here. Gx1's LK hit couldn't have been in September 1968 for two reasons. The first is that in Sept 1968 he had recently smashed the AEI/Llandaff university plan (by using smear methods) so it wasn't necessary to kill me then, I was firmly back on the 'ship to Australia' route (without a degree). The second is that when the LK hit took place I did not have the lower part of my left leg encased in plaster, which I did in Sept 1968. So the LK hit did not take place in Sept 1968. As for Sept 1966 well at this time Gx1 had me on the 'ship to Australia' route and there was nothing troubling him, so there was no need for him to kill me then. The same applies to Sept 1969, I was on the ship out route, he'd flattened the AEI/Llandaff plan a year earlier, so there was no need to kill me then either. It was the shock he got when he first heard about the AEI/Llandaff plans in early 1967 that jolted then into action and his immediate response was to plan to kill me in the coming months, i.e. the September 1967 LK hit (an attempt to kill me using the 'accident' method).

Before now I did not really think AEI had closed their Cardiff office to get me to go on a full time university course, so I hadn't looked closely at these pieces in the jigsaw to see if they would fit together. My understanding had been that a few hundred people across the country employed by AEI lost their jobs when the company reorganised the business in 1968, and surely this hadn't happened simply in order to close the Cardiff office. But for the pieces in this area to fit together this is what happened, as I said, "believe it or not". Perhaps I was mistaken and only a few tens of people across the country lost their jobs, or perhaps a restructuring had long been planned and our area manager knew about it and decided to close the Cardiff office as part of it. Our Cardiff office only numbered about thirteen people so the act of closing the office, taken on it's own, could not be called a big event, the area manager and his second in charge (both in the Cardiff office) would no doubt have moved to some other office in AEI's Cables and Lines Division. And the same applies to our chief draughtsman (I don't know what happened to him).

If we say that the office closure had nothing to do with me then these pieces I've talked about don't fit together, because it would mean AEI/Llandaff did not form a university plan for me in 1967. Then why Gx1s LK hit in Sept 1967? Why the installation of Summers, the funeral home, into the drawing office in the months before then? And why did he proceed in February 1968 with new plans for smearing/dirtying and killing me later that year (the BD hit)? As I say these pieces can only be explained, fitted in, when it is accepted that AEI/Llandaff formed and commenced a plan in 1967 that was meant to result in my going to university in 1968, and in Gx1's mind he had to stop that happening, and killing me would stop it (I've told you he was warped many times before now).

Two Years Prior to Sept 1968 (2)

[I'll give you something else that supports my statement that AEI and Llandaff had me on route for starting a university course in September 1968.] At the end of the 1967/68 rugby season our Llandaff Tech rugby club was going well. I was elected captain and we entered a team in a local seven-a-side competition in which I scored a try from inside our twenty five, but in a close game we didn't get past the first round. My father was present. The team had a good bit of enthusiasm in it and this meant we had early start plans for the next season.

College rugby usually starts when the lectures start, which is at the beginning of October, but we managed to get our team together as soon as the new season started, at the beginning of September '68. Our first game was on about 4th September. It was in the days before this first game when I met our college lecturer who arranged our fixtures. You would have expected him to look happy, I mean there was me, the new captain, getting things organised and we had a team ready to go into our first game of the season weeks before lectures started, an achievement in itself. But no, he did not seem to be happy, I didn't know why. I didn't ask him what was troubling him and he never told me. When I'd last seen him, some months earlier, he was fine.

I'll add a bit more. In the previous season, the season I started playing for Llandaff Tech, the team was, even in November (well into the season) having difficulty getting a full team together, more than once we had to play a game a couple of players short. By January though things were a lot better. This illustrates that in the space of one year the college rugby team had seen a vast improvement. So when I say our fixture lecturer should have been happy when I met him at the beginning of September that's exactly what I mean, he knew the team was in a much better state than it had been a year earlier. But no, as I said, he was unhappy about something.

So what was troubling our fixture lecturer? The answer is now apparent from what I've said earlier. He did not expect to see me at the college. The college's plan was for me to be enrolling on a university course at this September time, and he was disappointed to see that I was not doing this. I think it's most unlikely that he knew much about why I wasn't starting a university course, all he'd probably been told was that some people higher up had decided I was not going to university.

[Another small but significant point has just come to mind.] One of my lecturers at Llandaff Tech wanted to meet me at a pub early one evening. We met and had a talk for ten minutes or so. I don't recall what we talked about, which means the conversation was about nothing in particular. Before this happened I'd never met a lecturer in a pub. [Now I can't be sure about the date this occurred but I would place it in the 1966/67 ONC year, the year I got the 'fail', the postponed pass result. What would explain this meeting? Answer, there was talk about my future amongst staff at the college, talk of me going to university after a one year postponement of the ONC pass, and this was their way of showing it. In other words the one year postponement, which the college put into practice, supports my statement that Llandaff Tech had plans for me to go on a full time university course.]

Two Years Prior to Sept 1968 (3)

[In this paragraph and the next I'll give you a few more details that support my statement that things were going well for me at AEI and Llandaff.] In September/October 1967 I organised a chess competition and a darts competition for the staff in our AEI Cardiff office, some of our site engineers, who called in to our offices occasionally, also took part. There was approximately sixteen people in the darts competition, perhaps twelve in the chess competition. I won both of them. And in our annual dinner dance, in about November 1967, our area manager selected me to sit on his table of eight. I didn't have a girlfriend at this time so just for the night I went with a girl who done clerical work with us. One of the other AEI employees on the table was our area's best cable jointer (with his wife), he was believed to be well paid (our company laid 132kv cables etc remember). At this time the thoughts in my mind were that nine months on from here I'd go from being a trainee draughtsman to being a draughtsman (with a pay rise), and that, because I appreciated the job, was okay with me.

In June 1968 at Llandaff Tech, with me having in recent months been elected captain of the rugby team, the college had an end of academic year dance that was attended by the principal of the college. He presented college ties to a number of students, and one of them went to me.

You could call these two occurrences, on the area manager's table and the principal's presentation, a fine ending to my years with AEI and Llandaff Tech. Both of them, apparently, thought it was a university degree course for me next.

And then along comes Gx1 with his warped mind and the 'butcher' meeting, which I've told you about (in TCF6 and 9). I said it was to 'tell me' he was going to 'butcher' my rugby at Llandaff Tech, yes, that's what he did, but it seems, from what I've told you, he was 'saying'

90

more than this, he was 'saying', 'I'm going to butcher your Llandaff rugby and the Llandaff/AEI university plan'.

Two Years Prior to Sept 1968 (4)

It was about February 1968 when we in the drawing office were told the office was closing in two months. [At this time and indeed in May 1968 I had no university ideas in my head, this is illustrated by the following.] My rugby at Llandaff Tech was going well and the season finished with me getting the captaincy. At this point I was encouraging the team to get together in late August ready for the start of the new season (weeks before lectures began at the start of October). I was out of work and thinking I'd find some job in the coming months and continue studying one day a week at the college in the autumn. Even if I didn't carry on with a part-time course at the college or couldn't find a job it wouldn't make any difference to my playing rugby for the college because the team was open to ex-students. A few words of explanation here. Llandaff Tech, as a guess, had about fifteen hundred part time students (three hundred each day of the week) and one hundred full time students. The rugby team comprised of about four full timers with the others being either part-timers, ex-students or friends. Which means I didn't have to be studying at the college in the autumn of 1968 for me to play for the team.

It was the end of June when I went for an interview at Cardiff university about my starting a degree course there in the autumn. [This has to be a little surprising, simply because I was keen on playing for Llandaff Tech when the new season started, and studying at Cardiff university would mean I'd play rugby there and not at Llandaff Tech. Well all I can say is that somehow, near the end of June, AEI/Llandaff must have got the idea of going for the university route given to me, and so that's what I did.]

But as we know by the start of September Gx1, using dirt activities, had blocked university and he had me lined up for an electronics technician job in the second half of September. Here is where the dirt that was Gx1 really shows up again. His blocking the university route was one thing, it illustrates his warped attitude to life (which he got from higher up), but that wasn't enough for him. Now, in the first two weeks of September, he stopped my Llandaff Tech rugby as well, by using a planned accident to put me on crutches for two months.

Gx1, in stopping me going to university, was following a covert directive, issued by the people who ran the country. How did Gx1's mind connect this to also stopping my rugby? The answer is linked to the plan to murder my father and the plan to ship me out. If I became too successful playing rugby it could interfere with or stop both of these plans. It's apparent that some lecturers at Llandaff Tech thought I should soon be playing for Cardiff RFC (the greyhound joke in effect tells us this), a season spent captaining the Llandaff Tech rugby team before heading for a Cardiff trial would have been a perfectly good route to take. In Gx1's mind he would have looked at it like this, 'if he has a season captaining Llandaff Tech that'll make his move to Cardiff even more definite, so hit his rugby now'.

Yes Gx1 was acting on a covert directive in stopping me go to university and shipping me out, did this same directive cover murdering workers and their sons, my father and me, and the carpenter's son (see later in this book)? Or were the murder plans Gx1 doing his own thing?

Gx1 Hits a Passenger Ship in 1972

As you know in June 1972 I went to Australia. I had a one way ticket from London to Perth. Travelling on a charter plane from Gatwick to Singapore and there it was straight from the airport to the dockside to get on a passenger ship for Perth. The ship, about 12,000 tons, with perhaps a hundred and fifty passengers, would take eight days to get to Perth. It was about the fourth day out when I awoke in the morning at 7am to find the ship in a permanent lean, it had rolled to one side with the decks at an angle of, well not that far off thirty degrees, say about twenty six degrees. I went up on deck (the shared cabin I was in was at sea level) and saw that the ship was continuing to travel onward in a calm sea.

We, the passengers, were told that during the night a main water tank in the lower parts of the ship had fractured/holed and it's contents had flooded out. Presumably the ship's water tank was situated to one side of the ship. The use of water was to be restricted, for example the showers were now out of action and would only be turned on for an hour in the evening.

The ship made a detour to the nearest port, Geraldton, Australia, two hundred and sixty miles north of Perth, where we docked, about one and a half days after the tank had holed. We were there for six hours taking on water. Then, with the ship back on an even keel, we sailed on to Perth.

How many ships does this happen to? Very, very few is the answer. Now did I just happen to be on the one voyage in 500,000 where the ship had a holed main water tank? No. This was Gx1 at work, it was an extension of his 'weigh him down on one side' joke that I've told you about, his 'put a bullet in his head' joke.

The question to ask is, was this a real 'bullet', a real attempt to kill me, along with hundreds of other people? When Gx1 planned this he had no way of knowing what the weather would be like at the time the ship was hit (by one of their hit men). There is no doubt that if the sea was rough the ship could capsize. Gx1, assuming he considered this capsize possibility at the planning stage, perhaps said to himself, 'it'll be a nice job if it does go over', and, 'if it's calm it might go over anyway'. So my answer to the question about killing me is yes it's possible that Gx1 hoped this would kill me. The fact that the hit man hit the ship in the early hours of the morning, when all the passengers were in bed, supports this, it was the prime time to cause a maximum number of deaths. Perhaps Gx1 knew I'd be on a sea level deck (with only a port hole) because I had the cheapest ticket, but whether he considered this or not isn't important because passengers in bed on any deck would be in big trouble if the ship started to capsize in darkness. With passengers, in bed and asleep, not realising what was happening till the boat was half way over. And when the ship reached the upside down on the surface position there would be no way out for them. Drowned by the incoming sea.

But let's check this. Did Gx1 plan this as a small extension of his 'weigh him down on one side' joke, with no one getting killed? Perhaps he told their hit man to hit the ship and it was the hit man's decision to do the job in the early hours because it was the only time he could do it with no one else around. But a severe list in a rough sea. That, surely they knew, could be a capsize. Did Gx1 tell the hit man not to do it if the wind was up and the sea rough? I don't know. But I do know that Gx1 had a warped mind and on this basis alone what I said in the last paragraph looks valid.

Sudbury Court Rugby Club to Wasps in 1971

[Here's more on what happened on the rugby scene in 1971 and 1972. Again the idea is to give you a better understanding of what was going on.] When I started the job at St Bartholomew's Hospital in March 1971 I moved into a fairly basic guest house in east London (Bart's being on that side of London). Within a month or so I found out that a friend of mine who had played for Llandaff Tech's rugby team had bought a flat in north west London. And around the end of April I moved to his place.

I'd been doing a one day a week course at Glamorgan Polytechnic before moving to London and so when I started at Bart's I straight-away joined a similar course at Central London Polytechnic. I played for their rugby club and at the end of the season played in their sevens team (I scored but we lost in the first round).

With the approach of a new rugby season ('71/72) my friend in the north west London flat reckoned we should join Sudbury Court rugby club, it was only a mile or so from our flat. And in August we started pre-season training with them. It was still a week or two before the season began when I changed from training with Sudbury Court to training with the nearby Wasps rugby club. My friend stayed at Sudbury Court.

[Let's look at this more closely. Why did I move from Sudbury Court to the Wasps?] I knew that my friend and I had played some good rugby in training games at Sudbury Court and it seemed to me that it would be of interest to see how I got on at the Wasps (one of the best teams in the country for those that don't know much about rugby). The fact that the Wasps ground, like Sudbury Court's, was close to our flat was a key consideration. Getting to and from training in the evenings was no problem. [Fine, those were my thoughts at the time, but I now know that it was our performance in training at Sudbury Court that got the inner minds of the club working. Two new players from Wales and one of them looked like he should play at a higher level. Excuse me speaking like this but I have to tell you the facts because there's no one else here to do it. One night after training I noticed a London Welsh player in the bar. The club had called him over to have a look at the new players. Anyway one way or the other the club evidently decided to push me to the nearby Wasps rugby club. Perhaps they realised, like I did, that the close proximity of the Wasps to where I lived was a big point in it's favour. London Welsh, in south west London, would have been a lot more awkward to get to, and from, for twice a week evening training.]

Now you already know that for the first game of the season I was selected to play in the Wasps second team. I'll tell you more about this. I made no mistakes in the game (no missed tackles, dropped balls, etc) and scored a decent try (a fairly straightforward run in from twenty five yards out). So for the next game, at Leicester, I was again selected for the second team. In this game I once again made no mistakes and put in an exceptional try saving tackle eight yards out which I'll tell you about. The Leicester second team was feeding the ball along their threequarter line from a lineout on the left of the field and I was of course paying particular attention to my opposite winger (I was on the right wing), it was him I had to blot out when the ball got to him. Their full back had come into the line between the outside centre and the wing and this meant that I now had an unmarked man with the ball just to the left of me heading for the try line. If I slowly moved to tackle him he would pass the ball to the wing and he'd have an unopposed short run to the try line. So what I did was to move toward my opposite wing, this encouraged the full back to hold on to the ball and go for the line (he was only ten yards out), as he did so I suddenly switched my direction and got to him before he had a chance to pass the ball, I made sure I brought him and the ball down. Other players caught up and we got the ball away, no try. Apart from this it was a quiet game for me, I only received one pass, from our scrum half from a lineout that was ten yards out from our line, I kicked the ball into touch.

[Let's examine something I've only briefly mentioned before now. The Leicester game and their team.] In the Leicester clubhouse before the game I looked at a noticeboard and saw their team for the game against us. The wing opposite me was, originally as selected, the England winger Keith Fielding. But his name had been crossed out and another name inserted next to it. [What was going on here? I ask the question knowing of course that Gx1 had plans for me and my father and he didn't want anything to get in the way. Bear in mind that Gx1 had known about my rugby potential for some years, he had already hit me a number of times to stop my progress in the game. He knew I was fast and a very good tackler. What if I played against the England winger and neutralized him, stopped him whenever he got the ball? Being an England winger the Leicester team would have tried to get the ball to him as much as possible. Answer, it would be rave reviews for me amongst the Wasps selection people and straight into the first team. And that would mean Gx1's plans for me would be smashed, well if not smashed he'd certainly have a lot more difficulty shipping me out of the country nine months on from here. So all this adds up to tell us what? That Gx1 made sure the England winger was taken out of the game before it started, to make sure I didn't get any rave reviews. This is very much the same sort of reason he had for hitting me in the Cardiff trial game, he knew without hitting me I would, or at least could, get selected to stay at the club and he wouldn't take the risk.]

Why was the England left wing going to play in the second team? Perhaps it was his first game of the season, having just come back from holiday, and the selectors wanted to give him an easy game.

As it was my try saving tackle on an 'ordinary' club player in this Leicester game, coupled to a faultless game, was enough to get me recommended for the Wasps first team. Especially since in the previous game (the first game of the season) I'd also made no mistakes and scored a try. It's obvious that Wasps wanted to play me in the first team or at the very least keep me in the second team (and not drop me) because for what other reason would Gx1 have gone to the trouble of arranging to get me into the Bart's stupid on call job a few weeks on from this game (the job that he used to stop my training)?

My social life in London was very quiet, I hardly went anywhere. The same applies to my rugby with the Wasps, we played the games and then went our own separate ways. There was just one occasion when one of our team got me to go to a party one night after a game. It was a sensible/quiet affair with not many people there. A girl I considered to be very attractive was present, Miss R, she was with a girlfriend. [I won't go into details here, I'll just tell you that a Wasps official arranged this night in the hope that I'd take up a relationship with Miss R, if I did the Wasps could use it as leverage to get the covert Gx1 block on my playing in the first/second teams removed. I met her a second time a week or so later but we didn't get a relationship started. Gx1 was I believe aware of what was going on and he used his dirt activities to ensure the relationship didn't materialise.]

Near the end of the '71/72 season Sudbury Court rugby club picked a special invitation team to play against a nearby town's side. The team contained a number of their present players together with former players and guest players some of whom were playing first team rugby for a first class club (such as the Wasps outside half). They selected me to play in the game. [I think the Sudbury Court people (officials and players) couldn't understand why I was only playing in the fourth team at the Wasps. They didn't know about Gx1 did they!]

What I said at the end of the last paragraph is perhaps a slightly incorrect assumption. It could be that Sudbury Court officials found out something about Gx1. Let's just suppose that a Sudbury Court official asked a Wasps official why I was only in their fourth team. Well if he'd spoken to a person who knew what was going on he would have got, 'someone in Cardiff has told us to keep him out of the first/second teams because there are other plans of some sort for him, we don't like doing it but ...'. I leave it to you to fill in the words.

Let's look at what could so easily have taken place in the 1971/72 rugby season if Gx1 had not been around. I could have stayed in the first/second team area at the Wasps. I could have had a very good relation-ship with a female (there was Miss L, the Bart's nurse, Miss R or Miss H, I tell you about Miss H in the 2017 chapter). And then, near the end of the season, there was the job with Hewlett Packard (they supplied a car with the job). The job would have been based at their offices west of London, about ten miles from the Wasps, which means I could have got to mid-week training. And perhaps I could have returned to my friends flat a half mile from the Wasps ground. Include Gx1 in the equation and you get all this obliterated, he stopped the lot.

What Gx1 done to me at the Wasps was a disaster for my rugby, but was it any worse than what he done to me at Cardiff RFC in 1969 (poisoned me prior to the trial game)? Or what he done to me at the start of the 1968/69 season (hit me, put me on crutches, to stop my rugby for some months because I was becoming too successful in the game)?

The following occurrences all indicate that I would have played for Cardiff in the 1969/70 season if Gx1 hadn't stopped it happening:

(i)   At Llandaff Tech there was is it seems two lecturers pushing me toward Cardiff rugby club.

(ii)   The fact that Gx1 found it necessary to hit me in the Cardiff trial game tells us he'd been told I'd probably be selected to stay at the club.

(iii)   The greyhound joke confirms what I say in (i) and (ii).

(iv)   At Sudbury Court the club pushed me to the Wasps rugby club.

(v)   At the Wasps the selectors wanted me to stay in the first/second team area.

(vi)   Gx1 arranging the 'on call' job for me at Bart's (to stop me training at the Wasps) confirms (v).

The last three paragraphs are, on their own, presumably enough to convince you that Gx1 was dirt.

[A few paragraphs back I gave you details of the two second team games I played for the Wasps before Gx1 got me stopped, put down. While I'm in this area I'll go over again, giving you a few more details this time, the one first team game I played for Penarth in 1969. And for people who don't know much about rugby I'll say that at this time Penarth were considered to be a first class club, they had an annual fixture with the Barbarians, one of the best teams in the country. Since then they have moved to a lower category. Back to where I was, the first team game I played for Penarth.] I've previously mentioned that I only received a pass once in the game and I put in an acceptable up and under, I was near the half way line when I kicked, the other side got to the ball first and made it safe. My opposing winger received the ball twice and on both occasions tried to run past me. The first time he was about thirty yards out and I brought him down as he went to one side of me. The second time was from a scrum that was about fifteen yards from the touchline and five yards from our line. Their scrum half got the ball and went to the blind side, to the winger who was opposite me. At this time the scoreline was level and there was only minutes to go and the other team, playing at home, were pressing hard to get the winning points. The scrum half passed to the winger and as he went for the line I tackled him. And we got the ball away. At the final whistle it was a draw. I hadn't made a single mistake in the game. And what happened next? I never again played for the first team. [We now know why of course. Time and time again crazy/odd occurrences point to Gx1 and his dirt activities. He made sure I was kept out of the first team from here on because he had plans to ship me out of the country and murder my father.]

Gx1's Plan to Murder My Father

Gx1 planned to murder my father. The murder plan was probably also known about by another Group X person, the "overweight man" at the butcher meeting. When Gx1 got my father hit in 1973 it was the first part of a two part plan to murder him. The hit was in the planned accident/natural causes category which means no foul play was suspected by my parents. The second part of Gx1's plan to murder my father was to kill him using a slow acting poison (over a period of weeks).

Let me give you a bit more detail here. The basis of the murder plan was really quite simple. Get my father into hospital (the UHW), by covertly knifing him, and arrange for him to be given a false diagnosis of cancer. The slow death using poison sometime after would then be questioned by no one. This was very much the way Gx1 did things, wherever possible he used quiet/surreptitious methods to get what he wanted. And what he wanted here was my mother free (no marriage ties with my father dead) and a fully paid for house in her name. An 'accidental'/'natural' death was infinitely better than a violent death, for example where someone kills a person by shooting him or using a knife. A violent death such as that would be more difficult for him to arrange to start with, in that getting someone to do it would not be easy, and such a death would bring with it a police investigation, okay his position meant he could ensure the investigation got nowhere but it could nevertheless give him a few small problems, so the openly violent method was to be avoided whenever possible.

I considered what happened to my father in 1973 to be very surprising to the extent that I had my doubts, 'was something odd going on?' My father was fit and healthy, his work kept him like that, cancer? Never. But what could I do about my views, tell the hospital staff? Well I knew what I'd get if I did ('there it is, you have to accept it'), so I said nothing. [It wasn't till two years later that I first became aware of Group X dirt activities (when I was sure they had got me stopped at Swansea university in 1975).]

The hospital operation meant my father had to spend months afterwards with long hours in bed recovering. My mother stopped work to look after him. Months later both my parents reached retirement age. My father returned to work in about 1975 for his old employer on a part time basis. My mother never returned to work.

My parents had a fifteen year mortgage on their house. The last payment had been made some months before my father had to stop work. [This meant he had no mortgage payment problems to contend with after he was hit. Now someone at the time might have said, 'well at least he had a bit of luck, having to stop work after he had finished the mortgage', yes it did seem that way, but this was just a part of Gx1 planning. When he had my father killed he wanted a fully paid for house passed on to my mother. If he'd hit him (put him out of work) whilst mortgage payments were ongoing it could have meant the house purchase would have fallen through with the result that there would be no house for him to pass on to my mother. All along, from when Gx1 first thought up the plan to kill my father, it had been, 'hit him when the house is paid for'.]

My father's mortgage was with the corporation. [The term "the corporation" is not used much these days. It's now usually called the local council, local government in other words. The Cardiff City Hall was their main office base in the 1960s and 1970s. Gx1 was an employee in the city hall, he knew all about the mortgage.]

What did Gx1 plan to do after he murdered my father? It could be:

(i)   He was going to marry his widow, after quietly getting rid of his wife (poison). Or

(ii)   A friend of Gx1 was to marry his widow, quietly murder her, then sell the house with the money being spilt two ways. Or

(iii)   Somehow ship his widow and me to Australia.

I was in a book club. They sent me a very low price book every month with details of other books they had on sale for that month, which were at a normal price. Two low price books they sent me in about 1976 were "Arigo, the Surgeon with the Rusty Knife" and "Dr Frigo". I kept them. [Around 1980, when I realised that my father had been hit by Group X in 1973, I interpreted these books to mean, 'the cancer diagnosis that wasn't' - the surgeon with the rusty knife. And, 'the person who was to give the kill poison at a later date' - the frigo/fridge doctor. The books were Gx1 signs', they 'advertised' what he had arranged to have done to my father. The rusty/dirty knife part of it would have been the small operation my father had first, the operation that gave a false diagnosis of cancer, he then had a second operation a week later to remove the so called 'cancerous area'.]

The final part of Gx1's plan to murder my father did not take place. Why? The answer is that too many things started to happen that, according to his plans, shouldn't have happened. First of all my one way ticket to Australia, where I was supposed to be living when he had my father covertly knifed, hadn't come off, I'd returned.

Soon after the knifing, he got me going with Miss D. He pushed hard for me to marry her because when I did this he could complete the plan to murder my father. And it seems he still had plans to ship me to Australia, with her when I married her.

His marriage plans were on track when he got me stopped at the end of his 'one year and out' arrangement at UCS in 1975, forcing me back to Cardiff and Miss D. But within days he saw his plans go into disarray, I had managed to continue my university study at Cardiff university (UCC). This

99

was a disaster for him. After his shocked initial attempts to get me off the UCC course came to nothing he found himself having to concentrate his efforts on me (getting me hit and feeding dirt/smear information into UCC). When I passed my end of academic year exams at UCC in June 1976 but was 'failed'/stopped (because of his dirt activities), he realised I had some UCC lecturers on my side, people who were against my being stopped who wanted my position improved in some way. And my father and his employer were starting to become more aware of what was going on ('why is he not on a course and out of a job?').

If I had not started at UCC I would had to have gone on to the pointless polytechnic course, and that was exactly what Gx1 wanted, me 'failed' at UCS, going nowhere in career terms, with Miss D pushed in front of me five days a week (the polytechnic was ten miles north west of Cardiff, Miss D's home six miles north of Cardiff, a three mile detour to her place). Gx1 knew I wasn't really interested in her but nevertheless he thought the regular journeys to the polytechnic would do the job of making the relationship permanent (marriage). By studying in Cardiff, and not at the polytechnic, my lack of interest in her could continue, and if that happened his marriage plans could fall through.

CN, who admitted me to the UCC course, together with my advisor of studies, made sure I stayed on it in spite of pressure from Gx1 to get me stopped that was applied openly within the confines of UCC (perhaps via UCS) about two weeks after I started. Bear in mind that it was at this time that Gx1 stopped my UCC rugby by getting an electron gun man to hit me (a planned accident/injury). CN and my advisor of studies have to be two of the best people I've ever met.

Gx1 was a warped official, he got covert government employees, or perhaps I should say government employees who do covert things, to do some terrible things over the years to us (me and my family). I also know that he hit five other people, using the planned accident (or natural occurrence) routine. I tell you about these later in the book (the carpenter's son, Mr HC, the lad in the 1973 car 'accident', the Cardiff RFC player and the musician).

In 1972/73 Gx1 Fixes a Rugby Team and Hits Me Again

In this section I tell you about the period immediately after my return from Australia in September 1972. Bear in mind that this was an important time for Gx1, he had for a number of years planned to hit my father in 1973 and the hit was now only months away. He had shipped me to Australia on a one way ticket in June 1972, I was supposed to stop there as far as he was concerned, out of the way, and I'd come back! And, worse still, in 1971 I'd played two games for the Wasps second team before he'd managed to stop/de-escalate things there. And so what was I going to do on the rugby front now? Cause him more trouble?

I'd only been back at the University Hospital of Wales electronics job a few days when someone told me the hospital was starting up a new rugby team, it was going to be called Cardiff Hospitals RFC (the UHW had in recent years become the main hospital for Cardiff but there were also a few older hospitals in the area). It was going to get fixtures with teams that were mostly in or near Cardiff. My playing for the new rugby team seemed the obvious thing to do.

A week or so after the first game it was decided, by whoever ran the team, that the team's home ground was going to be in a mental hospital in Cardiff. There was a field in the grounds of the mental hospital and posts would soon be put up and a pitch marked out. When this was done we changed and showered in the mental hospital and played on the nearby pitch.

Have you ever heard of a rugby team with it's ground in a mental hospital? This was a result of Gx1 influence. He was doing a dirty/smear job on the team, rubbishing it. In earlier years he'd hit my rugby many times to make sure I stayed on the 'ship him out' route, now he was again worried about my rugby, it could interfere with the plan to hit my father in 1973.

There is no doubt that the new rugby team was started up because I had returned to Cardiff. I'll explain why I say this. Who started up the team? There are two possible answers.

(i) In the past I had played rugby a few times with Miss N's brother and he was a doctor in Cardiff hospitals. He had, I will assume, been told about my playing at the Wasps (I phoned Miss N when I'd just played a second team game for them). He could have started the team up on the basis that he thought it would be a step toward my playing for Cardiff RFC.

(ii) Gx1 used his influence to start the team. He had for years known that I could be, should be, playing for Cardiff RFC. My return to Cardiff meant I could again go to Cardiff RFC, so before this happened he got in first with the new team. My playing for Cardiff RFC in the months prior to having my father hit was far too much for him to take. Killing the father of someone who was playing for Cardiff RFC was more difficult for him to arrange (he might not get it passed). So he brought in the new team to stop me going to Cardiff RFC.

If Miss N's brother got the team started up then it means Gx1 stepped in within days with his 'dirty the team' plans. The team's first game was played at home on a parks pitch (pitches run by the local council) and I'm quite sure the team would have continued to use a parks pitch for it's home ground if Gx1 hadn't fixed things (made it move to the mental hospital pitch). If Gx1 got the team started up it follows that the mental hospital pitch was part of his start up plan.

101

There was a very odd occurrence that took place during a game I played for Cardiff Hospitals in this 72/73 season, it was about March '73. I was on the left wing. There was some loose play, a number of forwards from both sides were involved, about fifteen yards out from our line in the centre of the pitch. The other side got the ball and it was passed to their right wing, the player I had to mark. He went to run outside me, he was still two yards away in front of me and I was slowly turning to my left as he went that way (I hadn't started running yet, I'd tackle him from the side as he went past) when I got a sharp pain in the upper part of my left leg which immediately made me stop, he continued to the line and scored. It was very much like having a 240 volt electric wire touch my leg. After the sharp pain, the shock, there was no pain in my leg, it was okay, I was okay, and I carried on playing with no injury stoppage.

No winger ever got round me on the outside, I was fast enough to get to all of them and bring them down, this was known by various people and Gx1, it was one of the reasons why "various people" had, in earlier years, lined me up for Cardiff RFC. What appears to have happened here in this shock incident is that a Cardiff RFC selector had been invited by one of our team to watch me at this game, a good game for me meant I'd be asked to play a game for them. Gx1 knew about this and made sure I didn't have a good game. When it mattered one of his hit men put a stop on my movements. I was made to look hopeless. How was this done? I answer this by saying an electron gun, or something similar like a laser gun was used. The hit man was standing on the touchline on my side of the field and he fired the electron/laser beam at me at the appropriate time.

The game was against Cardiff High School Old Boys, on their ground. Could you see a Cardiff RFC selector being invited to our ground?

So I didn't get asked to play for Cardiff. Gx1 was pleased, he could now get on with the plan to hit my father a few months on from here.

The Gx1 October 1975 Electron 'Bullet'

This section connects to the last section in that Gx1 appears to have used the same method to hit me here.

I had, just to remind you, about two weeks before this October 1975 hit, started at UCC. My studying at UCC was, according to Gx1 plans, not supposed to happen. Playing rugby for the college, with the UW included (I'd repeatedly flattened a UW winger in a training game), and then it could be Cardiff RFC, were awful thoughts in his mind, if these things happened he would probably have the final part of the plan to murder my father blocked. So once again he was desperate to stop my progress in rugby.

[Gx1 hit me in the first game I played for the UCC first team (the second game of the season) as follows.] The game was away against a team in Cheltenham. I had just been involved in tackling someone and I was on the ground sitting up, about to get up, when I suddenly got a severe but brief pain in my chest for no apparent reason, I mean I hadn't been kicked or hit in the chest. I got up, the pain had gone, and I carried on playing.

When we got back to Cardiff I went to the infirmary's accident department and saw a doctor. There was no bruising and no pain in my chest, there was just a bit of soreness in one small area. I thought I'd go for a check anyway. After an x-ray he said there was no bone damage but that I should not play for three months.

Gx1 had got what he wanted, he'd stopped my rugby. Someone on the touchline had fired an electron/laser bullet at me. And he had the doctor ready for my arrival with the 'stop rugby' words. You might say, 'but what if you hadn't gone to the hospital?' I can answer this by saying he would have done the same, got me hit me in the chest, in the next game, and kept hitting me till I went to hospital, or perhaps he'd have got me poisoned (to lay me up for a few weeks), he'd have stopped my rugby somehow, in his warped mind he had to stop my rugby.

Another 1975 to 66 'Sign'

In the third edition of "The Cathays Files" I first explained to you how the forgery at Swansea university (UCS) in May/June 1975 produced Group X's 66 'sign'. In the 'sign' was Gx1's reason for arranging the forgery (TCF9 page 152, TCF6 page 225), it was to 'say' he had me on route for marrying Miss D, she lived at a 66, and that meant me out of Swansea and back to Cardiff. There is another 66 'sign' I can tell you about.

In September 1975 I sat the re-sit exam for Pure Mathematics at UCS. A day or two later I was told about a very good car that was on sale at a very cheap price at a car repair place in Swansea. I went to have a look at it. There was good sales talk and a test drive (the garage bloke drove) and I bought it. The car was a Sprint 2600 (made by Alfa Romeo).

This car purchase was arranged by Gx1 to give a 'sign' that said, 'sprint 26', which is 'sprint 66'. Meaning run fast to 66, to Miss D. He was the car signs 'expert' (his boot number plate visit in 1969 and other car related 'signs'). Well working backwards from this sprint 26 'sign' it follows that he was the one who thought up and arranged the 'sign' that matched it, the forgery 66 'sign' that appeared three months earlier. Which reinforces what I said in previous editions, that it was probably Gx1 that thought up the forgery plans. His influential position, his secret position, enabled him to get the forged question papers dished out to me in the two part examination. He was it seems the director in a criminal conspiracy with staff at UCS to make and use forged documents that involved three people, himself and the two lecturers, four people if it was another person in UCS that made the forged documents (and not one of the lecturers), five if he got a person in the college administration offices to arrange all of it.

I found out later that the bodywork of the car was in very poor condition. And I had problems with the engine. It was off the road for most of the time. I got rid of it, for nothing, in 1978.

More on the Gx1 1976 Taxi Poisoning

At this time, February/March '76, I was on the Cardiff university course. Gx1 had been told by staff at the college that I was doing okay, which meant it looked like I'd be proceeding to the next year of the course in September 1976. This was contrary to his plans and he was working overtime on getting me off the course, the taxi poisoning was part of this. Details in TCF6 pages 235/6 and TCF9 pages 161/2.

A week or so before this poisoning took place I saw the barrister who was Miss D's Group X member's friend. I hadn't seen him since 1973. He was in a pub I was in near UCC. We didn't say hello. A month earlier I'd finished with Miss D. In the weeks after I was poisoned I thought to myself that the barrister could have been in the pub to point me out to the bloke who was to poison me.

Gx1 as he often did when carrying out a hit, placed 'signs' into this poisoning. Both the name of the pub where I was poisoned and the place their hit man/support man got out of the taxi were the 'signs'. The name of the pub 'said' the poisoning was being carried out by the people who hit my father in 1973. Or to put it another way, Gx1, who hit my father, was 'saying' he was now poisoning me. He was poisoning me because I was troubling him on two counts, (i) my study, success, on the road to a degree, was interfering with the plan to murder my father (the final part of which he wanted to get done as soon as possible) and (ii) me, a worker, a commie in his mind, get a degree? No, he didn't want that to happen.

Yes Gx1 had, in the weeks before this hit, dished up a 'sign' that said he was intent on avenging Miss D (the Avenger taxi I drove), hitting me because I'd finished with her (the wonderful virgin remember), but this was only a 'front', the reason he fed into UCC that would help to get me stopped. The real reasons he had for getting me out of university were (i) and (ii) as stated in the last paragraph, but of course these were definitely not reasons for getting me stopped that he could input to the university.

Gx1 Attempts to Murder Me in 1977 on a Cross Country Walk

As I told you in The Cathays Files 9th edition page 168 I was on a long distance cross country walk in 1977 when I got a severe headache. Thinking about this now, when writing this chapter, it reminds me of what happened to a perfectly healthy lad aged about fifteen in 1969/70. He died, when walking near his home, of a brain haemorrhage. His father, a carpenter, worked for the same company my father was working with. Did the person who planned to have me poisoned on this 1977 walk, Gx1, have the same idea in mind? Yes he had succeeded in getting me stopped at university but some UCC staff were it seems pressing to get things put right for me, perhaps get me back into the college. One way of making sure this didn't happen would have been to kill me, using the planned accident routine of course, death by natural causes. And no doubt he was still hoping to clear the way for the final hit of my father, (me out of the way, no university problems, would clear the way).

There were a number of small groups on the walk, each group took it's own route to a mid-way checkpoint, then back to the start. The distance covered would be about fifteen miles. [The friend I sometimes went on training runs with was with me, Mr G, he wouldn't have poisoned me. A person I'd never met before, Mr Z, was with us, he done it. There was only the three of us in our group. What I tell you next is more detailed than what I said in TCF6 and 9 and it varies slightly, take this as the accurate description.]

Mr Z was aged about thirty eight and he was, so Mr G told me, a surgeon at the UHW.

We were about half way through the walk when I began to feel unwell. I decided to leave the other two and head toward a main road (I had a map and compass), my intention being to perhaps get a bus back to our starting point which was in a village.

It was when I was on my way to the main road that the severe headache hit me, it was no ordinary headache, it lasted about twenty minutes and for five minutes of this it was agonizing. I kept on walking, I actually thought 'if I stop, sit down or lay down I'll never get up'. It was that bad. By the time I got to the main road it had eased. I saw no buses and walked back to the village.

When I reached the village the headache had gone and I was feeling okay again. I went to the pub that was our return venue. On entering I saw Mr G and Mr Z along with some other people who had been on the walk. Mr Z looked as if he was amazed to see me. [Why was he amazed to see me? There is only one answer. He had poisoned me and thought I'd be laid out flat somewhere in the country, dead. At the time it did not occur to me that I had been poisoned.]

A poison intended to give me a brain haemorrhage makes sense from what I experienced. About a half hour after being given the poison it really got to work on me by causing a pressure build up in the blood supply to my head, the twenty minutes severe headache, this is when the haemorrhage should have occurred. But it didn't, probably for two reasons, (i) physically I'm well made which means that my body's natural ability to counter anything that shouldn't happen to it is no doubt better than the average persons (ii) I carried on walking through the intense pain period, this would have kept my blood flowing at a good rate with the result that the poison got diluted/neutralised quite quickly. If I'd sat down, rested, my blood flow would have slowed and given the poison more time to fracture blood vessels.

[It appears that Mr Z had a back up story in place, just in case one or two people made it known that they were extremely surprised that I had died a natural death as a result of a brain haemorrhage. He put the snake bite angle into the events.] **For a part of the walk, about forty yards, Mr Z led the way through dense undergrowth when he could easily have gone round it (I followed him).** [This it seems was to create the snake bite story. The walk was in open country, from a base level of about 900 feet to one or two hills at 2,000 feet, a lot of it flat, with short grass covering almost all of it. Perhaps the poison he gave me contained some snake venom so that if tests were made on me after my death the cause of death could have been placed there. Only one species of british snake is lethal and even then the death of a man or woman as a result of being bitten by it is a very rare occurrence.]

It's likely that Gx1 gave the surgeon the idea of the snake bite get out clause in order to help to get him to do it, i.e. 'I'll make sure no questions are asked but if some are here's your way out, so you're safe whatever happens'. It's possible but less likely that Mr Z thought up the get out clause himself.

An official version of events, if some questions had been asked, would say, 'on this occasion the snake bite had the excessive effect of a brain haemorrhage, which caused the death'.

A small point, there were no snake bite marks on my legs. You figure out how Gx1 would have covered this angle. And here's another thing to look at, the UHW, where Mr Z worked, had an animal house, where small animals were kept for the purpose of testing drugs. Did it contain Britain's poisonous snake? With the venom being used to poison me?

When in conversation in the pub I heard Mr Z say he enjoyed seeing army personnel suffering when he was in charge of them on training exercises/runs. [This remark could have been literally correct, with no inference/'sign' intended, but army connects to Miss D (via her name), which means he could have been 'saying' he had poisoned me because I'd finished with Miss D and she was suffering/heartbroken. Again he could have been fed this stuff by Gx1 in order to get him to do it, i.e.

'you will be doing the right thing because he has ruined a virgin's life'. Gx1 knew it was rubbish/crap of course but as you know he'd say anything to get what he wanted.]

There is no doubt that this 1977 poisoning was meant to kill me. Killing was quite obviously part of Gx1's activities, as seen in his 1967/68 attempts to kill me and the part completed plan to kill my father.

While I'm at this point I'll say that I'm quite sure the 1976 taxi poisoning was not meant to kill me. The intention was only to lay me up in bed for a few days, it was a sort of warning sign if you like 'saying' he, Gx1, was working on making sure my study at UCC would soon be stopped. And as for the 1979 poisoning in Spain, well again that was not meant to kill me, the kill was to take place from the high roof, the poison was to get me there in a rough condition.

Let me say a few more words about the lad who died in 1969/70. I met him once when me and my father did a small roof job on his parents house in Penarth. He was quiet and sensible. In 1969/70 I was with Penarth rugby club and Gx1 hit me to make sure I didn't play for their first team. Did he murder the lad as one of his 'signs'? A 'sign' that said he had 'put the poison in', dirtied me, at Penarth rugby club. With his thinking being, 'the lad is the son a carpenter, so he's a worker/commie, which means it's right for me to kill him'.

Another way of looking at what happened to the carpenter's son is to say that it is very, very rare for a healthy teenager to die of a brain haemorrhage. Was this a chance in 500,000? Or was it because Gx1 was in the vicinity? I know what I'd choose, without any doubt at all. Gx1 murdered him.

2011

The Oxford Trip in 1972

When I was working at St Bartholomew's hospital (1971/72) I applied for a job with an electronics company who were based at Slough, about ten miles west of where I used to live in north west London (near the Wasps ground). A few days before the interview for the job I phoned the ex-Bart's nurse I had been going out with for a short while three/four months earlier. [Miss P.] I hadn't seen her since she'd left London. She was now working in a hospital in Oxford, which was about thirty miles from Slough where I was to have the interview (I'd be driving). I arranged to meet her at about six o'clock on the day of the job interview.

I had the interview then drove to Oxford. She had told me I could go to her room in the hospital's nurses home. I went to her room and she was there. We stayed in her room for a while, she wanted to read to me from a book, I said okay. I listened to her for five minutes perhaps more. The book was "The Hobbit".

Let's stop immediately here. "The Hobbit"! There are a number of big words in the vocabulary that Gx1 used for me, and "hoppit" is definitely one of them (usually written as 'hop it'). It was hoppit for me in 1968 when he used the planned accident routine to stop my rugby. He put me on crutches with my lower left leg encased in plaster.

"Hoppit" has another meaning that is equally relevant to Gx1 activities. It means shove off, leave. That's exactly what he had been doing to my life for some years, arranging to ship me to Australia. And on this particular occasion, my meeting with Miss P, it was no doubt used to 'say', 'shove off, the relationship is going nowhere because you will soon be leaving the country'. I knew nothing about Gx1 plans to ship me to Australia, it wasn't until 1975 that I first became aware of Group X warped 'fix him' activities.

What happened on this Oxford trip yes tells us that Gx1 was stopping my relationship with Miss P, but more than that it reinforces what I said earlier in the book, that it was probably Gx1 that got her moved out of the Bart's job, to stop our relationship at that time.

This 'hoppit' meeting is more evidence that Gx1 was closely monitoring my life. Which in turn supports my statement earlier in the book that he almost certainly put the block on my getting the Hewlett Packard job (this interview I went to). An objective assessment states without any doubt that I should have got the job. I knew one of their field engineers (the job I was applying for) quite well, he had an ONC, I had an ONC. I knew their products, often having worked on them. And I had spent a week on a course with them at their factory three years earlier (I was employed at the UHW at the time, the hospital had bought a lot of their equipment).

Miss P was perhaps slightly too tall for me (she was about my height) but we got on with each other very well. Our conversation was always interesting. She was a genuine girl and knew nothing about outsiders stopping our relationship. But, someone says, 'if she wasn't a Gx1 'yes sir, no sir' girl how did he get her to read The Hobbit to you? How did he know you were going to see her?' There's no need to go into possible answers here, what matters right now is that there is no doubt that her reading The Hobbit was a result of Gx1 activities.

When she'd finished reading to me we drove to a pub for an hour or so for a drink. At about nine I took her back to the hospital and returned to London. This meeting with her in Oxford was the last time I saw her.

Gx1 used a very similar 'sign' routine in 1974 when he got Miss D to, no not read to me, but play the piano and sing a song to me, the song 'said' he was quietly killing my father and me. He also used books for 'signs' at other times, i.e. the frigo and rusty knife books (killing my father), and the cowboy books (Miss D for me, one year and out of Swansea).

A Job Stopped in Australia in 1972

Here's something that might interest the australian government with regard to what british Group X type people can and can't arrange in other countries.

As you know I went to Australia in June 1972 on a one way ticket with the intention of finding work to get the money for my return air fare three months later in September. For a while I had a job that was going okay, it was laying kerbing and paving slabs. It was a small two man business. One day they told me they were stopping work, not permanently, just temporarily. I didn't work for them again. What caused them to stop work? Petrol rationing. There was a strike at one or some petrol refineries in Australia and the government introduced petrol rationing. People had to get petrol coupons and use them to buy petrol, and they couldn't get the coupons to cover the amount of petrol they wanted.

Now again here is what would, for Gx1, have been a very satisfactory occurrence. He knew I'd spent what money I had on a one way ticket to Australia and he also knew I had the intention of returning to this country in September for my friends wedding. My returning was of course very much against his plans. Was Gx1 in luck here, the money I got from this job stopped by the strike, or did he arrange the strike? I leave it to you to decide. But I will add one or two things. In Britain, since 1945, there has never been a time when the government has had to introduce petrol rationing. Can the same be said about Australia, with the single exception being in 1973? I don't know. If the answer is yes it would indicate that the strike was arranged by Gx1.

There's also the Sydney poisoning to look at. I'll just briefly say that Gx1 got me poisoned when I was at a hotel in Sydney the night before my return flight to Britain to keep me off the flight. For details see page 143 of The Cathays Files 9th edition.

The North Wales Walk

This took place in about March 1973. Gx1 had, for some years now, lined up 1973 for carrying out the first part of the plan to murder my father. I'd returned to Cardiff from Australia in September 1972 and Gx1 was very unhappy about this, he'd shipped me there on a one way ticket. He was worried that, having played rugby at the Wasps in the 1971/72 season, I might continue playing by going to Cardiff RFC. "Worried" because he wanted to keep my profile low, that way it was easier for him to proceed with the plan to murder my father.

In the "2009/10" chapter, section "In 1972/73 Gx1 Fixes a Rugby Team and Hits Me Again", I told you about some of Gx1's activities in the 1972/73 rugby season. The North Wales walk is another one of them.

Mr E, who worked in the same part of the department I was in at the UHW wanted me to go on a trip with him to North Wales. Driving there (would take about three hours), camping out the night, going on a walk the following morning in the mountainous Snowdon area (3,500 feet) and then driving back the same day. I said okay.

Let's go straight to the point, Gx1 gave this walk idea to Mr E, there can be no doubt about it. It's the only time I went on any sort of walk with him, and I never went on walks in mountains. Mr E was a Gx1 'yes sir, no sir' man, he was as you know used by him on later dates. And the timing of the walk tells us it was a Gx1 arrangement. It took place when he was worried that I might go to Cardiff RFC. And what opportunity does a walk in a mountainous area present? In Gx1's mind it presented an opportunity for a fall, laying me up injured for months with a broken/sprained limb would help to stop me going to Cardiff RFC.

This 'fall trip' presumably took place in the weeks before the Cardiff

110

Hospitals rugby game that Gx1 knew was going to be used as a Cardiff RFC trial game for me (I don't have exact dates). Gx1 did not get his fall, though I was very close to it, which meant he had to find another way of stopping me proceeding to Cardiff RFC. And he did this, as stated earlier in the book, by getting an electron/laser gun man to fire at me, put a stop on my movements, make me look hopeless, at a crucial time in the hospitals game that was watched by a Cardiff selector. So I wasn't invited to Cardiff RFC. Gx1 had got what he wanted.

The Rugby Meeting in 1976

It was about April 1976, in the middle of my 1975/76 year at UCC, when this happened. One of the rugby team lads, the good outside half that I got on well with, found me in the college one morning and told me he wanted me to go to a rugby meeting at lunchtime. Apparently CN, who had a particular interest in the rugby team, had told him to get hold of some of the players. At the meeting about eight were present. CN, who didn't look happy, said the topic he wanted to bring up couldn't be discussed because there wasn't a quorum (enough people present to make a decision). The meeting finished, it wasn't re-arranged for a later date.

What we had here, I didn't know this at the time of course, was CN 'sending' a message to me. Quorum is close to queer (quor). Gx1 had fed 'he is queer' into the college as part of his efforts to get me stopped, and CN was 'telling' me this. I'd finished with Miss D a few months earlier in January and Gx1 was trying to use this fact to get me stopped, i.e. he fed into the college,. 'he's finished a relationship with a wonderful girl, she is very disappointed, stopping his study will push him back to her, he's queer'. Gx1 knew the 'wonderful girl' and 'he's queer' stuff was rubbish.

The Unemployment Figures are Going Up in 1976

This would be in May 1976. One weekday lunchtime I had walked into town and I was heading back to the college when I accidentally met Miss D. She was on her own and said her car was parked nearby and she'd give me a lift back to the college. This wasn't particularly useful to me because the college was only about six hundred yards away, anyway I said yes to the lift. She had recently bought a new car, it was about three years old and quite smart. In our drive of about three hundred yards we somehow got onto the topic of unemployment and as I got out of the car she was saying 'the unemployment figures are going up'.

This was a Gx1 covertly arranged meeting without any doubt. He had a couple of reasons for arranging it. He wanted me to see the new car, it was meant to impress me, encourage me to go back with her. He also built a 'sign' in here. The 'sign' was 'the unemployment figures are going up'. Let's say her mother told her to say this, acting on Gx1 instructions. This 'sign' was to 'say' I'd soon find myself unemployed, four months on from here, in September, when my university study would be stopped. Yes, at this time, May 1975, Gx1 had it seems done enough to get me stopped and he knew it, i.e. the college agreed, before any exams had been sat, that they would stop me, fail me, in the June exams.

I don't think Gx1 expected me to go back with her at the time of this meeting just because of the new car. The car was meant to be of use when the big push took place in September (when I'd be 'failed' and was expected to bounce to her).

[I'll give you a bit more that I can place in this section. It's Gx1 making use, again, of his 66 'sign'. By this time, April/May '76, he was getting some co-operation out of UCC.] One of the subjects I was doing was the Social Structure of Modern Britain. It was the weekly tutorial for the subject. A tutorial is where a small number of students who were doing the subject met in a room to discuss the recent lecture on the subject and generate some homework for it. The tutorials were chaired either by the subject's lecturer or more usually by a post graduate student. Well this tutorial I have referred to was chaired by a post graduate student. There were about six of us in the room. He set some homework, we should do an essay on a book and he gave us the titles of perhaps two books, we could choose the book to read and do the essay on. One of the books was 'Zen and the Art of Motorcycle Maintenance'. It sounded to me like a very odd book to read and do an essay on. Motorcycle maintenance? What did that have to do with the subject? I didn't look for the book and therefore didn't read it. I did the homework on the other book.

To this day I haven't read Zen and the Art of Motorcycle Maintenance but I've known for many years what it's about because I've seen it talked about in the press a couple of times. It's the story of a journey made by a man and his son on a motorbike across much of the USA. Most if not all of the journey was on Route 66.

Recently I've looked up a few more details on the book. It's not about motorcycle maintenance at all. It was published in 1974 and for some reason it sold in large numbers. And this is presumably how Gx1 got to hear about it. He knew it was a Route 66 book and therefore a 'sign' he could use. He had the book fed into UCC, i.e. told a contact to get it referred to in my presence. This would as far as he was concerned 'attach' 66 to me. It was going to be out of UCC and back to Miss D for me.

112

West Wales for Two Months in 1976

I've mentioned earlier in the book that in the summer of 1976 I was in west Wales for two months. Here's more on it. It could actually have been more like six/seven weeks but I'll continue to refer to it as two months.

For two or three weeks I worked on a farm. The farmer had a son who was about my age and he told me I could meet him and some friends of his at a pub one night (a Fri/Sat).

I turned up at the pub. There was a dance there and the farmer's son introduced me to a girl and I danced with her. It was just a few dances and conversation. She told me her name, I was surprised to hear that it was the same as Miss D (first name).

This 'same name' meeting was arranged by Gx1 of course to push Miss D to the front of my mind, when I got back to Cardiff it was Miss D for me. Gx1 knew where I was (what's new?) and he told the farmer to tell his son to introduce me to this girl. She was uncomfortable in my presence, a result of being told to give me a false name. It was the only time I went for a drink with the farmers son. I lived a very quiet life for the few weeks I was in west Wales.

In the last section I told you about Miss D's new car. It was brightly coloured in a sort of light blue. Well whilst I was in west Wales for these two months I saw perhaps four cars that were identical to it. [A coincidence or Gx1 at work? My answer is Gx1 at work. We know he used his influence to place cars and he was here using Miss D's new car as another way of pushing her in front of me. In readiness for the big push that was coming up soon.]

West Wales for two months, when I could stay in Cardiff at my parents house (the college flat, where I had been staying, was only available to mid-June). How interesting, why go to west Wales when I knew no one there? Do you know what the answer is? Gx1 used his influence/ connections to get me there. Why did he do this? What did I do in the previous year when I was in Swansea waiting to return to UCS? I went to Swansea rugby club for pre-season training. Gx1 was now, in 1976, worried that I might, whilst waiting to return to UCC, go to Cardiff rugby club for pre-season training. Shipping me to west Wales for the summer would ensure I didn't go to Cardiff rugby club.

Gx1 was, and had been for years, putting a block on my rugby, and my education in the form of a degree was also, as far as he was concerned, a no go area. He had given the green light however to Miss D, because he knew she was trouble. Did he consider her to be a way to killing me via the uncovering of her secret sex life?

113

The Gx1 1977 Cut Strap

In 1976 I bought a sailing dinghy, it was about eight years old. I hadn't done much sailing but it interested me. The first time I used it, in July '76 on a river in west Wales, the mast broke. [See the section "Gx1 Breaks the Mast of My Sailing Dinghy in 1976" later in this book.] I had insured the boat so I claimed on the insurance for a new mast. Getting the claim processed took months. It was about January 1977 when I knew I could have the money to buy a new mast. And then it was another long wait getting the mast made and delivered to a boat dealers in Cardiff from where I picked it up toward the end of 1977.

It was a dry grey winter's morning in Nov/Dec 1977 when I took my sailing dinghy to Llandegfedd reservoir (located twenty miles north east of Cardiff). I had Mr G as the crew, the second man. The reservoir is used for sailing and it has quite a few dinghies stored there in a dinghy park alongside the water.

There was no one around when we got the dinghy onto the water in a light breeze. In south Wales the wind more often than not is from the south west and this was the case on this day. The dinghy park was in a small bay on the south side of the reservoir and we sailed north west from the launch area alongside a low lying hill on our left which reduced the wind force on the surface of the water. This meant that we sailed quite slowly. After about a minute we got to the end of the hill, the headland, and the wind increased because it now had a clear blow in from the south west.

I put my feet under the foot strap so that when I steered more into the wind to increase the boat's speed I could lean backwards using my weight to control the tilt angle of the boat

As soon as I steered closer to the wind the tilt increased and I leaned back to decrease it. Suddenly the foot strap broke. Mr G didn't use the strap, he was sat further up the boat. I went backwards into the water and with my weight removed from the boat it immediately, from the force of the wind on the sail, capsized and within ten seconds it was completely upside down. I couldn't see Mr G so I shouted to him asking if he was okay, he could have been under the dinghy or on the other side of it. He replied saying 'I'm okay', he was on the other side. We were wearing buoyancy jackets so we had no problem staying afloat.

I had never been in a capsize with the boat before but obviously I knew what to do. Right it by putting my weight on the side of the boat and then as it rolled grab the centre board and pull that over. But my pressing down on the side of the dinghy had very little effect. It was a big dinghy with a large sail area and with the sail now under water it was acting as a drag on any righting movement. I tried this for a while and having realised it was no use knew I had to get up onto the hull to get hold of the centre board and pull it over. I was getting tired fast, the water was very cold and it was draining my energy. I managed to get out of the water and onto the hull and by pulling the centre board over I could see that slowly I was making the boat rotate and eventually the sail came to the surface. I was now stood on the centre board which was horizontal and the boat quickly flipped the last ninety degrees to the upright position. I got into the boat as it righted itself. I then helped Mr G climb into the boat.

I pulled the mainsail down because I didn't want to be blown over again. With the foot strap broke I knew I couldn't sail the boat properly. Before I'd thought about what to do next I saw a man about hundred and fifty yards away in a small outboard motor powered boat heading toward us. He had just motored out from behind the headland, the dinghy park was around there which was obviously where he'd come from. I was surprised to see this boat coming toward us because up to this point I hadn't seen anyone (apart from Mr G) at the reservoir. He towed us back to the dinghy park then left. There was still no one else around. We got the dinghy onto my trailer, attached it to my car and drove back to Cardiff.

That night I was thinking about what had happened. The foot strap had broken. What? But I'd fitted a new strap myself sometime earlier and it was in first class condition. The strap was about three inches wide by an eighth of an inch and it was made of a woven polyester type material. It was about three feet long and held at each end by a metal plate that was placed over the strap, screws went through the plate and the strap and into the boat. They were long screws and the wood at the bottom of the boat into which the screws went was solid and part of the main frame of the boat. I had sealed the ends of the strap by melting the polyester material, this means the ends were very hard and there was no chance of the strap's weaving un-raveling. The strap was immensely strong, you could probably hang 600lb or more on it, for it to break from what could have been no more than 30lb was an impossibility. So how had this solid foot strap broken?

The dinghy was in the garage at the back of my parents house. I had a close look at the strap and it's fittings. Both metal plates at the ends of the strap were firmly in place, fixed to the bottom of the boat. One end of the strap, the end that had broken away, had a straight clean end to it. It had been cut by a sharp knife right next to the metal plate. There was no doubt about it. The last three quarters of an inch or so of the strap was still under the metal plate. Someone had got at the boat to ensure that it capsized when I sailed it.

In more detail. The strap was cut right across it next to the metal plate, the plate was loosened by unscrewing it's two securing screws a few turns, and the cut end was placed under the plate, pushed up against the screws, and the screws were tightened. This would mean the end of the strap would be held by the plate but with only about a quarter of an inch of it under the plate and no screws going through it a 20lb pull would pull it out.

Doing the job in this way was better than another way of doing it, i.e. cut across the strap leaving a few strands uncut, so that the strap done it's job for a while but soon broke. This other way of doing it wasn't as good because if I'd happened to have glanced at the strap before the capsize I would have seen the partly cut end and stopped sailing. Whereas using the first method the cut end was hidden under the metal plate. It was evident that the first method had been used because as I've said the broken strap had a "straight clean end". The other way of doing it would have left the broken strap with a few loose stretched strands on the end of it.

Who had done it and why? I didn't know and thought no more about it.

Why didn't I think that Group X had arranged to get the strap cut? Because I thought they'd finished having a go at me. They'd achieved the most important part of what they wanted, me out of the two universities, failed, and that, I thought, was the end of it (their efforts to get me married to their Miss D hadn't come off).

In late 1977, when this dinghy capsize took place, I had not connected what had happened to my father in 1973 to what Group X had done to me in the universities. It was sometime later when I realised that Group X had hit my father in 1973 and that they planned to murder him.

Now however I know that Gx1 arranged the capsize. Why did he do it? Was it another attempt to kill me? The first answer here is yes basing it on the fact that in this same year, 1977, he tried to kill me on the Black Mountains cross country walk. The walk poisoning had failed so he tried this capsize kill method.

A person in very cold water can only survive for perhaps an hour, then it's death by hypothermia (the heart stops), the efforts I was making were rapidly draining my energy and presumably reducing this hour. Gx1 presumably thought I wouldn't be able to get the boat upright (see the next paragraph) which would mean my death by hypothermia in forty five minutes and Mr G's death soon after.

The dinghy was sixteen feet long had a big mainsail and a sizeable centre board, it was in other words a large dinghy and it was quite heavily constructed in wood. The fore and aft areas were covered over and the sides had buoyancy built into them (which made the sides fifteen inches or so wide). This explains why, when I tried pushing down the side of the boat when I was in the water, I had little effect on it, I was trying to push down a large buoyancy chamber. The only way to get a boat like that righted is to do what I eventually did, climb onto the hull and then with my feet/weight on top of a side buoyancy chamber, lift the other side of the dinghy up by pulling the centre board over. Gx1 perhaps thought I wouldn't climb onto the hull. I should have called Mr G, who was new to sailing, to my side of the boat to help me but somehow I didn't think of this.

Some of you might think that capsizing is a fairly regular occurrence with sailing dinghies, having seen them often capsized on inland water or on the coast, yes but the dinghies you've seen capsized would usually be small/light/medium sized dinghies that easily flip over and back up again. My dinghy was, as I've said, big and quite heavy and dinghies like that don't go over very often. I sailed the dinghy many times after this happened, on the sea as well as the reservoir, and I never capsized it. Big sailing dinghies are, with their large centre boards, slow to roll when the wind is coming from across the boat which gives the helmsman ample time to correct the roll if it becomes too much (by letting the mainsail out, or using the rudder to alter course, or moving his weight).

But there's a few questions to ask here. Gx1 had done his background work for this hit of course, he knew the reservoir was empty on a Sunday morning in winter, there would have been no point in doing it with other dinghies out on the water that could help us. The reservoir has a sailing club based there and every sailing club has a small rescue boat that's out on the water when the club has it's sessions. It seems the club has it's sessions on a Sunday afternoon in winter. When we arrived at the reservoir, it was probably about 11am, I saw no one. How come the man in the small outboard motor powered boat appeared when no one was expected to be out sailing? The boat he was in was I assume the sailing club's rescue boat because only dinghy sailing was allowed at the reservoir.

Let's first try and answer the question I've just asked by using the pure chance angle, i.e. the man in the small boat just happened to be at the reservoir and he had no connection with Gx1. As I said there was no one round when we launched our dinghy. Did he live in a house by the dinghy park? There are no houses in the area. The club sailing session started at 2pm, why was he there at 11-15am? If we say he was doing some work on a boat in the dinghy park and I didn't see him how did he know we had capsized when the place we capsized at couldn't be seen from the dinghy park, the low headland was in the way? So the pure chance angle does not produce a satisfactory answer for his appearance. Which means more questions have to be asked.

It appears to me that he was he acting on the instructions of Gx1. He was sitting in his boat watching and waiting for what he knew was going to happen, the capsize? By staying out of sight, watching my unsuccessful attempts to right the boat, all he had to do was let time take it's course with the result that before one hour was up I'd be dead by hypothermia, with Mr G perhaps also expected to die. If this is all he had to do then why did he watch and wait at all, his presence wasn't necessary? The answer here would be that Gx1 thought we could, having given up trying to right the boat, attempt to swim to the shore, and if we did this he was to move in, intercept us and make sure I finished up dead. How would he do this? Place his boat between me and Mr G, reach over to me first and push me underwater, keeping me down for a minute or more. My being halfway to death by hypothermia when he got to me meant I wouldn't have put up much of a fight. Mr G, unable to see what was going on, would be told he had difficulty getting me out of the water. End result my death by a combination of hypothermia and drowning, an 'accident'. It could be that Gx1 thought I might swim to shore on my own to get help and leave Mr G by the boat, which would make things easier for the hit man.

Someone reading this says, in response to what I said in the last paragraph, 'you've got it wrong, people don't do such terrible things, okay Gx1 had told the man in the boat what was going to happen, the capsize, but they also told him to make sure you were both okay, that is watch what happened and if we couldn't right the dinghy to come over to us after twenty minutes or so and pull us out of the water'. I reply with, 'you mean Gx1 went to all that trouble (getting someone to cut the strap and then getting this man out in the boat) just to find out if I could right the dinghy? What was the point of that?' No, this reader's theory doesn't make much sense. By far the most obvious reason for getting the strap cut was that he wanted me dead, something that's verified by the attempt to kill me earlier in the year, and the capsize was a way to do it by 'accident'.

At the time the rescue boat appeared I hadn't decided what to do. Presumably it would have occurred to me that we could pull the mainsail up a bit and use it to take us downwind (when running before the wind a dinghy doesn't roll to one side so the foot strap isn't used). The nearest shore of the reservoir was about hundred and fifty yards away but it wasn't downwind so we couldn't go that way, downwind the shore was about a mile away.

Why did the man in the boat, having seen the dinghy righted and both of us in it, motor out from behind the headland, proceed over to us and tow us in if he was part of the Gx1 hit? Yes a bit odd. Perhaps he said to himself, 'I can't kill one of them by accident now, so it's job off, if they sit there till 2pm, when the club members arrive, they'll get towed in, so I might as well do it now.'

I sold the dinghy in 1980 because I was short of money.

Gx1's Thinking in 1977

The motives Gx1 had for killing me in 1977 are as follows:

(i)   He made extensive efforts to get me off the degree course at UCC in 1975/76, he eventually succeeded, however some lecturers, knowing I'd passed the exams, wanted me back in the college to finish a degree. He did not want that to happen, my death would ensure it didn't happen. Bear in mind that in 1967/68 he tried twice to kill me (by 'accident') to stop me going to university in September 1968.

(ii)   Perhaps he was worried that one or two UCC lecturers could, or were, asking some questions at UCS about why I hadn't stayed there. He didn't want any noises made at UCS because he'd got staff at the college to give me forged/altered examination question papers when I was studying there, as part of his 'stop him' activities. My 'accidental' death would put an end to the subject.

(iii)   He didn't want my position enhanced in any way (like continuing at UCC to finish a degree) because he was in the middle of a part completed plan to murder my father. In fact you could say he wanted to have a go at me, kill me, for interrupting this plan. Perhaps with me out of the way he could get on with the second part of killing my father.

(iv)   He had tried hard to get me to marry his Miss D, knowing that she was trouble. I didn't marry her. The Miss D part of Group X would have wanted me dead because I had stopped the relationship, I'd disappointed her.

1977 to the 1980 Town Hall Electron 'Bullet'

Gx1 tried to kill me in 1977, and failed. He didn't try to kill me in 1978, why? At the start of 1978 I moved to a place fifteen miles west of Cardiff and this appears to have, let's say, placed me outside his area of control, or at least it was more difficult for him to arrange things for me when I was living there. I moved back to my parents house in Cardiff in mid-1978, which was good for him, but at the same time I formally started things happening at UCC by writing to their registrar about what had happened in 1976. This meant that killing me (by 'accident') from this point on would have looked suspicious, i.e. 'he wrote to UCC stating his case, complaining, and then he got killed'. Hence no Gx1 attempt to kill me in 1978, he just had to live with the fact that enquiries were now officially being made and he had to fend them off as best he could.

But then we arrive at another death by 'accident' arrangement in the form of what happened to me in Spain in 1979/80. It appears that whoever planned these events in Spain and then used their authority to get them carried out hoped for one of the following:

(i)   I'd die by a genuine suicide, helped along by the poison I was given beforehand and the guidance to the high roof.

(ii)   Someone was supposed to throw an un-suspecting me off the roof, with it being made out as 'suicide', and at the last minute it was called off.

Whichever applies it seems the suicide way of killing me got replaced in 1980 by, 'let him live but destroy the support UCC is giving him'. Hence the Swansea Town Hall meeting in October 1980 when an electron/laser beam, in effect like a metal bullet from a silenced gun when it first hit me, was used to 'kill' my UCC support in the 'under wraps' official enquiries.

I'll go over my "UCC support" again. The Prime Minister had apparently told Gx1 he could continue to run things. Some UCC staff, knowing I'd passed the exams in 1976, wanted me to return to the college to finish the course or get the merchant bank financial compensation job. If Gx1 told UCC that I could not do either of these things UCC would not have accepted it. So Gx1 arranged to covertly hit me at the town hall to ensure I lost the support of UCC. He then said to UCC, 'recently, when under pressure at a public meeting in Swansea Town Hall, he became struck dumb, collapsed, so it was right to stop his study, therefore he should not return to the college to complete the course or be given the financial compensation job'. UCC, knowing nothing about the covert government 'bullet' fired into me at the meeting accepted the position.

More on Spain in 1979/80

[Let's look at a few more things that happened on my 'holiday' in Spain.] As I said I got a hire car on arrival at Malaga airport. I stayed in Fuengirola, about eight miles away, for a few days then booked out of the hotel I was in and drove down the coast to Algeciras (about sixty miles), stopping a couple of times on route to have a look at places.

At a cafe in Algeciras a british bloke talked to me. I told him I was on a day trip drive and I'd soon, in an hour or so, be heading back to Malaga. He told me there was a good place to stay at if I wanted to break my return journey. It was about fifteen miles from Malaga and just off the main road, it was called the El Paraiso hotel.

I started back to Malaga. I decided to have a look at the place the bloke had talked about. It was a big, fairly new, upmarket hotel

120

located in countryside about a mile off the main road. I booked in for the night. The next day I left the place, drove to Torremolinos, a couple of miles from Malaga, booked in to a fairly basic hotel and returned the hire car to the airport.

Now what do we have here? Let me tell you. El Paraiso, it's quite easy to see that if we rearrange the letters we obtain the word paralise, usually spelt paralyse. This was the british officials, who were monitoring my presence in Spain, 'saying' that it was paralyse for me. I'd soon be dead.

[Continuing to look for Group X type 'signs' I find what definitely appears to have been another one here.] There was a noticeboard in the El Paraiso's reception area advertising a free buffet at lunchtime on the day after I arrived. I was only staying the one night but there was no pressure to vacate the room because the hotel, being the off season, was nearly empty. I went to it, about ten people were there. It was in a large sized room near the top of a tower block that was at the back of the hotel. The main hotel building, where the reception area was located, was a low level building. My room was in this low level building.

What does this free buffet remind us of? When I started at UCS in 1974 I saw a sign in the department I was in advertising a free coffee meeting for new students (in TCF6 and 9). Was this El Paraiso free buffet arranged with the intention of bringing the UCS free coffee meeting into the picture? I think it was. It was to 'say' that what happened at UCS was connected to the forthcoming 'paralyse'. I was right about what had happened at UCC and the authorities didn't want it to get into the public domain because it could bring out the UCS forgery. Gx1 could quite easily be identified as the cause of the UCC fraud and the UCS forgery because staff at both colleges knew he'd arranged, fixed, things, and that would go a long way to uncovering the part completed plan to murder my father.

Let me take you through a few points again here. My letter had gone to UCC in August 1978 about passing exams and being improperly stopped. UCC investigated what had happened to me and apparently (from this El Paraiso buffet) they also investigated, asked questions, at UCS about why I hadn't stayed there, and in this latter process they found out about the UCS examination irregularities. They then went to the Welsh Office with 'what shall we do about it?' My job with the Welsh Office in early 1979 illustrates that they were in on the situation. The Welsh Office did their own investigation and soon connected what had happened to me at the two universities to what had been done to my father. And they found out that it was Gx1 that had caused all of it. They put a stop on any ideas that Gx1 still had of completing the plan to murder my father. But, problem, Gx1 was a senior official.

The Welsh Office sent "the problem" to higher authorities. 'What is to be done about it?' they asked. The higher authorities was it seems the Prime Minister. My job in her constituency which I'd started in October 1979, a few months before the 'holiday' in Spain, illustrates that she knew about the situation. And the Queen could also have been involved here because she was named as the adjudicator for disputes in Welsh universities. The higher authorities were it seems still acting on Gx1 advice, allowing him to do what he wanted. The decision to paralyse me came from Gx1 or the higher authorities.

Someone says, 'the british officials who were monitoring you in Spain had to know about the UCS coffee meeting to be able to use it as a UCS 'indicator', how did they get to know about it?' Well SV took a big part in my year at UCS. And where did I first meet him? At the UCS free coffee meeting, where he entered the room, looked round, saw me and headed straight for me. He was one of the UCS 'fix it' people, he had been told to make sure I stuck to the 'one year and out' plan. And at the end of the academic year I believe SV was involved in the forged documents activities. The UCC investigation into what had happened at UCS would very soon have pin pointed SV and the free coffee meeting.

The UCS staff would have been willing participants in the UCC investigation because their frame of mind was that they had a right to do whatever they wanted to do. But presumably they'd realised they'd overdone it when they had fixed/altered a student's end of academic year examination question papers (I'm quite sure that neither their college nor UW regulations say they can make and use forged documents). In answering questions about what they'd done they would in fact have been confessing to the acts of forgery and using forged documents, but they no doubt didn't think of it like that. Gx1 however knew it was forgery in 1975 when he got the UCS staff to give me the altered question papers. It was the basis of his '66 sign'. The 'sign' that 'said' me to Miss D and out of Swansea. The 66 being derived from section six of the Forgery Act being breached twice.

The Welsh Office, who, by the start of 1979, had found out that Gx1 had arranged what had happened at UCS, UCC and the UHW, was not aware, as far as I know, of the many other Gx1 covert dirt activities that he'd got carried out. But I'd say that by 1981, when I met Michael Roberts in the Welsh Office, and certainly by 1983, they had found out more about Gx1's numerous covert activities (from my civil court proceedings and their own enquiries) to the extent they now considered him to be 'dirt'. It was in 1983 I found out about the forgery and reported it to the police. So did a prosecution start with Gx1 in the dock for at least some of what he had done to us? No.

In 1983 the police were in an awkward position. They knew that Gx1 with, apparently, the backing of the Prime Minister, had, in October 1980, covered it all up.

2013

The Gx1 Plan to Murder My Father - More 'Signs'

When I returned from Australia in September 1972 my parents had two cars at their house, the Triumph Herald we'd bought when I was seventeen [With it's 'you to Australia' Gx1 'sign'.] and the Ford Cortina we'd bought in 1969. [With the 'your rugby is dead' number plate Gx1 'sign'.] My father was using the Cortina, I'd sold it to him three/four months earlier to get the money to go to Australia, so I used the Herald.

In June/July 1973 I bought an MGB, a sports car, it was about three years old. I traded in the Triumph Herald and got a loan from my bank for the extra (I was working at the UHW). I also at this time applied for a job as a field engineer based in Cardiff with International Computers Limited.

The garage I bought the MGB from was called the Three Horse Shoes garage, near it was two pubs, the Three Horse Shoes and the Cross Inn. The Cross Inn is the start of the Manor Way, a dual carriageway going north west out of Cardiff. [All these were Gx1 'signs' that referred to the plan to murder my father. Yes the MGB was another car he got me to buy, using his covert methods.]

I'll explain the 'signs'. Three horse shoes (the pub and the garage) gives three sevens. Three sevens is 73 backwards. Cross inn gives a sword (like a cross) or knife in someone. Manor Way connects to Manorbier, a place in west Wales that Gx1 had sent my father and mother to for a night in a tent in the summer of 1972. A bier is a trolley for carrying a dead man/woman. Way gives WAT, my father's initials. Is that enough for you? This load of Gx1 'signs' says the knife is going into WAT's back in 1973 and he will end up dead as a result of it. Two months later Gx1 got a hit man to knife my father

A fortnight or so before I bought the MGB I'd seen it at a car sales place in Llandough (near Cardiff). [Having got me interested in the car Gx1 moved it to a small garage by the two pubs so that my buying it there would produce his 'signs'.] The small garage I bought the car from was a car repair place, not a sales place at all. When I went to see the car it was parked outside on the road, a bloke who owned the garage took me for a test drive in it (he drove) with the roof down, it was a warm evening, and then he sold it to me.

Yes in 1972 my parents camped on a farm at Manorbier west Wales for a night or two. They used a six foot high ridge tent that my brother bought in the early 1950s (or my parents bought it for him). I had camped out in it a number of times in the '60s with friends of mine. In September 1972 when I'd just returned from Australia my father told me that a week or so earlier he and my mother had camped out for a couple of days at a place called Manorbier. I was very surprised at what he said because my parents had never camped out before. [This camping trip was a Gx1 trip, somehow he'd got my father to go on it. He wanted it as a death 'sign', i.e. he was going to murder him.]

[Gx1 also used this Manorbier camping trip as a sort of introduction to 1973, when the first part of his plan to murder my father would be implemented. I'll explain.] My parents never went on an overnight stay or week long holiday. Yes, never while I was alive anyway, when they got married they stayed in a hotel for a few days but that was about it as far as I know. The reason my parents never went on week long holidays is because my father never got paid for days he didn't work. That was standard practice in the building industry, workers got their weekly wage packet and any days they didn't work they didn't get paid for. He simply could never afford to take a week off work, a week with no money. What we did as a family in the summer when I was young was go on day trips on a Sunday or bank holiday to a seaside place near Cardiff that we could easily get to on the train (bus once I think). That means it was Barry or Porthcawl. In those days this was common practice for workers in South Wales, the trains/buses would be packed and sometimes the beaches were as well. [Gx1 had, in 1972, evidently decided that the best place to hit my father in 1973 would be when he was on holiday. But as I say he never went on holiday. So he thought up this 1972 Manorbier trip which as well as creating one of his 'signs' would make my parents think of going on holiday in 1973.]

[Gx1 used his contacts to get the 1973 caravan holiday arranged.] In about January 1973 my mother, who worked in a department store in town, was encouraged to go on the holiday by one or two women she worked with and they probably helped her book it, a two week stay in August in a caravan in Paignton. Even if my father lost two weeks pay she probably thought they could still pay the bills. And it could be that she knew she'd get paid for holiday leave. My father, when he told his employer about the two weeks holiday that his wife wanted, got the surprising reply that he'd get paid for the two weeks off. Never before had he been paid for days

off. [This last bit, my father getting paid for two weeks holiday, was no doubt arranged by Gx1 to make sure he didn't object to my mother's idea of a two week holiday for them. I mean my father having two weeks without pay was a good reason for not going on holiday, but with pay he'd say okay to it.]

The 1973 False Hospital Diagnosis

The interview for the ICL job that I'd recently applied for was in August 1973 in south west London. The day before it was due to take place I drove to the interview in my MGB and stayed a night in a hotel near the venue. It was a morning interview and after it I drove to see my parents who were on holiday in a caravan in Paignton. It was I think the Tuesday or Wednesday of their second week. I went to their caravan site and eventually found them. It was just a social visit, they were fine. I stayed with them for about two hours and then returned to Cardiff, I was due in work at the UHW the next day.

When my father and mother returned from their two week holiday my father told me he had a problem that had just occurred, there was blood in his stools, and he went to his general practitioner straight-away.

What happened here was the start of part one of the Gx1 plan to murder my father. During the last night of his holiday my father was knifed in the back, in the anal canal or rectum, by a hit man in the early hours of the morning when he was asleep and drugged (anaesthetised, to keep him asleep).

My father, when he awoke, knew nothing about a knifing. I didn't get any exact details from him but as well as blood in his stools there was most probably also blood on his bed. He and my mother no doubt assumed it was piles, a well known problem in the human body.

Surreptitiously drugging my father in preparation for the knifing had problems attached to it. The Gx1 hit men had to make sure he drank/eat something with the drug in it say one hour before bedtime (let's assume the drug took three hours to take effect), and they had to ensure my mother, who would be sleeping alongside him, also took the drug. Perhaps they did this, but they could have used a different way of inducing a deep sleep in my parents, by feeding a sleeping gas into the caravan two hours or so after they went to bed. Then, having entered the caravan, the hit man applied another gas to my father that created a general anaesthetic in him prior to the knifing. Gases that induce sleep and switch off a persons nerve system have been around for eighty years or more, usually they are used in hospitals of course.

For part one of the two part murder plan to be successful Gx1 had to get a diagnosis of cancer attached to my father. The second part, killing him using poison, could then be carried out at a later date with no questions asked by anyone because it would be 'death by natural causes, death caused by cancer'.

Let's first look at the gp. What would have happened if my father had seen a 'clean' gp, i.e. not connected to Gx1?

The gp's thoughts, on talking to my father, would have been piles. Blood in the stools is a fairly common problem that's treated by gps (initial measures consist of increasing fibre intake and drinking more fluids). And he would have examined my father for piles, more properly called haemorrhoids. These are like small blood filled sacks in the anal canal (the last two inches or so of the digestive tract) that have become enlarged and leak blood, caused by hard stools. He would have found no haemorrhoids, because of course there weren't any. If the knife cut had stopped leaking blood he could have told my father that things looked okay and to come back in a few days for a check. And the check up would have been okay. That would have been part one of the murder plan stopped, before it went any further.

But what if the cut was still leaking blood? Would he have done an enema or would he have sent my father straight to the hospital? An enema is where the anal canal and rectum are washed out using water and a handheld instrument is used to look at their inner surfaces. If he had done this he could have seen the source of the blood, the cut.

Gx1 had given the murder arrangements a lot of thought, for years he had been dishing out secret signs that 'advertised' what he was going to do. He knew that a clean gp could ruin the murder plan (as in the last two paragraphs). So he had to get my father sent to a gp who was one of his 'yes sir, no sir' people, i.e. a gp who would send my father to the hospital no matter what he saw.

My father's health was excellent, and that means he hadn't been to a gp for years. In fact I had never known him go to one. He injured his left wrist and it stopped him working for a while and he must have gone to a gp then but I think that was about 1950, when I was aged two. Anyway this would explain why, when he went to his gp on return from the holiday, a Dr Hurley in Woodville Road, he told me that he had died and he went to a gp, Dr J, who was a few streets away, where he was told to go to the hospital for tests.

My father must have proceeded as follows. He first went to where Dr Hurley had his surgery. When a gp retires or dies his practice/business (and that includes his list of patients) is usually taken over by another gp at the same address. If this was the case the receptionist telling my father to go to Dr J's would be very odd indeed. It could only be explained by saying that Gx1 had got her instructed to do this because the gp who had taken

126

over Dr Hurley's business was not 'their' man. Or, my father, when he went to Dr Hurley's, found a building with no doctor's business in it at all, and someone in the building or perhaps next door, having been readied by Gx1, told my father about Dr J.

It's apparent that Gx1 got my father knifed on the last night of his holiday, not earlier in his two week stay, because he didn't want him to go to a gp in Paignton. He had the gp and hospital fixed up for him in Cardiff, not in Paignton.

Now we get to the hospital, the UHW. We know that Gx1 had the false diagnosis of cancer lined up and waiting for him here.

Was the cut still leaking blood when he entered the hospital or had it stopped bleeding? Under these circumstances, the Gx1 murder plan, it would have made no difference either way. Because he would have made sure that the hospital doctor who saw my father would proceed on the false diagnosis route. Presumably, to make things 'look' right the doctor arranged to have an enema done. Then using an instrument he would have seen a healthy anal canal and rectum, did he see the cut? These things were however irrelevant to him because he was proceeding on the false diagnosis route regardless of what he saw.

My father was told he had to have a barium meal. [This is where an x-ray detectable food/substance was fed to my father. His digestive tract could then be looked at in an x-ray type procedure. This meant that any tumours in the tract would show up in the x-rays. My father, in excellent health, had no tumours in his digestive tract of course. Did the doctor have his x-rays tampered with, switched, to show x-rays with tumours? Could be but I don't think this was necessary. All he had to do was carry on with the investigation process to the point where the false diagnosis label could easily be attached to my father, which was the next step.]

The hospital doctor, now together with a surgeon, told my father that a biopsy, a minor operation, was necessary. [This is where a small piece of flesh/tissue was cut out of his digestive tract (anal canal, rectum or intestine) and sent to a laboratory in the hospital for examination under a microscope. And here it is, the place to insert the false diagnosis of cancer. The laboratory technician said in his report, 'the small piece of flesh has a cancer in it'. He lied in other words, there was no cancer. So the Gx1 directed false diagnosis of cancer had been produced.]

My mother and I were told that my father had cancer and a major operation was necessary to prolong his life, if he didn't have it he would die within a year or so. The operation would be to remove his large intestine, rectum and anal canal. We said yes to having it done. After the operation my father spent months in bed at home with my mother looking after him. She never returned to her job.

What happened to my father was, in criminal law terms, grievous bodily

127

harm, a conspiracy, that was intended to result, at a later date, in an early death, using poison, murder.

The Gx1 Car 'Accident' in 1973

Here we have a problem. I know all about this Gx1 car 'accident', that means I know exactly what he did and how he did it. And I've written it out. But I can't give it to you here because this is a book for the public to read (and you are a member of the public) and Gx1 in this 'accident' used methods that are officially, in government terms, covert/secret, i.e. not for the public to know. This isn't the only time Gx1 used covert methods of course but in this car 'accident' he relied heavily on them which makes it impossible for me to give you a reasonable description of it. So all I can do is briefly tell you about the 'accident'. I can however explain to you why he arranged it.

Gx1 had tried to get me to go out with Miss D in April 1973 (the meal at Mr E's house). But I had no interest in her. Four months went by and he decided to try again, this time he pushed Miss D (via her mother) into having talks with me in work. In September 1973 I thought okay I'd ask her out and have a closer look at her. At the end of the month I left the UHW job and started the ICL job.

Why did Gx1 wait till April 1973 to try to get me to go out with Miss D? Bearing in mind that I'd returned to my job at the UHW in September 1972 (when I got back from Australia) and she was working in the department I was in then. The answer is tied in with the problems he were having with me on the rugby front. Some people thought I should go to Cardiff rugby club, if I did a pretty good female should be found for me, and Miss D, with her gawky teeth, was not in that category. So as long as my move to Cardiff rugby club was in the pending tray he couldn't push her onto me.

The 1972/73 season that I played with the Cardiff Hospitals rugby team is covered in "In 1972/73 Gx1 Fixes a Rugby Team and Hits Me Again" in the "2009/10" chapter. I'll refer to the "Hit Me Again" part of it here because it's the Gx1 hit that led straightaway to his pushing Miss D onto me. In March/April 1973 I played on the left wing for Cardiff Hospitals in a game that was watched by a Cardiff rugby club official. If I had a good game I'd get invited to play a game for Cardiff rugby club. It was very important to Gx1 that this did not happen (he'd already stopped me playing for Cardiff once, at the start of the 1969 season, and he'd stopped/inhibited my rugby on many other occasions). During the game he got an electron/laser beam fired at me when I was about to make a crucial try saving tackle on my opposing winger fifteen yards out. The beam momentarily stunned me, I was stopped in my tracks, and the winger ran easily to the try line. Result,

128

'when it matters he misses a tackle', so I was not invited to Cardiff rugby club. For Gx1 it was pressure off, the first part of the murder could proceed as planned, and it was 'get him to Miss D' time. Within a week or two he pushed Miss D at me.

Gx1 knew all about Miss D and he wanted a bit of it (the rear sex) and he could get a bit if I was married to her ('when married you can live in a flat at a house we run', he did part-time work in an office that was on the ground floor of the house). My marrying her was also a route to carrying out the second and final part of his plan to murder my father, and it seems to killing me (the 'killing me softly', piano song). But he probably thought there was little chance of marriage as far as my own personal thinking was concerned (because of her gawky teeth). So how was he going to make me marry her? He was going to arrange a car accident that would leave me and Miss D with upper body, facial, injuries. And after it I would feel bound to stay with her, marry her.

In the car accident, which took place in December 1973, a lad (18-22) was seriously injured and he perhaps died. Myself and Miss D however escaped with no injuries.

[Although as I've said I can't give you extensive details of the car 'accident' I can tell you about one vital factor in it.] The accident took place on a main road going north out of Cardiff about a quarter of an hour before midnight. Along the road there were tall main road lights, these ended where the road left the perimeter of Cardiff. The last three hundred yards or so of road lights were off. In other words this stretch of road, still within Cardiff with housing either side of it, was in darkness (blacked out). If these road lights had been on, as they should have been, the accident would not have happened. [Who got the road lights switched off? Gx1. He worked in the city hall, and getting the council's road lighting people to switch them off ready for his 'accident' was easy for him to arrange.]

It was about two weeks after this car accident that the wife of Gx1 (one of my father's sisters) called at our house. As I've said elsewhere visits to our house by her or her husband were very rare occurrences. It was during the day and I met her when I walked into the living room, she was in the room with my mother (my mother had stopped work to look after my father who was in bed in the house recovering from the September 1973 operation). I was in the room for only a minute or so and while I was there no mention was made of the recent car accident. She perhaps said to me, 'how's your relationship with Miss D going?' I would have said okay, nothing more than that. If she did say that I would have assumed my mother had told her about Miss D because I hadn't seen her for ages (maybe three years). Anyway the bit that stuck in my mind was where she said, 'when you get married to her there's a flat I have you can live in'. I found it an astonishing thing to say because I had only been going with Miss D for about three months and marriage hadn't been mentioned by anyone. I said nothing and left to go wherever I was going. [This was where Gx1 had planned, prior to the 'accident', to use the big line, 'you have to marry her now as a result of the serious injuries you both suffered in the accident'. But in this respect the 'accident' had failed, neither me nor Miss D were injured, so Gx1 couldn't get his wife to feed this line to me, my mother and father, the best she could be told to do was just say, 'when married there's a flat you can have'. Words that were feeble by comparison. Instead of being a hard hitting, 'you have to', it was, as far as I was concerned, a silly (and astonishing) thing to say. When I first went out with Miss D I had my doubts about her and I still had doubts about her.]

It could be that my father's sister, as referred to in the last paragraph, called at the house to see him a few times in this period following his operation. I however, as I've told you, only saw her once. She was a genuine women's tea meetings do good sort of female. It was her husband who was the warped one. She didn't know this of course, he kept his dirt activities to himself and his tight circle of work associates.

[Yes part of Gx1's car 'accident' had failed dismally, I hadn't received facial injuries to match Miss D's protruding teeth. So the problem remained, how was he going to make me marry her?] Here, January/February 1974, we get to Miss D's overnight stay in the dental hospital in Cardiff when her teeth were done. [Gx1 presumably arranged it to clear the way for marriage.] I had assumed that her protruding top front teeth could not be straightened and that she just had to live with it. But when I saw her after the hospital job her front teeth looked normal. [Did the hospital somehow manage to straighten the teeth (make them vertical)? Or did they extract them and insert false teeth? I don't know, nobody told me and I never asked any questions.]

Some weeks later I became sure that Miss D was in a secret sexual relationship with her brother. I said nothing about it to her, and I told no one else about it either. I had never really got on with her, she didn't seem to be a clean thinker, her secret relationship was obviously one reason for this. I knew I had to finish with her, but I could see that finishing could bring me problems, with her mother saying, 'how dare he finish with my daughter'. Her mother and their Group X friend were no doubt very pleased they'd found a job for her in a university and in so doing they'd presented her as 'a living at home innocent young church going virgin'. I had started going out with her, and if I now dropped her? Yes it definitely looked like it would be trouble for me. [I was right about her secret relationship and I was right about problems for me when I finished with her. When I did stop her Gx1 used it in 1976 as an excuse to hit me off the course I was on at UCC.]

The 1979 Boundary Change

In early 1979 I was reading the local evening newspaper when I was surprised to see that our house was involved in a boundary change that would soon be made to some MPs constituencies in Cardiff. The house was on the edge of one constituency and when the change took place it would be in another constituency. I wondered if the change had anything to do with what was going on at UCC (I had written to the registrar of the college in August 1978 about what had happened when I was at the college and the problem was unresolved).

Constituency boundary changes are rare occurrences, they usually go unchanged for decades. A boundary change affecting where I lived a few months after my letter to UCC?

In TCF9 I said that my parents house in Cathays, where I was living in 1979, was situated in Michael Roberts constituency. I said this as a result of looking at the internet when I was writing TCF9 in 2013. I didn't say it because I recalled it from 1979. In early 1979 I had not thought of writing to my MP so I made no particular note of who my MP was.

However in 2016, when I looked at the internet again on this subject, I saw something different. The MP for where I was living in early 1979 could have been someone else. I put it like this because the information I saw was different to what I'd seen 2013 and this 'new' information didn't go into sufficient detail (boundary maps, etc) to be able to be sure about it. So was Michael Roberts my MP in early 1979?

Gx1 knew there was more to it than just the 1976 UCC dispute. He knew that as well as getting me stopped at UCC he had also arranged at UCS in 1975 to have fixed question papers given to me as part of his 'stop him' activities when I was at that college, and, that in 1973 he had got the UHW to issue a false cancer diagnosis applicable to my father, the first part of his two part plan to murder him. He also knew that for many years he'd been hitting me (numerous times) to keep me down. He didn't want something done about the UCC dispute because it could uncover some or all of his other criminal activities, to stay in the clear he had to keep it under wraps. And to keep it under wraps he had to destroy the winning position I was in. I was right about the false results and some UCC lecturers knew I was right. We should bear all this in mind when we look at the boundary change.

And when do constituency boundary changes get implemented? When an election takes place. And what arrives on the scene in May 1979? A general election, brought in about six months before it's time, because the Callaghan government had become unpopular. Was the unpopularity created by the people that ran this country to obtain the early general election? I answer the question with yes. Did Mr Callaghan deliberately make some bad decisions to get the election brought forward?

Mr Callaghan had his constituency in Cardiff, which means he knew the people who ran Cardiff and that means he knew Gx1.

The boundary change becomes even more notable, in fact odd, when I say that, as far as I recall from looking at the evening paper, it wasn't a case of an entire ward being moved to another constituency, it was just a small area around our house (perhaps a couple of hundred houses) that was being moved to another constituency.

In June 1979 I wrote to my MP, Ian Grist, about the dispute. He replied with, 'you can tell me about it when I see you in five months time'. A five months wait to see my MP? [This odd response from him illustrates that strange things were going on in the background, in the Group X area.]

The boundary change and the early election appear to have been arranged to ensure the UCC dispute, which was heading for an MP, was not dealt with by my pre-boundary change MP. But instead by Mr Grist.

Whilst waiting to see Mr Grist I started the insurance sales job working for a broker who was based in Mrs Thatcher's constituency. And then, three months into the job, we get to the December 1979 government poison I was given in Spain that made me ill ready for my arrival on a high roof. But there was no 'suicide', no one turned up to throw me off. Then we get to the government's electron beam that hit me at the Swansea Town Hall meeting in October 1980. The hit that planted false evidence into the unresolved dispute. The hit that made me look stupid. The result was that UCC, knowing nothing about the government's covert town hall hit and the false evidence it created (a smear, dirt covertly applied to me), stopped supporting me, to say in other words, 'okay, we accept that nothing will be done about it, he's stupid'.

Gx1 had got what he wanted, what he'd done at UCC would stay under wraps. And that meant what he'd done at UCS and the UHW would also be kept under wraps. He had enlisted the help of Mrs Thatcher (and her MP Mr Grist) to that effect.

Did Mrs Thatcher and other people that ran this country in 1979/80 know about all of Gx1's activities of earlier years or just some of them? Either way, all or some, she should not have allowed government officials to line me up for 'suicide' from a high roof or plant false evidence into the dispute at the town hall.

In 1975 Gx1 Again Poisons Me

By here expanding on some things in the Swansea year that I told you about in TCF9 you will obtain a better understanding of the situation.

Within a week or so of my moving to Swansea in October 1974 I moved into a room in a house with a shared kitchen that I'd been told about by the university accommodation office. A couple of weeks later I met Mr S by accident at the college sports ground, he was a friend of Miss N's brother (I was going with Miss N from mid-1969 to Sept 1971). [I haven't attached a letter to Miss N's brother in TCF so I'll do that here, I'll call him Mr Y.] I'd sometimes played rugby with Mr S and Mr Y when we were all working/studying in Cardiff hospitals. When I first met them they were students but by this time they were doctors and Mr S was working in the hospital that was alongside the university. It was his idea that we went out for a drink and this became a weekly occurrence. One night he wanted to go to a dance, where we met Miss K, he knew her because she worked in the hospital. I thought she was perhaps his girlfriend but no that didn't seem to be the case.

In our conversation a week or two later Mr S said that Miss K's father was the secretary of the Welsh Rugby Union. Her surname was the same as the secretary's surname (his name was in the programmes for internationals), but I didn't really believe him, I didn't say this though. But the odd thing was that Mr S was an honest sober sort of person and he hadn't attempted to make a joke of it. Anyway I left it at that and neither of us mentioned the subject again.

Sometimes when me and Mr S went out in the night Miss K was present. She was an attractive and decent female, perhaps a couple of years younger than me. I couldn't understand why she always seemed to be on her own, I mean with a girlfriend yes but never a male. Why wasn't Mr S going out with her?

Lectures finished at the university a week or so before Christmas. I could have returned to my parents house in Cardiff straightaway but no I chose to stay in Swansea right up to when I drove home at about 4pm Christmas eve. My hurrying to Cardiff to see Miss D didn't come into it, she was, in my books, on the way out. I had all but finished with here. For reasons stated earlier I knew it would be better/safer if she finished with me. In the days before Christmas I joined Mr S and Miss K for a pre-Christmas gathering/party in the hospital they worked in. It was a quiet and sensible affair. And the three of us, as far as I could see, remained single throughout.

About a week after returning to Swansea in January I attended an interview in the college. I was questioned by a lecturer and a professor. I think a few others on my course were also interviewed. Apparently it was to discuss the pre-Christmas examinations/tests we had sat. [I explain why I tell you about this later on.]

One night, it was January/February 1975, Miss K had a party at where she was living. Mr S had picked me up from my place earlier in the evening and we drove in his car to the party on the west side of Swansea. The party was okay, there was a lot of singing of rugby songs and of course that meant, my being into rugby and trained into welsh rugby songs at numerous Arms Park internationals, that I quite enjoyed myself. At the end of the night it was apparent that Miss K was on her own. And so was I, as for Mr S, well I didn't know what had happened to him, he'd left without telling me. So how was I going to get back to my place? Miss K said I could stay the night in a spare bedroom, which surprised me a bit, I thought it was good of her to make the offer. She slept in the main bedroom with a girlfriend. I left early in the morning without seeing them. I walked to the main road then got a bus into Swansea.

Let me go over a few things here. First my use of the term Group X in this book. I have used it as a collective term for a number of people, such as Gx1 (who had been close to my family since the 1930s) and some people I came into contact with in the late 1960s and the 70s.

Gx1 was the person who arranged many covert dirt activities, such as planning to murder my father and getting him hit, attempting to murder me, etc. He used his position, a high level government job, to get what he wanted done by 'yes sir, no sir' people, who, on many occasions, could be called 'hit men'.

I talk about Group X here because Mr Q, a policeman, Miss N's father, was in Group X, and he is very much involved in what I tell you in this section. He was not in the part of Group X where the dirt activities were planned. His way of thinking was respectable, which means he only accepted decent instructions.

Mr Q knew I had played rugby at the Wasps, and he also knew that

Gx1 had fixed things to ensure I didn't play in their first team (which they wanted me to). And, being a rugby man, he was unhappy about it. And he decided to try to correct things for me (he didn't say this to me, it's obvious from what I tell you here).

He arranged for Mr S to get a job in the hospital that was next to Swansea university and got him to meet me and start a once a week night out together. The purpose being to get me introduced to Miss K. Mr Q thought that if I started a relationship with her the next step would be my playing for Swansea RFC.

Let's look at the position of Gx1 in this 1974/5 Swansea year. In 1973 he had got me going out with Miss D. He knew she was trouble for me, which was in line with his plans to murder my father and ship me out. I had uncovered some of the Miss D "trouble", i.e. she was in a secret sexual relationship with her brother. And for this reason, and others, I was quietly trying to get rid of her. Gx1, however, did not know that I knew about her secret sexual relationship. Not even Miss D knew I was aware of it. I had said nothing about it to her because I knew that if I did it would create problems. She would most probably tell her mother about what I'd said, and then I'd have her getting at me, saying that I'd done a terrible thing in accusing her innocent church going daughter of such an awful act. Gx1 perhaps realised that I didn't seem to be very keen on Miss D, but nothing more than that, and so he thought he could push through the marriage to Miss D plan.

The appearance on the scene of Miss K was a major obstacle to his plans and he was closely monitoring the situation. If I started a relationship with her it looked like I'd finish with Miss D (which of course I would have done). So when he heard that a Miss K and me close relationship could happen, or was about to happen, he knew he had to move in to stop it to keep his long term plans alive.

Let's now move on a few weeks to something that happened in March/April 1975. I had not seen Miss K since the party at her house. And the same applied to Mr S (I had the impression that he had left his job in the hospital and gone to work in another part of the country). Swansea rugby club had a Saturday afternoon home game with some other team and I was to meet Miss K and a girlfriend of her's outside a pub that was next to Swansea's ground at 2pm (an hour before the kick off).

I don't know how this pub meeting was arranged. It definitely wasn't my idea. I only went to one Swansea game in the entire year I was in Swansea and I had no intention of going to this one. When I say, "I hadn't seen Miss K since the party" what I mean is I don't recall having met her since then, but I must have briefly met her in the few days before this pub meeting for it to have been arranged (I was not on the phone). The hospital where she worked was between the college and the college sports ground, and I often walked across the front of the hospital when going to or from the sports ground. Anyway however I met her she must have stopped me and asked me to meet her and her friend outside the pub and I just said okay.

The two of them were standing outside the pub when I arrived, waiting for me. We went in, it was crowded. They sat down and I stood at the bar trying to get served. After a long wait I got served, and found a seat some distance from them (about thirty feet), they were sat in the middle of a number of girlfriends and talking to them. I became hot and uncomfortable for no apparent reason, and I felt odd. I was talking to no one, well I didn't know anyone there apart from Miss K and her girlfriend. After about five minutes they got up to leave. I left with them. Outside the pub Miss K told me they had stand tickets for the game and that's where they were going. I went wherever I was going (not to the rugby game). It seemed like a bit of an odd meeting, why did Miss K want me to meet them at the pub?

This meeting was a Gx1 hit arrangement from start to finish. Presumably he got some plausible reason for the meeting fed to Miss K. He then got her to meet me 'accidentally' a couple of days before the game when she asked me to meet her and her friend outside the pub. The plausible reason could have been based on the stand tickets that she and her girlfriend had for the game, with her intending to give a spare one to me to sit with them, assuming the pub meeting went okay.

You could say that after the party my relationship with Miss K was in the pending tray, was I going to ask her out? And in this pub meeting Gx1 made sure that if I did the answer would be no. He had my drink poisoned by the barman. The drink made me hot and flushed (red faced). The result was what he wanted. Miss K, when she left the pub, saw an odd looking individual in front of her, me, and called off her original intentions, didn't offer me the ticket.

There is a possible alternative here. Miss K could have assumed, when she asked me to meet her and her friend outside the pub, that I would be going to the game, and that I would be buying the usual terrace/standing ticket. And she and her friend were intending to buy the same tickets and watch the game with me. But when, on leaving the pub, she saw that I was flushed, she changed her mind, and decided that she would not go with me to the game. And saying they had stand tickets was a way of ending the meeting.

Getting a poison dished out was par for the course for Gx1, it was one of his 'fix it so things go the way I want them to go' routines.

Let's look at a few more things here. Yes Mr Q knew about my Wasps rugby and that it had been blocked by Gx1. Did he know that

136

Gx1 had done a number of other things to stop/inhibit my rugby in the pre-Swansea years? For example did he know:

(i)   That in 1968 Gx1 had destroyed my captaincy of the Llandaff Technical College rugby team when he crippled me (put me on crutches for two months using the 'accident' method) to stop my rugby because I was getting too successful for his liking. Probably not because he didn't become a member of Group X till 1969 (when I started to go out with his daughter)?

(ii)   That Gx1 made me incapable of playing rugby when he had me doped/poisoned in the trial game I played in at Cardiff RFC at the start of the 1969 season?

(iii)   That Gx1 had stopped me playing for the Penarth first team in 1969 (after one very good game I played for them)?

(iv)   That Gx1 hit me (electron gun) in the game I played that was watched by a Cardiff selector in 1973 to again ensure I didn't go to Cardiff RFC?

Was Miss K's father the secretary of the Welsh Rugby Union? Yes I now think he was, I haven't received any new information on this, what I'm going on here is the rugby singing at her party, which I never started, I just joined in, and her stand tickets for the rugby game. And of course as I've said Mr S wasn't the type to give me false information. My not believing it does at least illustrate that my appreciating her was based on what I thought of her and not on any connections she might have. I eventually did manage to ask her out. I met her by accident as I walked across the front of the hospital she worked at. But this was some weeks after Gx1 had stopped our relationship at the pub meeting, so you know what the answer was, 'no'.

Why didn't I accept what Mr S had told me about Miss K's father? I'll give you a few things here to explain this. In my own mind I was confident and sure of my ability on the rugby field, no one got past me and I scored quite a few tries. But selectors apparently had players who were better than me. At the Wasps even though I'd played two faultless games in their second team (and scored) they dropped me to the fourth team (and kept me there), and at Penarth having played a very good game for them, they dropped me to the second team (and kept me there). I was mystified as to what happened at these two clubs, but anyway the result was that I apparently wasn't in their opinions a particularly good player. So how could an ordinary player, like me, get introduced to the secretary of the Welsh Rugby Union's daughter? Well it just didn't figure, and hence I didn't believe him. You see in 1974, when I was told about Miss K's father, I had no idea that Group X had, for years, been fixing/stopping my rugby. It was September 1975 when I started to become aware of Group X 'fix him' activities.

The interview in the college that took place in January 1975 that I mentioned earlier. What was that about? One of the two people that interviewed me was a lecturer on my course, the other was a professor I'd never seen before. Both of them were selected by Gx1 to be in front of me on this occasion. How can I say this? Because the lecturer's surname quite obviously contained my brother's initials, and the professor got his academic qualifications in Australia. These facts cannot be coincidences when you bear in mind that Gx1 had through the sixties and early seventies been restricting my life to ensure I could be easily shipped to Australia (one way). In 1972 he got me there, but, after a stay of three months, I returned, which, according to the Gx1 plans was not supposed to happen. Now, at this interview he was again 'saying', 'I have you on route for Australia'. And that meant 'I am going to stop you and Miss K', because Miss K is not a ship out candidate, i.e. if I did start a relationship with her and perhaps stay with her he could not get me and her shipped to Australia, and perhaps it would also mean that the final part of his plan to murder my father would fall through.

It follows from what I said in the last paragraph that Miss D was a ship to Australia candidate. So by getting me to marry her Gx1 could eventually push through the 'you to Australia' plan (with her going with me) and carry out the final part of his plan to murder my father.

Gx1 could get the staff at Swansea university to react to him on a 'yes sir, no sir' basis. It's of interest to note that later on when I was at Cardiff university he could not, in October '75, get the staff there to do what he wanted, stop me (he fed an open 'stop him' request into the college, perhaps he got someone at UCS to do this). So he immediately got me hit by an electron gun man, to stop my rugby. Then from January '76 on, having been told by UCC that I was doing well on the course (good essay/homework marks), he fed bits of rubbish into the college (to dirty me) and arranged covert hits (taxi poisoning etc).

Gx1 Closes In With His Miss D in 1975

There's more Gx1 dirt that took place in this Swansea year that I haven't told you about. Since I started at the university I'd been living at a house about a mile from the college. Gx1 got me out of this place at the start of the Easter break (no need to go into details), and when I returned to Swansea after Easter he got me located in bed and breakfast accommodation.

The woman who ran the place seemed to take an interest in me. At breakfast everyday she always had a lot to say. Her husband had something to do with UCS. I was for most of my two weeks there the only guest. The girlfriend I had in Cardiff, Miss D, got into the conversation somehow and she thought she should come to stay with me at the guest house for a night. And, she said, she could stay for free, and, she thought I should marry her. Uh! She knew nothing about her and hadn't even seen her. I didn't want to offend the woman, I said nothing. Miss D stayed for a night.

You can see the Gx1 angle, it stands out a mile. He was using Miss D as an excuse for getting me stopped at UCS (he did the same at UCC a year later). No doubt he was dishing out, 'she was a seventeen year old church going virgin living at home when he started to go out with her so he should, has to, marry her'. Gx1 knew the virgin stuff was rubbish, he knew she was secretly having sex with her brother before I started going with her. He'd use anything to get what he wanted.

Gx1 produced even more dirt at this guest house but in public terms it's not easy to give you the details.

At the start of my UCS study Gx1 had set me up for a 'one year and out' stay, a hit ('stick a failed label on him'), to put me down and push me to Miss D. Now, April '75, he was making arrangements with the UCS staff to have the 66 'sign' given to me at the start of June - the end of academic year examination forged Pure Mathematics question papers.

The Autograph Book

My brother was the age for getting autographs, about 10/15 in 1946/51, when he collected rugby player's autographs in a small notebook. My father went to watch Cardiff games at the Arms Park in those years and he took him to some of them and encouraged his interest in rugby.

When I was 10/15 in 1958/63 I never went to watch Cardiff games with my father because he'd stopped going to them some years earlier.

I was sixteen, 1964, when I started going to Cardiff rugby club games at the Arms Park with my mate (DC) who was the same age as me. At that age I was past the autographs age (I have never asked a rugby player for his autograph). We went to all the home games, and a few of the away games in my car (which I got soon after my seventeenth birthday), Gloucester, Llanelli and Bridgend I recall going to. We also went on the train to a Wales game at Murrayfield and in my car to a Wales game at Twickenham. You could say the nearest I got to asking for an autograph was when the french number eight Spanghero was outside the Royal hotel in Cardiff one evening after an international signing autographs, it was about 1967. I just looked on.

Because we had difficulty obtaining tickets for Arms Park internationals we bought Cardiff rugby club season tickets a couple of times in these years, which guaranteed that we'd get tickets for internationals.

I began to play rugby for the Llandaff Technical College team in 1967, where I was studying part-time. This meant that my regular attendance at the Cardiff home games ceased because I was playing for the college on a Saturday afternoon. My rugby supporter mate, who was also on a part-time course at the college, joined me in playing for them.

One day not long after I'd started playing for Llandaff Tech I said to the lecturer who had an interest in the team, he arranged the fixtures, that I wasn't sure what to do, play for the college on a Saturday afternoon or watch Cardiff. He said it would be best if I played the game while I was the age for it because I could always, in later years, watch the game. [He was I believe some months on from here involved in pushing me toward university and to Cardiff rugby club, playing for Cardiff rugby club.]

I didn't play rugby after I left school in 1963 till 1967 because there was no one to play for, well it seemed like that. I was in a full time study year at Llandaff Tech in 1963/64 then started work with AEI in 1964 and went onto a part-time course at Llandaff Tech but in these years I was too young for their rugby team, they just had the one team and it had adult fixtures, the players were aged 19 and above. In 1967, when I started to play for them, I was aged nineteen.

My work as a trainee draughtsman, my study at Llandaff Tech and my rugby were all going very well in 1967/68. Far too well for Gx1 and it worried him. His plans, formed years earlier, were to murder my father when he'd finished paying the house mortgage and ship me to Australia. Success for me in a big way, going on to a full time course at a university or playing rugby for Cardiff, both of which were on the cards (AEI management and Llandaff Tech staff had me en route for these things) would almost certainly stop his shipping me to Australia and it would create serious problems for his plan to murder my father. He was far too pig ignorant to revise the plans he had in the light of the expectations that had been pinned to me and instead he made additional plans, plans to destroy me. And yes that's literally correct. He made plans to murder me, by 'accident'. Quite simply in his warped mind if I was dead he'd have no problem proceeding with the plan to murder my father.

The first Gx1 attempt to kill me by 'accident' in these 1967/68 years didn't succeed and he made a second attempt, it also ended in failure. So he went for other ways of stopping my potential achievements, these included dirtying/smearing me and physically inhibiting me. He used the 'accident' method to put me on crutches for two months. It put me out of rugby for almost a full season.

If there was ever a correct/ideal route to be on for someone to eventually arrive as a player for Cardiff rugby club I was on it. I lived in Cardiff and the Arms Park (Cardiff's ground) had been part of our family's life for decades. In my 16 to 19 years I was regularly at the Arms Park for club games and internationals. I played rugby for a college in Cardiff, and captained the side when aged 20. The next step was playing for Cardiff. And this was where Gx1 moved in, he hit me to stop me going to the club because it would force him to alter plans he had, in other words he knew that if he didn't hit me I'd play for Cardiff. We have what is in effect confirmation of this in what happened to me at the Wasps in 1971/72. Having seen me play the Wasps selectors wanted me to play for their first team. And here again Gx1 moved in to stop it.

The Spire in 1959/60

I said in The Cathays Files that I didn't know exactly when Group X formed their plan to murder my father but that the plan existed in 1966. I'll tell you why I said this.

In the summer of 1966 I went on a two week holiday in Paignton with some lads. My mate and a couple of other friends travelled in my car (Triumph Herald) and four more friends travelled in another car. We stayed in two caravans.

One day soon after we'd arrived, I found that my car boot lid had a fault. When it was opened it wouldn't stay open. It had a stay on one side of it and the stay had come away from the lid of the boot. Perhaps you could say it had broken away but it would be more accurate to say that the method of securing the stay to the lid had gone missing (it was like a nut and bolt). Anyway I decided to get a garage in Paignton to repair it and at the same time get a basic service done on the car.

This car boot lid fault was Gx1 issuing one of his 'signs'. He got someone to remove the fitting at the top of the boot stay. He planned to carry out the first part of the plan to murder my father a few years on from here and by highlighting the boot stay he created a 'sign' that detailed the initial stage of the hit. I will explain, as follows.

The boot stay worked on the sword in a scabbard principle. One rod sliding within another with a click device in the middle that kept the rods extended until it was clicked again to release them back to the closed position.

A "sword in a scabbard" is what Gx1 got done to my father in 1973, he had a knife put in to his rectum whilst he was doped/anaesthetised at night when he was sleeping.

And yes, as you may recall from having read the relevant parts in The Cathays Files, the holiday location matched. My father was hit when he was in a caravan in Paignton, and here was I, in 1966, in a caravan in Paignton.

And one more 'sign' that Gx1 undoubtedly had in mind here, the 'sword' was in the car boot. Boot gives, in Group X language, WT. The B gives the W and t gives T, my father's initials. So we have 'sword/knife in WT' in Paignton.

You'd like to know how Gx1 managed to get us lads to go on this holiday. Some of you may already have ideas on how he done this. I'll just give you here a possible route. Perhaps, having got the caravans lined up, he had someone tell one of us lads that we could have the two of them for a special/reduced price. And that did it, the offer was taken up. Me and my rugby mate had a friend that sometimes joined us for nights out (the two of us usually went to the cinema once a week and he joined us now and then) and it was he who told us about the holiday offer, he worked with one or two of the other lads. How on earth did Gx1 find the time to pay such close attention to things? An answer is that he did all or much of his 'arranging/fixing' in work hours. Gx1 did 'office work' in the city hall, i.e. he was paid out of local taxpayers money!

There is something that indicates that the Gx1 plan to murder my father existed before 1966. What follows in this section explains it.

The rear of our house in Cardiff was on a main road and on the other side of the road was the main entrance to a large cemetery. The school I started at in 1959 when aged eleven was on the other side of the cemetery. I either cycled around the cemetery to get to school or walked round it or walked through it. There was an entrance/exit gate on the other side of the cemetery near the school.

The entrance to the cemetery at the rear of our house had large iron gates and there were/are church buildings built in natural stone that were just inside, about eighty yards away from, the entrance. These buildings comprised of two chapels with between them a structure that supported a spire. Archways linked the chapels to the central structure. The tall spire made the buildings look attractive and respectable. [It was the standard sort of spire you see on churches all over the country. By that I mean it wasn't amongst the tallest you see but it was a good heigth, say about a hundred and forty feet.]

Well it was either the end of 1959 or 1960 when I saw scaffolding erected around the spire. Presumably they were doing a small job near the top of it I thought. Within days the spire was taken down, demolished. And replaced with a spire that had a copper roof that was less than half the height of the original one. I was amazed, the new spire looked hopeless/awful in comparison to the one they'd demolished. It ruined the overall appearance of the buildings. After a while, from the effects of the weather, the copper took on a dark green colour. From good looking church buildings they now looked like something out of a witches handbook. I talked to no one about this, it was just my own personal thinking when I looked at the spire. [I'll return to the subject of the spire after I've given you some other details.]

In 1968, in the last few weeks of my job as a trainee draughtsman, the chief draughtsman gave me some work to do that was quite out of the ordinary. He gave me a CEGB (Central Electricity Generating Board) drawing of an electricity pylon and he wanted me to make a new drawing of it, copy it if you like, on a new scale. All my work up to this point had been the construction/drawing of plans that showed where our high voltage underground cables had been laid. Pylons never concerned us because they were manufactured and owned by the CEGB. The closest we got to them in our drawings was illustrating the terminal posts, where our cables ended. Occasionally these terminal posts were situated on the base of a pylon, usually they were on small iron structures in electricity sub-stations, or our cables terminated by jointing to existing underground cables.

I have no doubt in saying that this pylon drawing was arranged by Gx1, it was one of his 'signs'. He had decided on how he was going to murder my father and this 'sign' was indicating it. Stage one would be a 'natural' piles for him, haemorrhoids, a knife in his rectum, which would lead to a stage two no questions asked 'natural death', poisoned, sometime later. Piles, in Group X language, is easily seen in pylon. It was pile(s) on for my father. He was on course for stage one.

Here are some more Gx1 'it's going to be piles' 'signs'. He tried to get me to go out with a girl who lived in Pyle (about twenty miles west of Cardiff). Here's how he introduced me to her. When I started work at the infirmary in 1968 he, as I've told you earlier, got a commie 'sign' put in place (he'd made sure I didn't go to university) by getting a Mr McCarthy employed alongside me (Senator McCarthy). Well he arranged for him to do some research work in another department of the hospital and the girl from Pyle, who worked in that department, would help him. Because of this when I occasionally met her in the hospital we said hello to each other. I got the impression that I could have asked her out but I didn't. So the Gx1 'fix him up with a Pyle female' didn't come off.

In the 1960s the planning and building of the M4 motorway near Cardiff took place. Look at junction 37 on a map. It's the Pyle turnoff. Did Gx1 arrange to have the Pyle turnoff numbered 37 to give one of his 'signs'? To 'say' that in 1973 my father would be covertly knifed in the back, 37 backwards, pyles. In M4 there is WT (my father). I think it's more than likely

143

he did. He used 37 at other times, i.e. the 37 caravan, and the 37 pub, both of which indicated his plan to hit my father.

As the construction of the M4 approached Cardiff the council's planning/highways department would have stated how many junctions they wanted into Cardiff. It appears to me that they obtained more junctions than was necessary. I say this because today, decades after the motorway was built, junction 31 is not present. Which means that in later years the council's planning people did not think it was necessary to use, build a junction, at 31.

[It was May/June 1974 when Gx1, using surreptitious methods, got me to sell the MGB I'd bought in 1973 and by buying a cheaper car I'd get some spare money out of the deal.] The bloke I bought the new/secondhand car from lived in Swansea and on the phone we had chosen Pyle as our meeting point because it was mid way between Cardiff and Swansea. He had driven to Pyle in the car and he sold it to me saying everything was okay with it. He then got into a friend's car and returned to Swansea. I also had someone with me (Miss D) and she drove the car I'd arrived in back to Cardiff and I drove the new car back. The clutch had a big problem, it was difficult to get the car into gear. Within days I knew it couldn't be put right by adjustment. A new clutch was required and it would be an expensive garage job. It was a rear wheel drive car and that meant the gearbox or the engine had to be taken out to get at the clutch. I wasn't surprised when I found I couldn't contact the bloke I'd bought the car from. I'd been done, it was a con job, the amount I'd paid him was for a car that was going okay, and it certainly was not going okay. It later became apparent that part of a clutch lever, where it entered the gearbox housing, had broken.

I've always, since about 1980, considered this purchase of a car in Pyle to be a Gx1 X fix up, hit, from having a decent car he put me onto a car that was almost unusable, I was cheated out of a substantial amount of money. It was typical of his 'create problems for him ... keep him down' routine. But now, 2014, on looking at this again, I can see that Gx1 had a lot more than this in mind. Pyle for him meant piles, knife into a rectum. The bloke came from Swansea. And what did I do a few months after this trip to Pyle? I started at Swansea university. Well, well, what a coincidence. No chance with Gx1 around. In this car purchase he was 'saying' it would soon be Swansea and 'piles' for me, he was going to 'knife me' in Swansea. After one year at the college I'd be out failed, 'knifed', my education/career history would be very severely dented. And in such a position I certainly wouldn't be too good for his Miss D, and I'd be far more likely to grasp her.

This Pyle car fix up adds weight to my saying years ago in The Cathays Files that it looks like Gx1 got in at the beginning of my year in Swansea by telling the lecturer I met to only accept me onto a one year course that was prior to the standard three year degree course. Something I considered to be odd at the time. Yes Gx1 knew it was going to be one year and out. He knew he could tell the college staff what to do.

I think that part of Gx1 thinking at the time of the Pyle car fix up was that I didn't appear to be particularly keen on his Miss D and it looked a bit like she wasn't good enough for me. So, using a phrase I've used before, it was 'take him down a few pegs', which would make me more suitable for her. He wanted me to marry her because when that happened he could complete the murder of my father (get the second stage carried out). Recall here that five months or so before this Pyle car purchase he arranged a car 'accident' where I was supposed to end up with upper body, facial, injuries, but I escaped uninjured. So, because the 'accident' didn't do what it was meant to do, 'put me down', he arranged a different way of doing it, this Pyle car purchase was the lead in to it, I'd be 'put down', 'knifed', in Swansea (one year and out failed).

Let's now return to the spire that I talked about earlier in this section. Spire in Group X language is piles. It's easy to see this, put the s on the other end and get the l out of the r. Gx1 destroyed a good spire, to issue one of his 'signs'? Yes. Who runs the cemetery? The local council do, and where was he located at the time? In an office in the local council. I have no doubt in saying that he got it done. So this destruction of the spire tells us that the piles for my father plan (the first part of a plan to murder him) existed in 1959/60.

2015

Miss W 'Killed' in 1969

There's another Gx1 arrangement that I've known about since the eighties and now I'm looking closely at it and putting it into print for the first time. I'll include a few things you already know about, it'll help you to get a complete picture of this part of the jigsaw.

During my 16 to 19 years my mate, DC, and I bought our season tickets for Cardiff RFC games at an office in their clubhouse. When we were over 18 we, after a Cardiff home game, went into the clubhouse bar for a drink one or two times. It was only one or two times because after a game it was very crowded and difficult to get served. And anyway five o'clock on a Saturday afternoon was for me time to go home for one of my mother's great meals. By the way we did not drink, go into bars, until we were over 18 (with I think only two exceptions as far as I was concerned when I drank almost nothing). We had enough to do in our pre-18 lives without going into bars.

In Oct 1967, when DC and I were both aged 19, we stopped going regularly to Cardiff home games and started playing rugby for Llandaff Technical College on a Saturday afternoon instead.

In my 1967/68 season with Llandaff Tech Gx1 let me play rugby without hitting me. It was only when he knew I was going to go places in the game that he made plans to hit me, stop me, and this became apparent to him at the end of the season. New plans that is, bearing in mind that when aged 11 my rugby ability had been recognised and he acted to ensure I got nowhere in the game in those years. But anyway I'm now talking about the 1967/68 season, at the end of it I was made captain of the Llandaff Tech club (for the next season). This disturbed Gx1 a lot. It looked like I was on course for playing for Cardiff RFC and he didn't want that to happen.

In the next three months Gx1 decided what to do about the new problem. At the start of the 1968/69 season he hit me, put me on crutches for two months, an 'accident' of course, and took me out of the game for the rest of the season.

[Now I come to the part I haven't told you about before.] After DC and I stopped going regularly to Cardiff games in Oct 1967 we went to very few of them, perhaps only two in the 1967/68 season, none in the first part of the 1968 season and perhaps one more after that. On this occasion I'm talking about here we had been to a Cardiff home game. It was near the end of the 1968/69 season. After the game we went into the clubhouse bar where we met Mr V and a couple of his friends, he and one of his friends played in the Llandaff Tech team. [At other times we never went out with them for a drink, it could be that DC arranged this meeting or I had somehow met Mr V in the days before the game and arranged it.] In the bar I saw Miss W, she was with a rugby player who I think had played for Cardiff's 2nd team (but not the 1st team). Because she was with someone I didn't go over to her to say hello. After a half hour or so DC and I left Mr V and his friends in the bar, we had no plans to meet them later that night (5pm was for me back home for a meal time).

Even after watching an international at the Arms Park me and DC, probably without exception, went home straightaway for our evening meals and out again at 7-30 or 8. If we went back into town at that time the post match 'nearly impossible to get a drink' surge at the pubs had gone and things were a lot better.

It was months later when I next saw Mr V, I met him by accident, he told me that after our meeting at the Cardiff clubhouse he'd had a crash in his car near the Plaza (a cinema in the suburbs of Cardiff) and a woman in another car had been killed. [I haven't seen him since then. This is unbelievable, we have an Australia Road here. The Plaza is near Australia Road. And we know very well that Australia Road was for me, in Gx1 terms, what it was all about. Which means Gx1 arranged this clubhouse meeting and car 'accident' to reiterate one of his 'signs'. A car crash just to give a 'sign'? What! Bear in mind here that he arranged a car 'accident' in 1973 in which a lad was most probably killed.]

To believe that Mr V just happened, by pure chance, to have a crash near Australia Road is not on. Not when we know Gx1 was around, 'accidents', of all sorts, was his speciality.

Let's look at a new angle here. Did Gx1 somehow get Mr V to tell me he'd had a crash near the Plaza and a woman was killed when he never did? Tell him to lie to me in other words. Well how would he do this? Give the instructions to his father who then passed them on to Mr V is an answer. But Mr V was a friendly chatty sort of character, he wasn't the lying type. When he told me about it I believed him totally, he was serious and concerned about what he was saying.

This was the only time DC and I went in the clubhouse bar after we'd stopped going regularly to Cardiff games in Oct '67. And Mr V, as far as I know, didn't usually go to Cardiff games so this was for him also a rare visit. Two rare events, plus Miss W, and Australia Road 'say' without doubt that Gx1 arranged the meeting. So why did he arrange it, what was going on in his mind at the time?

I'll take the date of the meeting as near the end of the 1968/69 season. Gx1 had hit me to take me out of rugby at the start of the season and I hadn't re-commenced playing. Presumably the people at Llandaff Tech who had plans for me to go places in the game were pushing to get me back into the game, either by continuing with the Llandaff Tech club then going to Cardiff RFC or by going direct to Cardiff. Gx1 didn't want either to happen. If I continued with Llandaff Tech it would in effect nullify his start of season hit, he'd have to do it again. And if I went direct to Cardiff, well he'd have to think of a way to stop me there. It could be that it was about now that he formed a solution, he'd get the Llandaff Tech people off his back by saying, 'no, not a return to your team, send him direct to Cardiff', knowing that when I got there he'd covertly hit me in some way to ensure my playing for them was blocked. So the purpose of the Cardiff clubhouse meeting was to 'show' that this Llandaff Tech/Gx1 discussion was taking place. My meeting later on with Mr V was Gx1 giving me the result of the "discussion", it was, once again, Australia Road for me.

In the weeks before the 1969/70 season began I trained with Cardiff and played in their trial game. And here it is, another Gx1 hit, to make sure I didn't play for Cardiff. In the pre-season trial game he had me stupified/doped/poisoned, whatever you want to call it, I was useless on the pitch and of course Cardiff selectors didn't pick me to stay at the club. I went to Penarth RFC, played in their trial game and, undoped, they picked me for their 2nd team. Gx1 then fixed it again here, he arranged with the Penarth selectors for me not to play in their 1st team, but he didn't mind me playing in the shadows, in the 2nd team.

One of the reasons Gx1 didn't want me to play for Cardiff is that if I did he could find that some influential Cardiff rugby people would be able to stop his 'ship him to Australia' plan, i.e. the Cardiff people would form plans for my rugby here (staying in this country plans). So to ensure this didn't happen his stopping me play for Cardiff in the first place made sense to him.

Some words here on Miss W. I'd say that our Llandaff Tech fixture lecturer had me and Miss W lined up for going to Cardiff RFC. Miss W made it, I didn't. She didn't have warped Group X type people blocking her, I did. I've mentioned previously that our Llandaff Tech team had a good bit of team spirit going by the end of the 1967/68 season and this was illustrated by our 1968/69 pre-season training when we got our team all set up for going into the new season when this was four weeks or so before Llandaff Tech lectures started. I first noticed Miss W in the college after one of our training sessions. I'm not sure if it was near the end of the 1967/68 season or at the start of the 1968/69 season. She had an interest in the team. I thought she was very good, I mean quiet and attractive. And I wasn't going with anyone. But the possible relationship didn't happen because Gx1 stopped my rugby in Sept 1968. I'd say that if my rugby had continued I would have asked her out, and it's very likely she would have said yes.

What Mr V said to me when I met him sometime after the clubhouse meeting should be looked at again here. 'A woman was killed'. Whether a woman was killed in the car crash or not I don't know, I always thought he was telling me the truth, but he could have been told to lie to me (i.e. there was no death and no car crash). There is no doubt about what it meant to Gx1, it was one of his 'signs' that was directed at me, the woman that was killed, in metaphorical terms, was Miss W. I would not be going with her.

The 1963 Gx1 Heathway and St Malo 'Signs'

In 1963 I was 15. About a hundred yards up the street from where I lived was where GH lived, he was the same age as me. His father was a policeman. It was at this time that he moved to a road called Heathway, two and a half miles away. He invited me, DC and another friend (both lived near me and aged 15) to his house once a week in the evening to play board games. This continued for a few months. A couple of years later I lost touch with him. [Here again is Gx1 with his 'signs'. As you already know he was an ex-policemen in a senior government job. On this occasion he housed a policeman at a location that 'said' what he was going to arrange to have done to my father.]

In Heathway there is, in Group X language, WAT (the T is in the y), my father's initials. Heath connects to the Heath hospital (also known as the University Hospital of Wales). It was built in the 1963/69 period on a part of Heath park. So this 'sign', Heathway, places my father in the Heath hospital. And where did my father find himself ten years later when he was hit? In the Heath hospital.

Gx1 had another 'sign' in place at Heathway. St Malo Road joins Heathway a short distance from where GH lived. And what do we know about St Malo? It's a coastal town in northern France with a river running through it. The river's estuary has a barrier across it (the purpose of the barrier is to generate electricity). For Gx1 this was another 'sign' that indicated what he planned to have done to my father. A river running to it's estuary is comparable to the human digestive system. The estuary being the rectum. A barrier across my father's rectum would be 'necessary' after Gx1 had arranged for him to be given a false diagnosis of cancer applicable to his digestive system. The diagnosis being a result of his being covertly knifed in Paignton (using the 'accident/natural causes' method) two weeks earlier. The purpose of the false cancer diagnosis was, of course, to ensure no questions were asked when he was murdered sometime later using poison.

St Malo is near the island of Jersey, a ferry that connects them takes about twenty minutes. Jersey, the place where Gx1 went for his holiday every year. He knew about St Malo and it's barrier. He also, in 1963, when this Heathway 'sign' was produced, knew about the Heath hospital, it was in it's planning stages, and staff in the city hall, where he worked, were involved in it. I don't think I need to say any more here.

The Note on the Windscreen

Gx1 had, when I started at UCS in October 1974, fixed it for me to be there for just one (fail) year. It seems however that around May 1975 someone, let's say it was Mr Q (the positive part of Group X), was saying that perhaps I should stay at UCS and continue to the next year. And so a 'test' was arranged to see what I thought of Miss D. Group X knew that me and Miss D still had no long term plans in place and, more than that, I didn't seem to be particularly keen on her. Gx1, regardless of this, wanted me stopped at the end of the academic year, but he just had to go along with the 'test' idea.

It was about May 1975. I had driven from Swansea, where I was living, and was heading home to my parents place in Cardiff. It was a Friday at about 6pm. I was driving along a main road in Cardiff when I looked left down an adjoining side street. I saw Miss D's car parked about fifty feet from the junction. I stopped and parked and walked back to her car. I put a note on the windscreen saying, 'I was here, Haydn', and went back to my car and continued my journey home.

The reason I looked left down the side street, which I would not normally do when driving along a main road, is because about two weeks earlier Miss D was a passenger in my car as I drove along this road and at this spot she had said, 'Mr M lives there', referring to a house on the road. I said nothing (we were near the UHW and perhaps someone had told her he lived there as she drove past one day). Mr M worked in the same department at the UHW as she did, and he, if anyone in the department, was the most likely to go out with her, or knock her off on the side would be a way of putting it (I think he had a girlfriend). So, a couple of weeks later when I looked down the side street as I went past, I was looking to see if Miss D's car was there (parking on the main road was restricted to only on

150

one side of it). It was so she was at Mr M's place. And I left my note. Her being there didn't bother me at all, we never had any sort of 'only me only you' arrangement in place and so her being at his place was okay. Perhaps she'd soon finish with me, which is what I wanted anyway. I had no intention of knocking at his door to 'uncover' her.

Gx1 hoped I'd go knocking at Mr M's house to reprimand her, at least find out what she was up to. And she'd be there with say a couple of people from work which would make her being there okay. The 'test' result would then be, 'he was very concerned about her, he's keen on her', which would mean that, 'stop him at UCS and get him back to Cardiff for her', would stay in place. My lack of interest in her, I hadn't gone knocking at the door, supported Mr Q with his, 'keep him at UCS, and let his relationship with Miss D cease'. He had the idea, it seems, that I could start going with Miss K (see earlier in the book). For Gx1 the result of the test was a defeat.

We have previously seen in this book that when Gx1 lost an argument he brought in dirt methods to get his way. And this is what he did here. I won't detail this I'll just say that he got the result of the 'test' ignored/corrupted and another 'test' arranged. The new 'test', which took place about three weeks after the note on the windscreen, was improperly set up and no credence can be given to it's, 'he's keen on her', result. It was the result he wanted, so, 'stop him at UCS', could proceed.

Mr E Again Acts Covertly for Gx1

I was in the computer job with ICL in the summer of 1974 when this happened (having left the UHW job nine months earlier). Mr E phoned me one evening saying he wanted to meet me for a drink at lunchtime the next day. He wanted to meet, both in our cars, near the hospital, not at a pub. I said okay.

On meeting he told me he wanted us to drive to the nearby park where Miss D would be playing tennis. The department where he and Miss D worked had a tennis competition to see who was the best player in the department (it had one in 1973 when I was there, I played in it, Miss D didn't as far as I know). On this lunchtime she was playing someone in the competition. She had told me nothing about this. I'd never played tennis with her (I played the game in my 16 to 20 years with friends of mine and we had some good games), as far as I knew she was no good at it. I had no interest in going to see her but that's where he wanted to go, with me, and so in our cars we drove there.

We parked alongside the tennis courts and as soon as I got out of my car I could see that she was running toward me, she had stopped playing the game she was in, left the court and ran to me at my car. Uh! [There was no kiss or hug, we were never into that sort of thing when meeting, she just ran to me and said hello.] After a minute or so Mr E and I left to go to a pub and she went back to the tennis court to continue the game. I didn't see her play any tennis at all.

What was the Gx1 thinking, why did he use Mr E to get me to go here? Miss D was wearing a new tennis dress, I mean it was presumably new because she never played the game, because, as I've said, she was no good at it as far as I know. Gx1 knew she couldn't play the game and so he didn't want me to watch her play, he gave her, via her mother, the, 'stop playing as soon as you see him and run to him', bit. My leaving with Mr E after only a minute or so without seeing her play supports this. Gx1 had told him just to get me there and quickly leave. Perhaps he wanted to impress on the department that she was keen on me. Which would help him in his efforts to get me married to her (which apparently he wanted before carrying out the final part of the plan to kill my father). I say "impress on the department" because a number of the male members of the department had turned up to watch the game (about six of them were present, all under thirty, most of them married), to see her underwear of course. And Gx1 knew that would happen. Her new dress couldn't have been any shorter.

It could be that Gx1 was also thinking, knowing that I could play the game, that my seeing her in a tennis dress would make me like her more. Well if he thought this it would be an illustration of how thick he was.

At this time I believed that Miss D, the church going living at home seventeen year old 'virgin' when I started to go out with her nine months earlier in September '73, was a con job, she was in a covert sexual relationship with her brother? I had taken her up, started to go out with her, hence she was no longer a 'virgin', so it went. I was a few years older than her and in recent years had worked for a while in 'swinging' London, in her mother's mind that is. I could see that if I finished with her 'virgin' daughter, having 'taken advantage' of her, [Fixed up by Gx1 to 'kill' me is more accurate of course.] giving no reason for finishing, there was a good chance I'd find myself in trouble in some way or other. And of course if I accused her of sex with her brother and then finished with her that would obviously mean trouble. So this tennis incident perhaps helps to illustrate the awkward situation I was in. I thought the best way of dealing with it was to say nothing and quietly get out of the relationship somehow. [My moving to Swansea should have done it but it didn't.]

In the years before I met Miss D I had known some very good

clean thinking females. In the months that followed my starting with her I realised that she was not in the same category, her thinking had some oddities in it, you could say I thought, 'there's something up somewhere'. There was a couple of notable occurrences in this area but there was more, little things that people do/say, that don't usually get recorded in one's memory, help to form an opinion of a person. It was about March 1974 when I formed the opinion that she was in a covert sexual relationship with her brother.

Gx1 stopped my relationships with the "very good" females in the pre-'72 years because he had ship out plans for me, unmarried. In 1973, having against his plans returned from the 'ship out' destination (Australia), he got me going out with Miss D knowing that she was trouble. Bear in mind here the 1974 piano song, where he 'advertised' what he was doing, killing me and my father quietly.

More on 1968

My draughtsman's job with AEI finished in April 1968. It was probably early September when I had an interview for an electronics job at the Cardiff Royal Infirmary. The job came with one day a week off to study at a local college when the new academic year started in October, which is something I wanted, I'd go on a course at Llandaff Tech, I would also be captaining the college's rugby side.

Gx1 hit me in the second rugby game of the season, to stop my rugby, it was about 9th September. Part of what he arranged was a false diagnosis at the CRI, with the result that my lower left leg was put in plaster, this was his bullet in the greyhound's ear.

I started the CRI job in mid-September and turned up on crutches. The electronics technician who ran the small department (six including me and three mechanical engineering technicians) wasn't happy about this. But anyway the plaster on my leg didn't stop me sitting at a bench all day so I stayed at the job (no injury leave).

Three months earlier in June I'd sat the Ordinary National Certificate exams at Llandaff Tech and the result was a pass. The next stage was the first year of a two year Higher National Certificate course. In the last week or two of September I would have enrolled on it but the person who ran the department I was in at the CRI was, because I was on crutches, against this. He said I should not enrol on a course. This was contrary to what I had been told at the interview ('one day a week on a course'), getting round the college on crutches was my own problem not his, but anyway I didn't argue about it so there was no enrolment for me.

1968 was a big year for Gx1. In the first week of September 1968 I was

153

playing rugby for Llandaff Tech and I was the captain of the team, and I intended to enrol on a one day a week course at the college a couple of weeks later. By the end of September things were very different, he had smashed/stopped my rugby, stopped me enrolling on a one day a week course at Llandaff Tech, and in earlier weeks made sure I didn't start a full time university course.

I have an awful feeling that the Llandaff Tech rugby team folded, ceased to exist, within a year or so. Myself and DC had been major contributors to getting the team running well by the end of the 1967/68 season, in the first part of the season it usually couldn't get a full team together. September 1968, the start of a new season, saw the team in very good shape. When they lost me after two games the team took a heavy blow, and, as I say, I believe it folded in the 1970/71 season. Why am I not sure about this? Well after Gx1 hit me I did not play for the team again and did not at a later date continue to study at the college, and I saw very little of DC after it happened because he had started to go steady with a female (he later married her) with the result that we stopped going out together in the evenings. Since 1968 I have only seen him a few times and I have never thought of asking him about the team's 1968/69 season and later.

1969, Gx1 Completes the Destruction of My Llandaff Tech Life

In the 1968/69 academic year, I was not on a course at Llandaff Technical College. In about June 1969, nine months after starting the CRI job, I was moved to the newly built University Hospital of Wales, three miles away, where our department was opening a new department.

The job I was in offered one day a week off to go on a course at a college and October '69, the start of a new academic year, was approaching, what was I going to do? Well quite naturally I'd go to Llandaff Tech on the first year of the Higher National Certificate. [But when Gx1 was fixing things "naturally" was a word that never happened.]

Mr E, who was about my age, was already in the electronics department at the UHW when I arrived, he thought the two of us should go on the first year HNC course at Glamorgan Polytechnic which is about ten miles north of Cardiff, he said this because he lived eighteen miles north of Cardiff. And the head of our department said the two of us should go to the polytechnic. And so I enrolled on the polytechnic course and not at Llandaff Tech.

Oh dear me Gx1 covertly dominated/fixed my life didn't he. My life in our 'free' society. He had recently, in September 1968, destroyed my life at

154

Llandaff Tech and he didn't want me to re-start it, go back there, so in 1969, before I was moved to the UHW he installed Mr E in the new department ready for my arrival. He lived near, north of, Glamorgan Polytechnic, and Gx1 would use him to keep me away from Llandaff Tech. Without him I would never have even considered going to the polytechnic, and presumably the head of the department wouldn't have thought of it either.

It really was stupid for me to go to the polytechnic. What it did mean was me driving a lot of unnecessary miles, bear in mind that as well as the one day a week there, it was also two evenings a week at the place. Every trip, there and back to Cardiff, was 20 miles, when it could have been 3 miles to and from Llandaff Tech. Crazy, that was Gx1 for you. His activities, his arrangements, were either warped, criminal, corrupt or stupid. And he was a high level member of our society paid out of taxpayers money!

How did Gx1 find then place Mr E? Near the end of 1968 or the first few months of 1969 he must have gone to (phoned) the registrar's office at the polytechnic and got the names and addresses of the people who were on the final year of their ONC course, picked out those who lived north of the college and then in the weeks that followed got one of them to move from the job he was in to the UHW job. You must bear in mind that Gx1 to a large extent could tell management personnel what to do.

A Few Days in Threeseven in 1970

I started to go out with Miss N, Mr Q's daughter, in August 1969. I was working at the Cardiff Royal Infirmary and she worked in the offices there. In the summer of 1970 I stayed with her for a few days at her parents caravan in Tresaith, west Wales.

For those who don't know the welsh language "tre" is three and "saith" is seven. So the location would be called Threeseven in english. I've previously told you about Gx1 using 37 as a 'sign' (the three horse shoes, and junction 37) to 'indicate' when he was going to carry out the first part of the plan to murder my father. Another 37, Tresaith, would not be a coincidence. In 1973 Gx1 hit my father in the back, '73 backwards, 37. Gx1 got Mr Q in the latter part of 1969 or the first half of 1970 (after I started going out with his daughter) to buy/rent the caravan so he could use it as a 'sign' that would be attached to me when I went there.

The Gx1 Car Theft in 1971

Here is something that happened in 1971 when I was working at St Bartholomew's in London. My car was stolen. I was living in Sudbury and every work day I drove two and a half miles to Wembley Park tube station where I parked my car and got the train to Bart's in east central London. One day when I returned to the car at 6-15pm it wasn't there. A week or two later the car was found and I collected it from a police station in north London.

Up to today (2015) I haven't given what happened here much thought. But looking at this now there is no doubt that it requires closer consideration. What was going on at this time? I was playing rugby at the Wasps, in the first two games of the season I had played for the second team and scored, they wanted me to play in the first team, Gx1 wouldn't have it and he used his influence to get me pushed down out of sight into the Wasps fourth team. But there was pressure in the Wasps to get me back to the second/first team area. Was it a coincidence that this car theft, the only time in my life I've had my car stolen, happened at this time? I'd say no, it's almost a certainty that the theft was arranged by Gx1. And the reasoning goes like this. Gx1 knew that the car was very useful to me for my rugby. Two evenings a week I spent training at the Wasps ground which was near where I lived. The car was my transport from Wembley Park tube station to the Wasps for training. And it contained my rugby gear. Taking the car away from me would cause problems for my training sessions. And that is what he had in mind, he wanted to stop my training at the Wasps along with my second/first team rugby. So he arranged to have the car stolen. But the car was found after only two weeks, where did he go wrong?

A few days after the theft I was in Cardiff and I told Miss N about it. I was still seeing her but we had no long term plans. She presumably told her father Mr Q (a policeman) about the theft. [Did Mr Q make enquiries on the car that led to it being returned to me? It could be that Gx1 arranged the theft without telling the other Group X members about it. Mr Q, as I've told you before, was in Group X but he was a positive influence for me. When he was told by his daughter about the theft it could have been the first he heard of it and he made 'internal' enquiries, the whereabouts of the car was established (because it was an 'official' theft) and it was returned to me.]

The theft was probably part of Gx1's hurried response to my success at the Wasps, one of the things he could get done straight away to stop my progress (along with his getting a Wasps contact to have me dropped after my two faultless games in the second team, something he managed to arrange very quickly). He no doubt knew that it wouldn't cause problems for long, I'd get insurance money and I could get another car, but it would take weeks for the money to come through. So something more was required. And what did he come up with? He got the head of my department at Bart's to put me into a stupid (totally unnecessary) on call job which was coupled to my taking up accommodation near the hospital (moving out of the flat I was in at Sudbury). The job stopped my two nights a week training at the Wasps. The rest was easy for him, he said to the Wasps, 'he's stopped training so he must have lost interest in rugby, presumably you are now content to keep him in the fourth team'.

When Sudbury Court rugby club got me to move to the Wasps, who then selected me to play for their second team, it must have caused a bit of a stir in Gx1's mind. It confirmed that Llandaff Tech were right in 1968 when they said that I should play for Cardiff. When he destroyed my rugby in the 1968/70 years he now certainly knew, if confirmation was needed, that he had stopped a top level career in rugby. And what did he do? The dirt he had for brains thought up new ways to stop my rugby (the put down, the car theft and the on call job).

The Gx1 Coats Theft

Here's another theft that I pinned on Gx1 years back (early 80s). This happened in 1968 when he was worried about the success I was having in life (AEI and Llandaff Tech wanted me to go on a full time university course and my rugby was going well).

I had a really good sheepskin coat/jacket (my mother had bought it for me). [For Gx1 the coat would have looked too good, too impressive. And in his mind it was 'take it off him' time.] One evening I went into town with a friend of mine. He was wearing a very good knee length woollen overcoat. Both coats were stolen.

This theft was a small part in the Gx1 'keep him down' policy.

Poisoned by Gx1 Before a Cardiff Rugby Club Trial in 1969

I've told you about what happened here, I will now fill in some details.

The end of the 1967/68 rugby season was a big problem, a shock point, for Gx1. Rugby, for me, looked like it was on in a big way (Cardiff RFC was on the cards). And that, in his mind, was a direct challenge to the covert plan to murder my father, the first part of which was due to take place when his mortgage was finished a few years on from 1968. If I played in rugby's top level the plan might have to be called off, it would definitely make it more difficult for him to get it done. So, in his warped mind, he had to hit my rugby, make sure I didn't have any significant success in the game.

I'll briefly mention here, it's covered elsewhere, that in the summer of 1968 Gx1 tried to murder me, using the 'accident' method. This would certainly stop my rugby (and AEI university plans). But it didn't come off.

At the start of the 1968/69 season Gx1 took me out of rugby altogether, he used the planned accident method to cripple me, put me on crutches for two months. I didn't play for the rest of the season. He preceded this hit with the 'butcher' meeting that 'said' he was going to stop my rugby and the AEI/Llandaff university plan. And he also issued 'put a bullet in his ear'.

He probably thought it was a bit too much to arrange to have me crippled again at the start of the 1969/70 season (things would start to look a bit odd), instead he went for other ways of stopping me getting to rugby's top level.

The Gx1 PGN car number plate 'sign' appears in August 1969, one of his, 'your rugby is dead', signs. Together with the, 'u to Australia' sign (Autocar magazines).

It was presumably our Llandaff tech fixture lecturer that got me to go to the 1969 pre-season training sessions at Cardiff RFC. He perhaps knew Cardiff were looking for a wing and thought I'd get the place.

In the pre-season training sessions there was no Cardiff winger present (left or right wing), at least no established player. [Which indicates, as I've said, that they were looking for a wing.]

Gx1 knew what was going on and he was out to make sure I didn't get the Cardiff place. What he did was to get the Newport right wing to apply for a move to Cardiff, he would, being an established first team player, take precedence over me, i.e. he'd get the Cardiff place and I wouldn't. But it wasn't as simple as that, he knew that Cardiff might keep me at the club anyway.

A trial game was to take place. The Newport wing was due to appear in it (he hadn't attended the pre-season training sessions). I could play on the left or right wing but usually I'd play on the right wing. The Newport player was a right wing. [The trial game was divided into four sessions, at the end of the first three sessions team changes were made. Those who made it through to the last session would probably be kept on at the club.] I wasn't put on the field in the first two sessions. [Which shows that the selectors had me lined up as a probably keep player.] I was sent on to the field for the start of the third session, as a left wing, and the Newport player was the right wing on the other side, my opposing player in other words. [In selectors terms it was probably him or me to stay on at the club, hence they had us playing against each other to see who came off best.]

A lineout was being formed near the half way line on the right of the field, and that means, my being on the left wing, that I was standing near the middle of the field at the end of the threequarter line. The other side won the ball and they passed it along the line with no one holding on to it for long (perhaps they'd been told to get it out to their wing). When their right wing, the player I was to take out, received the ball, he was near the touchline, say about ten yards from it. And where was I? Twenty yards away. I had walked perhaps three or four steps from where I was standing when the lineout took place. I wasn't injured. I wasn't ill. I could not understand it. I never had the ball once. [It is now obvious of course that I'd been got at by Gx1 (fixed/doped/poisoned), but at the time these thoughts did not enter my head. It was 1975 when I first became aware of Group X dirt activities (at UCS).]

In such a condition it's of no surprise at all to say that I tackled no one in the time I was on the field. And as for someone passing the ball to me, well I was presumably never in the right place to receive it. I was able to stand up, walk round, but in other ways I was useless.

The sessions were each about ten minutes long. The one I was in seemed to be over in less than ten minutes. I was not selected to continue into the last session, and I was not kept on at the club.

It could be that the trial session I was in was terminated early because it had done it's job, shown that the Newport winger was the one to go for (and not me).

I must have looked hopeless walking round, I couldn't run. I felt a bit strange, light headed, but this meant nothing to me.

You could say the selectors should have realised that something was up. From the pre-season training sessions it was obvious I could play the game and then there was the Llandaff Tech recommend. But they, no doubt, were not thinking in terms of players being doped. In other words they presumably thought that what they'd seen was odd but they suspected nothing.

Gx1 knew that placing the Newport wing into the trial to take precedence over me could backfire. If I flattened him (he knew my tackling was exceptional) I'd get the Cardiff place. So, to take no chances, he got a hit man to poison me, dope me, to ensure the Newport player came out the winner.

Why do I say that it was Gx1 that got the Newport wing to apply for a move to Cardiff? Whenever he could he placed 'signs' into his arrangements. And the 'sign' he created here, using the Newport player, gave an almost exact indication of the plans he had for me. Newport gives 'ew' and 'ort'. the 'ew' gives 'u' and the 'ort' gives 'crt'. CRT is my brother's initials, so the sign says 'u to Australia'. By placing the Newport player in front of me (my opposing player), I was looking at the 'u to Australia' sign. Gx1 was stopping me play for Cardiff because in two/three years time he was going to ship me out of the country (one way), and playing for them could stop his ship out plan.

So Gx1 had made sure I didn't continue at Cardiff. But I was still willing and able to play the game. So he had to watch me, check that I didn't make progress in some other place.

Within a few days of the Cardiff trial I went to Penarth and played in their pre-season trial game. [I was okay here, I mean Gx1 done nothing to me.] The Penarth selectors picked me to continue with them. I played in their second team in the first game of the season. Then in the next game they picked me for their first team. I had a good game [Detailed in TCF6 and 9.]. And things were looking very good for me.

A number of Penarth fixtures were with some of the best teams in the country, meaning that I'd got into top level rugby. And what happened next? You can easily guess the answer. Gx1 moved in again to stop me.

In the next game I was selected as a reserve for Penarth's game against Cardiff (first teams). [This really was getting too much for Gx1, if I played against Cardiff I'd show the Cardiff selectors that something had gone drastically wrong in their trial game. Cardiff had bigger forwards and they'd get 75% of the ball and I'd have a great time tackling all over the place.]

At about 8am on the morning of the game against Cardiff a telegram was delivered to our house. It had been sent by Penarth rugby club and it said I might be playing in the Cardiff game later on that day (it was an early evening kick off). I considered the telegram to be odd. Why send me a telegram telling me what I already knew?

The telegram was a Gx1 'sign', he was repeating what he had already 'said' a number of times in the past year or so, 'top level rugby is a no go area for you'. He'd arranged with someone on the Penarth selection committee to have it sent to me (see below for an additional comment). And at the same time he 'put the poison in' at the club. Meaning that he fed some dirt/rubbish into the club to get a permanent block on my playing for the first team. After this telegram I never again played for the first team.

How do I know the telegram was a Gx1 sign? The first thing to say is that telegrams were not sent by rugby clubs, certainly not usually sent anyway. It's the only rugby telegram I've ever received. Now on to the next point. A telegram had a special significance for our family. My brother, living in Australia, sometimes sent one to us on the occasion of a birthday (we never received them from anyone else). And who knew about the Australia telegrams. Gx1. His wife was my father's sister, and my mother, when she occasionally called to see her, would have told her about a recently received telegram from Australia. So this Penarth telegram 'sign' points directly at Gx1. He knew all about our Australia telegrams. The Penarth telegram was to 'tell' me, again, 'u to Australia - top level rugby is dead'.

I'll say some more on the telegram. It's more than likely that Gx1, having come up with the telegram 'sign' idea, sent it himself. I mean why bother to ask/tell someone in the club to send me a telegram when the response he could get was, 'we don't send telegrams, if we want to contact a player quickly we phone him'. So, by sending it himself, he would avoid what could be an awkward response. Going to a post office and sending a

160

telegram saying it was from so and so would have been no problem in 1969.

Gx1, in the 1968/69 years, destroyed my rugby career when it was at a crucial stage. Age 20/21 was an ideal time to enter top level rugby. And in the years that followed he continued to hit/stop my rugby.

I have used the words 'the trial poisoning' in the title of this section. Some people would say it should be 'the trial doping', i.e. I was doped not poisoned. What I will say is that any substance that is covertly put in a person's drink/food with the intention of altering his normal behaviour (e.g. stupifying him) can be, and should be as far as I am concerned, called a poison. Because the substance is harmful/noxious to the persons natural bodily system.

2016

More Details on 1971/72

I first met Miss L in Cardiff, it was about January '71. She was the best friend of the girl DC was going out with. Both of them were nurses working in Cardiff hospitals. I met her when I had a drink in a pub with DC and his girlfriend. I then met her on one other occasion (just as a friend) before I left my job in Cardiff and went to work at St Bartholomew's in London in March '71. I found accommodation in a guest house in east London (a tube journey from Bart's). I was in this guest house for about six weeks and during this time I was told, presumably by DC, that Miss L had started a job as a nurse at the Hammersmith hospital in west London. I contacted her and we arranged to meet. I have a faded memory of my being in west London one weekend afternoon for an hour or so and this could have been when we first met in London. Other meetings with her stand out more clearly in my memory, as follows.

I was still staying at the guest house when she told me on the phone that she had some tickets for a dance at London Welsh rugby club. I drove to the club with two friends of mine that were my age, one was in the place I was staying at the other was staying a couple of doors away. Presumably she had told me that I could bring a friend or two with me. I met her and some female friends of her's in the rugby club (perhaps she posted the tickets to me). We had a drink and talk and that was about it. At the end of the night I drove with my two friends back to where we were staying.

Sometime later she phoned me to say she had some tickets for a classical music concert at the Royal Albert Hall, only one ticket for me this time. I met her with a female friend of her's outside the hall and we went in. She only had the cheapest tickets which meant we were standing on a top balcony, along with many others, and we didn't stay for the entire concert. But at least we could say we had been to the Royal Albert Hall.

On another occasion she had tickets for a piano and violin concert at the South Bank arts venue. I met her and her female friend at a tube station near the South Bank and we walked from there.

Another one of my faded memories is of meeting her to go to a pop concert at some place in London, it wasn't my idea, so again she must have got tickets for it and invited me. There was no dancing or drinking at the event, it was just a sort of serious listen to some live pop music. We only stayed for a bit of it.

For all this time we were good friends, nothing more than that. I remember that once I drove her back to her accommodation at Hammersmith hospital at the end of a night out and we just said good night (I mean there was no kissing).

The next time I saw her, It could have been the end of November '71, I drove to where she was living, it was now in a flat in west London, and we went out for a drink. At the end of the night we got closer to each other, i.e. kissing but she wouldn't let me proceed any further than that. It was about this time when she left her job as a nurse and started a job as an air hostess with BOAC.

When I saw her next it was January '72, she was now staying in a different place in west London with another girl who was in the same job as her. I drove to her place and after a drink in a pub we went to a quiet party in a large flat. Things were fine with us, as they had been all along. We left the party at about eleven and I took her back to her place. She was working on a flight that was due to leave Heathrow early the next morning which means she had to go to the airport at about midnight. I would have been quite happy to drive her there but she said some airline staff had already arranged to pick her up from her place. [This night was the last time I saw her.]

Let's now get into the close up area. The Group X covert area. And straightaway I find something that tells me that Gx1 was around. Miss L's nurse friend in London, the one who had been with us when we went to the concerts etc, went to a new job at the Walsgrave hospital in Coventry at about the same time as Miss L left her nurse's job. My father's first name (Walby usually called Wal) and grave. A coincidence? No of course not. Gx1 was 'saying' that his main concern was to put my father in a grave. In other words he arranged to have Miss L's friend moved to the Walsgrave hospital. For him it was a 'sign' and it means he was in the process of stopping my relationship with Miss L. Because putting my father in a grave was tied in with shipping me to Australia one way, and she was not a ship out candidate. And this 'quiet party' night was his 'stop the relationship' night.

Gx1 could see that my relationship with Miss L was going well and that it would soon become serious (with long term plans). I was playing rugby at the Wasps and that was very good as far as she was concerned because she appreciated rugby, which means she wouldn't have stopped it, and I was happy with her.

It's difficult to give you more details on the Gx1 'stop it' night because of his covert, non public, methods, but I think you can see that there is no doubt that he stopped my relationship with Miss L. It's a piece of the jigsaw that is an exact fit in the overall picture. The Gx1 'sign', Walsgrave, just confirms it.

[Let's go into a bit more detail on Miss P, the Bart's nurse.] One night, a week or so before Christmas '71, I went to a part of Bart's hospital where there was a bar and some dancing. It was the only time I went here. The reason for my going was that one of the people I worked with, he was a few years older than me and married, wanted me to go there with him. As I've mentioned previously I lived a quiet life in London as far as evenings out were concerned. At this place I met Miss P and we left together at the end of the night and decided to meet again sometime.

A couple of days later she wanted me to go with her to an evening carol service and I said okay. She was living in the hospital so it was easy for us to meet.

At about midday on the day before Christmas day I got her to look round the shops with me in central London. She had a nurse friend who's parents lived in west Wales and when I drove to Cardiff later in the day I took her with me and dropped her at Cardiff train station where she got a train to west Wales.

Having returned to my job at Bart's after Christmas Miss P wanted me to go with her to her parents place which was south of London. We drove there on a Saturday, stayed the night, her parents were there, and drove back to Bart's on Sunday evening. The trip was okay. A week or two later she left the Bart's accommodation and moved to a flat in north London (not far out). I saw her at this flat once, then soon after she left the Bart's job and started a job at a hospital in Oxford. Her move to Oxford meant that we stopped seeing each other. But I did see her once more, that was in about April '72 when I went to a job interview in Slough and after the interview I drove to Oxford to see her.

Some time back I said that my short relationship with Miss P was another relationship that Gx1 stopped. Well now you can see, from a few paragraphs back, that Gx1 in November/December '71, having formed his, 'stop him going with Miss L' plan, was not going to let anyone take her place. Which means he quickly formed, in January '72, his, 'stop him going with Miss P' plan, and he did this by moving her to a new job in Oxford. Here we again have confirmation of his involvement, it appears when I went to see her in Oxford in the form of his 'hoppit' 'sign' (details earlier in the book).

Miss P, evidently, was another female who was not a ship out candidate, i.e. if I formed a steady relationship with her, married her, I would have stayed in this country. And that as we know very well that was not what Gx1 wanted. My going steady with a non-ship out female when in London, heading for marriage, would also have meant the block on my first team rugby at the Wasps would had to have been removed, and he didn't want that either. For him it was 'ship him out' and hit anything that gets in the way.

Elsewhere in the book I have mentioned the girl the Wasps placed in the latter half of my season with them, hoping I would start a relationship with her, Miss R. Gx1 blocked her for the same reasons I've just given you, i.e. she was not a ship out candidate. And Miss H, who surprisingly appeared, started work, in London, was presumably also not a ship out candidate.

[I'll tell you how Miss N fitted in to the time I was working at Bart's.] I started to go out with Miss N in Cardiff in August '69. She was an attractive girl and we got on okay with each other. My moving to London in March '71 for the Bart's job and my staying in London on weekends to play rugby meant that my seeing her became a rare occurrence. This didn't bother me because I knew that really she was not my type, I didn't think I'd marry her. We went on holiday together for a week or so in the summer of '71 (we arranged it before I moved to London) and I saw her again a month or two later in September in Cardiff (when I told her about the car theft) but then our meetings again (with the new rugby season) became very infrequent to the extent that we just about finished with each other but neither of us actually said this. This coincided with my friendship with Miss L in London changing, in November '71, to a close relationship. Miss L was, or was about to be, my new girlfriend. [But Gx1 stepped in to block her, separate us, to make sure his plans stayed on track.]

On the 1967/68 Gx1 Attempts to Kill Me

I have said in this book that the reason Gx1 tried twice to kill me in the 1967/68 years was to stop me going to university in September 1968. Yes the September 1967 attempt on my life was to make sure I didn't go to university, because I was a 'commie' and it would interfere with the plans to murder my father. AEI and Llandaff Tech having in the previous months formed their plans for me to go to university. But the August 1968 attempt to kill me could have been for a different reason. I say this because in July 1968 Gx1 used his covert activities to apply some dirt to me, smear me, and this dirt could have been enough to ensure I wouldn't go to university. If this was the case why then did he, near the end of August 1968, try to kill me? Well the answer would be that it was to stop my rugby because

165

significant success for me in the game was on the cards and it would cause problems for the plan to murder my father (in the 1968/69 season I would be captaining the Llandaff Tech side and he'd been told I was on course for Cardiff RFC).

When the August 1968 attempt to kill me was not successful he, about two weeks later, 'accidentally' put me on crutches for two months, to stop my rugby.

The Welsh Office Job in 1979

Gx1 tried to have me killed in 1977 because he knew that what he'd got done to me in two universities in 1974/76 could backfire on him.

Pressure from my father and his old employer and the decent part of Group X got me into an electrical job with the Welsh National Opera in December 1977 (the decent part of Group X, Mr Q, knew about my Arms Park singing from the January '75 party and he thought it could be useful here). These people and/or UCC then got me to leave the opera job in August 1978 and write to the registrar of UCC about what had occurred when I was at UCC. This got UCC officially, and the Welsh Office, going on things. UCC knew they had stopped me in 1976 under pressure from outsiders (Gx1) and they wanted things corrected for me.

Gx1 realised he had to try to justify getting me stopped and, via the jobcentre, he got me, in December 1978, into an electronics job at a place a mile or so north of Llanbradach. He hoped I would call at Miss D's place on route to or from the job. I'll expand on this.

There is a mountain of about 900 feet height on the northern boundary of Cardiff and a road, steep going up, with a top flat bit of about ten yards that goes, again steeply, down to Caerphilly. Caerphilly is three miles from the northern boundary of Cardiff. Llanbradach is then two miles north of Caerphilly. The place where Miss D lived was east of Caerphilly about one mile down the road. Caerphilly, and Llanbradach are in a flat land area, separated from the Cardiff flat land by the mountain.

Gx1, as well as placing me into the job in Miss D's area, got a cousin of mine to move to, live in, Llanbradach. And he got him to call during the day, with his wife, at my parents house, where I was living, to see my father and mother (she was out), and me. He invited me to his house in Llanbradach. For Gx1 this was another way of getting me to go to Miss D. I never took up his offer, i.e. I didn't go to my cousin's house.

Gx1 also, would you believe, got me interested in moving to a house in Caerphilly. I didn't attempt to make the move.

Gx1 had told UCC in 1976, as part of his activities to get my study stopped, that I should marry Miss D because she was wonderful (I had recently finished with her), and stopping me would get me to go back to her. And so, in getting me into Miss D's area in 1978, he was trying to vindicate himself (hoped I'd go back with her). But he still lacked some important information. He didn't know that I had a very good reason for finishing with her and not going back with her (I'd told no one about it, not even Miss D), and besides my reason for finishing with her was supported by the fact that I'd never got on with her properly anyway. So, of course, in late 1978 and early 1979 I didn't try to get back with her. Which means the Welsh Office and UCC were left wondering about what had happened in 1976, and they decided to get me out of the Llanbradach job in January 1979 and straight into a temporary Welsh Office clerical job in Cardiff, and this was quickly followed by a temporary Inland Revenue job. The Welsh Office (and UCC) wanted something done about my study being improperly stopped in 1976.

In early 1979 Gx1 could see that the possible backfire was starting to happen. Staff at UCC and UCS knew that he had used his influence to get me stopped at both the colleges, knew in other words that he had got college staff to give me fixed question papers and false results.

I should again mention here that the covert activities carried out by Gx1 to get me stopped at UCC (the October '75 electron bullet, the February '76 poisoning, etc) were most probably still in the dark at this time, i.e. UCC didn't know about these hits and the Welsh Office had probably not yet found out about them. The Welsh Office did however know about his part completed plan to murder my father (they put a stop on it's completion).

Presumably, as I've said previously in this book, the Welsh Office forwarded the problem (what is to be done about it?) to the top level in the government, and that meant Mr Callaghan.

There is an extra bit of information I can give you here. I am inserting this paragraph into this section in 2018. In the past year or so I have become aware that Mr Callaghan, before he became an MP in 1945, worked in the Inland Revenue from 1929 to 1936 then for a few years he worked for an Inland Revenue trade union. So it would appear that the Welsh Office by moving me into a temporary job with the Inland Revenue were 'saying' that they had forwarded the dispute to Mr Callaghan. This paragraph reinforces what I've said previously.

You see what I'd said in my letter to UCC's registrar in 1978 was correct, I had indeed passed the 1976 end of academic year examinations and been given false fail results. And the, 'what is to be done about it', question was being passed from UCC to higher authorities.

And what happened in 1979? Mr Callaghan and his government left office. Let me mention the phrase "winter of discontent". The phrase was created by someone and used as a label in the media for the problems Mr Callaghan was having running the government in the 78/79 winter.

Problems that led to his calling an early general election in May '79 (six months or so before it was due).

But anyway Mr Callaghan, presumably because of the unfavourable media coverage his Labour government had received in recent months, lost the election, and he was replaced by Mrs Thatcher and her Conservative government.

Mrs Thatcher apparently took charge of the UCC dispute. And this was when I was poisoned and placed on a high roof, and months later hit by an electron/laser beam at Swansea Town Hall (false evidence planted into the situation by government officials). The government had stopped the dispute being resolved in my favour by covertly dirtying me (deceiving the people at UCC who supported what I said had happened).

"Winter of Discontent", gives w o d, Welsh Office discontent. A coincidence? I don't think so. The phrase was fed into the media to 'say' that the Welsh Office was unhappy about something. The Welsh Office apparently wanted to get the UCC dispute resolved in my favour but were not allowed to do so. It went to Mr Callaghan for him to deal with. Perhaps the people that ran this country said to him:

> 'yes Mr Thomas is correct but he has to lose the dispute because we cannot have a scandal like that get into the public's hands. To lose the dispute means that we get him to commit suicide, or we plant false evidence into it (have him dirtied)'.

Mr Callaghan could have responded by saying that if he couldn't resolve it in my favour he wouldn't have anything to do with authorizing the suicide or the plant. And so the people that ran this country got him out of the job as quickly as possible (by creating problems for him) and with a new PM in place, Mrs Thatcher, got her to give the go ahead on the suicide and the plant.

2017

<u>Two Early Gx1 Australia Road 'Signs'</u>

There's the walk I did in 1963 when aged fifteen with AR. He was in my class and he lived in Australia Road, which was near our school. It was a 15 mile walk with a night out in a tent for the Duke of Edinburgh's bronze award. [The headmaster, told what to do by Gx1, had picked him to go with me (just the two of us) to 'say' I was on Australia road, a long walk to Australia.]

The walk was on a Saturday afternoon in the summer. AR and I walked from Cardiff to Cowbridge common along the A48 road. Starting at 1pm and arriving around 6pm. We camped on the common (a field) for the night and at 8am the next day AR's father picked us up in his car and got us back to Cardiff.

I borrowed a rucksack from DC for the trip. He like me was in the scouts for a couple of years (not the same place as me). The tent we used for this night out was our (my parents) ridge tent. It packs into a fairly heavy sack and so I separated it into two parts for the walk, poles and pegs in one part, tent material in the other.

I only did the bronze, I didn't go on to do the silver and gold. I think you had to be 16 to do the gold and I left the school before I was 16 (to Llandaff Tech for a full time year) and anyway I wasn't interested in going beyond the bronze. Age 15 was the standard school leaving age at the time for "secondary modern" schools, where I was. O levels were done in other schools (grammar/high) where the leaving age was sixteen.

[This Australia road walk 'sign' is not the first definite 'you are on Australia road', 'you are going to be shipped out', 'sign', an earlier one is in 1956 when aged seven or eight (before we got the mortgage for the house in Cathays).] My mother took me to a dentist that was on North Road. [It was crt road in Group X language (my brother's initials are CRT), and more than that, Australia Road was nearby. Gx1 got someone to tell my mother about a 'good' dentist. The dentist hit me.] He made a sudden hard jab with a needle into the gums in my mouth that agonized me for a moment. [I had a dentist needle job in 1966/7 and that was nowhere near as painful. This latter dentist was doing a Llandaff Tech/AEI correction job and so he did a good/proper job, i.e. he didn't 'hit' me. It was a correction job on my front upper teeth which Gx1 had hit using acid in 1960/62 as part of his stop his rugby and dirty him activities. What did I say? See later.]

The Speedometer and the 1969 Engine Overheat Drive

Here is some more on the Triumph Herald car me and my parents purchased from a dealers in 1965. We bought it and when driving it home I noticed that the speedometer went full over, even when going slow. I took it apart in the evening, saw the problem, the rotate disc was sticking to the needle disc, caused by oil that had somehow got in there. I cleaned the oil out and it was okay then. [A bloke in the dealer's garage done it on the instructions of Gx1, squirted oil into the back of the speedo. Gx1 was 'saying' that Do, my mother's name (Doreen), from speedo, created a hard on (sex) for him, i.e. he wanted to have sex with my mother. The name of Gx1 contains o, i and l in that order, oil, which would, in Group X language, connect him to this speedo occurrence.]

At times it feels a bit silly when I am explaining Group X 'signs' to you. I've said it before and I will say it again here that giving out signs is not my way of going through life. What I am having to do here, and I've been doing it for sometime, is tell you about Group X 'signs', tell you about their way of thinking which used covert sign language.

[In this area there is also the engine overheat drive in the Cortina that took place in the middle of 1969. I didn't have a girlfriend.] I was working at the infirmary and there was a nurse that looked okay and I asked her out. [I will refer to her as Miss H.] I picked her up one evening from the nurses home and drove east out of Cardiff to have a drink at a pub out that way. I took what was perhaps known by some people as the old east road out. I didn't know the road well [It was either my first or second time on it.] but because the weather was good I thought I'd make a drive of it. About six miles out I turned left onto a road going north to go, hopefully, up to the A48 (the main east road out of Cardiff). I hadn't seen any pubs and so I thought I'd better get to the A48 where I knew there were pubs. I got to the A48 turned left and headed back toward Cardiff.

I was getting ready to pull over to the other side of the road to go into a pub's car park when for no apparent reason I looked at my speedometer and temperature gauge. The gauge was full over, overheated. I straightaway pulled into a layby that was on my left switched the engine off and waited for it to cool. The water was almost empty and the oil was empty. I didn't know what had caused it because things appeared to be okay. I phoned DC using a phone

170

box that was a hundred yards away and he drove out to me with a gallon of oil and some water. I put the oil in the engine and topped up the water. When I tried to start the engine it wouldn't turn over, parts in it had stuck together, seized. I got back to Cardiff with the girl in DC's car and left my car in the layby.

The next day I went to the car took the spark plugs out and put some lubricating fluid into each of the cylinders. The thinking was that the piston rings had in overheating stuck to the cylinder walls. I then put the car in gear and by pushing it backwards and forwards, in small movements, freed the engine. It started okay and I drove it back to Cardiff.

Oil was leaking out somewhere and with the car in the garage at my parents house I soon found the problem. It was leaking out where the oil filter can fitted to the engine. When the engine was stationary there was no leak, it was only when the engine was started and pressure was built up in the oil circulation system that the oil was pushed out, squirted out.

I took the oil filter can off the engine and found that two oil seals had been in place. There was only supposed to be one. One seal on top of the other meant they distorted each other and did not form a proper seal, so when the engine was running oil leaked out.

If the oil had leaked out quicker or if I had driven further before noticing the temperature gauge the engine would have seized and damaged itself beyond repair. But as it was it was still running okay. However it seemed necessary to check the engine by taking it apart to see what damage had been done. I did the job myself. Took the engine out of the car and on dismantling the engine found that the big end bearing shells had melted somewhat. I put new shells in. When the engine was back in the car it was fine.

The two oil seals were odd but I didn't give it much thought and left it at that.

Now things are a lot different of course. I know about Gx1 and his activities. This engine overheat night was another one of his car arrangements (there's a number of them, pgn number plate, 2600 forgery, the Herald at the beginning of this section, etc).

How and why did he do it? I'll take "how" first. He got one of his 'yes sir, no sir' people, a car mechanic on this occasion, to get at the car shortly before I went out that night. First of all to lift the car's bonnet required no access to the inside of the car (many or probably most cars were built like that in those days, i.e. no interior bonnet release lever), there was a bonnet release button at the top of the radiator grill. The mechanic took the oil filter off and put it back with a new seal on top of the old one. From start to finish the job would only take a few minutes.

I had arrived home at say 5-45pm parked the car on the street and gone

171

in the house for an evening meal. It was a fairly safe bet that I wouldn't return to the car till I went out at 7-45pm. Perhaps they got me on the phone (house land line) for five minutes when doing the job to make sure I didn't go to the car at that time.

The distance from where I lived to where Miss H was living was about a mile and a half. Some oil would leak out here but not enough to cause overheating. Then if I drove east out of Cardiff into the country, which Gx1 expected me to do, the rest of the oil would leak out and the engine would seize, blow up, which was quite obviously what he hoped would happen.

Miss H was living in the infirmary which is east of the city centre. It was usual for me to go to a country pub in such a situation. For example Miss C who I went out with for 6 months in 1966/7 lived on the west side of Cardiff and we always drove out of Cardiff to a pub.

Why did he do it? Well he done it because he wanted to ruin my first night out with her, stop the relationship starting. Yes but why did he want to stop it? The answer is, as is usually the case, connected to his intention to ship me to Australia (one way) and ensure I did not play top level rugby in this country.

Miss H was a decent, attractive, girl, and Gx1 knew that she was not a ship out female. In other words she was, for me, a stay in this country and play top level rugby female. So, to keep his plans intact, he stopped the relationship starting.

He used the car oil leak way of getting what he wanted because it gave a 'sign' that said, via the oil in his name, 'I did it'.

I have some more comments on this overheated engine night in a few paragraphs near the end of "The 1969 Lake Road East 'Accident'" later in this book.

Dancing Attracts

What I have told you about in the last section, Gx1 'saying' he wanted to have sex with my mother is something I haven't gone into before now. Let's look at more details in this area.

My father and mother, who got married in Cardiff in 1934, were great dancers, it was all ballroom dancing in the 1930s to '50s (waltz, quick step etc). They spent the latter part of the 30's living in Nottingham (my father had been offered a job there), and returned to Cardiff in 1940. My mother was slim and attractive and with her excellent dancing I think that Gx1 who was in Cardiff, and married to one of my father's sisters, decided to go after her.

"The Knife in the Trunk in 1946" section later in this book will tell you more about the 1940s.

It was about 1950 when my parents moved in to a semi-detached

172

council house in Cardiff, having previously lived in a privately rented flat. The council house was in Appledore Road. Well quite simply this in Group X language 'says' apple and dor (my mother). A coincidence? No, Gx1 was 'saying' that my mother was, 'good enough to eat, get your teeth into'. He was working in the city hall, and staff there allocated council houses. He arranged for my parents to get the house. Before he started work in the city hall he was, in the war years, a policeman.

Then in 1956 Gx1 helped to arrange the corporation mortgage on a house my parents moved into in Cardiff. He presumably got some money for this but I'd say a second reason for his doing this was to place himself firmly in my parents good books, i.e. get my mother to like him.

At about this time Gx1 became the local secretary of the Oddfellows, a sort of insurance society. It was an out of work hours part time job for him. He got my father to join it (pay a subscription for a small payout if out of work).

There was nothing that happened in the early years of my life (the 1950s and 60s) that indicated that Gx1 had a particular interest in my mother. I don't even remember seeing him till 1959 when I started at a school that was near his house. It's only since I have become aware of Group X sign language (say 1980 on) that I have known that some of Gx1's 'signs' were saying that he wanted to have sex with my mother.

And as for my father, well he occasionally did small maintenance jobs on Gx1's house, which indicates that he got on okay with him.

There is no doubt that Gx1 planned to get my father murdered, with 1973 being the hit year (his death then or soon after). The motive for the murder appears to be that he wanted to get hold of my, then 'available', mother, together with the fully paid for house she would have.

More on Gx1 Hitting My Brother in the 1950s

As I have said my parents enjoyed dancing, the '30s, '40s were dance band music days. It therefore follows that they bought my brother a sax when he was aged 13/14 in 1949. And he learnt to play it and read music. He played in a dance band in Cardiff when aged 16 but then within months gave it up. So what stopped his sax playing? The answer is Group X type people in the form of Gx1. He was working on the policy, as given to him by the people that ran this country, of keeping bright sons of original white workers down. And it was obvious to him that my brother was a very bright son of a worker. And so in these years he hit him a number of times.

As well as stopping my brother's sax playing he got him out of school early, only weeks before he was to sit the O level examinations. It was bound to be excellent exam results for him with 'he's really going

173

places', so in his mind it was time to stop him before things got out of hand.

And he also hit his rugby. He had to put up with his playing for Cardiff Boys because it had slowly developed from the previous few years but when he was told he was expected to play for the welsh boys it was, for him, stop him time. It could be that this was the initial reason for hitting him, i.e. the rugby hit came first and the other hits, the sax stop and the early school exit, followed in quick succession. In Gx1's warped mind the hits added up to a job well done.

My brother became ill days before the welsh boys trial game that he was due to play in. This was a hit carried out by Gx1, he poisoned him to make sure he didn't play for the welsh boys. My brother's health was excellent, a brilliant rugby player and athlete, and tennis player and cricket player. The reason 'ill' (a natural illness) was accepted/believed at the time by my parents, friends and school teachers, is that none of them suspected that warped officials such as Gx1 were in place in our society. As for any private individual making him ill, well he was a great lad, surely no one would do such a thing.

How he stopped his sax playing and got him out of school only weeks before the exams is not so easy for me to explain. All I can say is that he fed distorted information in at appropriate points.

That my brother was hit by Gx1 in these '50s years is, as I have said before, confirmed by a number of things. In the '60's Gx1 gave the map 'sign', which said my brother was 'in a grave', meaning that his '50s hits finished up by shipping him out, to Australia, never to be seen again, dead in metaphorical terms. Also in the '60s Gx1 gave another quite separate 'sign' that I haven't told you about before. This was based on engraving a compact (a woman's powder case, popular at the time). The sign said ct (my brother's initials, easily seen in compact), was 'in a grave' (from engraved). Then of course there is the fact that I came along and he did much the same to me. I was also expected to be very successful playing rugby and in education, and he made sure neither of them happened (hitting me not just once but numerous times over a period of years to get the 'keep him down' job done). And he tried to put me in a grave, metaphorically (ship me to Australia) and literally (murder me).

The Gx1 1960 Diamond Hit

As I have told you in my first year at my 11-15 school our physical education teacher was very impressed by my ability to play rugby and he thought I'd go places in the game (Cardiff Boys for a start). Gx1 was out to stop this. The first thing he arranged for this purpose was as follows.

The rugby season had finished and we were now, May 1960, starting the summer season sports. For the school this meant a baseball team and athletics (no cricket team). [The baseball game was/is only played in the Cardiff and Liverpool areas of the country. It is similar to the american game but it has two significant differences. The bowler delivers the ball using an underarm swing (in the american game the bowler throws the ball at the batsman, they say they 'pitch' the ball) and the bat has a flat face (the american bat is circular in cross section).]

It was a Wednesday afternoon sports day. The physical education teacher had a baseball game going for the 11 to 13s and he was trying out the new players in different positions to see how they got on. I was in the backstop position and doing well, my ability to catch the ball and throw it to base one was very good. [In baseball the key positions are the bowler, backstop and base one. He presumably put me in a key position because I was good at rugby.]

The bowler sent down a good ball at head height, the batsman missed it and it hit me on the forehead. The teacher stopped the game to see if I was okay. I was but to be on the safe side he took me out of the backstop position and didn't select me for the 11-13 baseball team (my batting was only ordinary). [Head protection gear was not worn by backstops in those days.]

Well, well. What a nice surprise for Gx1, just what he wanted, the physical education teacher's opinion of me lowered. "Surprise"? No chance. He done a dirty/smear job on me.

My missing the ball in that way had never happened before and nothing like it has happened since. It was a one off occurrence and here's how Gx1 did it. He had a man placed behind the bowler or behind me. His position was such that he was in line with the trajectory of the ball, in other words he could see if the ball, as it travelled to the batsman, was going to be good or bad, i.e. in the required zone when it reached the batsman or outside the zone. When the ball was travelling toward my head (a good ball), he operated a device that made me freeze. If the batsman hit the ball play proceeded as normal, if he missed the ball the required result was obtained.

In a bit more detail I'll say that the ideal good ball sent down by a bowler is meant to arrive about a foot to one side of the batsman's head. A backstop stands with his hands ready to catch the hoped for good ball, which means he stands in line with a good ball's trajectory with his hands up by his head with a gap of perhaps a foot between them, and he looks through the gap. When the ball proceeds toward his head he closes the gap between his hands and, if the batsman misses it, catches the ball in two hands. On this occasion I did not close the gap between my hands. I froze with my hands a foot apart. The batsman missed the ball and it came through to hit me on the forehead.

The "device" that was used to freeze me? For details ask Group X type people or the government. I'll just say it was an electron/laser beam similar to what they used on a number of occasions at later dates.

The diamond hit was useful for Gx1 but not enough. He decided he should do more to make sure the school's 'we have big plans for his rugby' got nowhere.

Enter the injection hit. It took place in what was probably my second year at the school.

Every twelve months or so a medical team visited the school to give injections/inoculations to the pupils. I had an injection and a half minute or so later fainted. I came round after what was apparently a minute or two with a couple of teachers by me. I was okay and nothing more was done about it.

How did Gx1 do this? He either got the person giving the injections to give me a 'special'. A dose of something that made me faint. Or a chloroform type of gas was released near my nose.

I'll link the details on the next two occurrences together because they are closely connected.

I was aged 12/13 when I first had styes on my upper and lower eyelids. Up to this point my eyes were fine. The styes were like small pimples. It wasn't just one or two, they continued for perhaps a year or more. I had small tubes of cream to put on them (I got the cream via a doctor) which had some effect but when one stye went a new one appeared. It was presumably these styes that caused my vision to deteriorate in that I began to have a bit of difficulty reading the blackboard. And when aged 14 I started to wear glasses.

It was in these same years when I first noticed a hole in the centre of my two front upper teeth. Up to this point my front teeth were fine (the dental job I had in 1956 was on back lower teeth). Why the hole arrived I didn't know, it sort of suddenly appeared. One day I saw it, before then it wasn't there. It perhaps had an eighth of an inch diameter and enlarged in later months to three sixteenths.

Both of these odd occurrences, the styes and the hole in the teeth, were Gx1 arrangements. The average person will probably say 'I don't believe it'. Let me convince you. A hole suddenly appears in the centre of two perfectly good upper front teeth. That has to be almost unheard of in ordinary dental decay terms. The most obvious reason for this happening, obvious when you know about Gx1 that is, is that a drop of acid was placed in the centre of the two teeth, which immediately created/burnt the hole. It was done at night when I was sleeping with chloroform vapours under my nose to ensure I stayed 'asleep' when my upper lip was lifted.

At the same time an infectious substance was placed, using a small pointed tool of some sort, on my eyelids. This continued for twelve months

176

or more at intervals of say two months. The acid on my teeth was perhaps only required a couple of times to create and enlarge the hole.

One odd occurrence would be enough to look for Gx1 involvement, two odd occurrences closely related and at the same time, makes Gx1 involvement even more likely. And of course we know all about his motives which were in existence at this time - 'keep him down and ship him out' which was coupled to his plan to murder my father (the spire tells us the murder plan was in place in 1959/60). In other words I have no doubt that Gx1 arranged to have my eyes and teeth hit.

My ability to see the rugby ball became a small problem in my 14/15 years (not the ball bouncing close to me, it obviously was the ball, but when a number of opposing players were some distance away from me it was not easy to tell which one had the ball when they were wearing dark shirts). But when I left school I stopped playing rugby so it didn't matter. And when I started to play the game again when aged 19 (for Llandaff Tech) contact lenses had arrived on the optical scene and I used them when I played rugby.

The baseball hit, the injection hit, the styes and the hole in my front teeth were meant to be enough to make the physical education teacher, who was the main source of the school's 'big plans for his rugby', lose faith in me. As a final step Gx1 got him moved out of the school to a job in another Cardiff school.

In my last rugby season at the school, the year for playing for Cardiff Boys, I was selected for a game that I now think was being used as a trial game for the Cardiff Boys team (I wasn't told about this at the time). There was an odd occurrence during the game which tells me that a Gx1 hit man was watching, and he made sure I missed a crucial tackle (to keep me out of the team).

The Gx1 'Stop Sex' Poison in 1971

When I was writing about the engine overheat drive earlier in this chapter it reminded me that I met Miss H again at a later date. I had forgotten about this second meeting with her and so didn't include her in earlier chapters when I was telling you about the females Gx1 blocked when I was in London. I'll tell you about it here.

It was Oct/Nov 1971. I was working at St Bartholomew's hospital in east central London and I had recently moved to a flat owned/rented by them that was near the hospital. [This was the move that was arranged by Gx1 to stop my two nights a week rugby training in north west London.]

I was surprised to hear one day that the girl that was with me on the car engine overheat night in Cardiff in 1969 [Miss H.] was working at a hospital in London. That night out in Cardiff was our first night out and of course the engine overheat meant that we didn't have the drink that we planned to have together. She had quietly sat through the experience and so you would have expected me to ask her out again to replace the drink we never had with a new evening out, but for some reason I hadn't done this. Which meant the engine overheat night was the last time I had seen her.

How I got this information about her starting in London I don't know. The best guess I can come up with is that DC, who knew I went out with her in 1969, had told his girlfriend who was a nurse that I'd gone out with her and she got him to phone me to tell me she had started working in London.

I phoned her and arranged a night out. I called at her place at about 8 one evening, it was on the west side of London. I was in my car. We went to a pub by the Thames that wasn't far from where she was living. We got on with each other okay, I thought she was pretty good, quiet and attractive. I took her back to her place at the end of the night, went in, and we proceeded toward sex. But here there was something wrong, I felt strange and sex was an impossibility for me. I left at about 11-30pm feeling like a bit of an idiot. I never saw here again.

I had been going with Miss N when I was in Cardiff but my moving to London in March '71 meant that our meetings became rare occurrences. And Sept '71 was the last time I saw her for sometime (about six months), we stayed on good terms. I usually had sex with her when I was with her. In other words I was okay at sex. So why was I not okay at sex on this night in west London? It was more than 'not okay', I couldn't even get to the sex stage. I, as I say, felt odd and disturbed for no apparent reason. I mean here was an attractive girl in front of me, a girl I quite liked, and I was useless. I could not understand it.

It was Gx1. You already know what was in his mind. He had me written in for shipping out in eight months time and a steady relationship with a female could inhibit or block the ship out plan. So he made sure I did not start a steady relationship with her.

As I've said on the engine overheat night she had been no problem at all and on this night in London she was again quiet and unassuming. She said nothing about my not having sex with her when she was obviously happy for it to take place. The fact that I didn't ask her out again was entirely due to my feeling odd near the end of the night and my thinking that somehow she was not for me.

Had things proceeded normally on this night, with no Gx1 interference, there is no doubt that we would have begun a steady relationship.

How did Gx1 get me into this 'sex is impossible' condition? Well the obvious answer is that a drink I was given at the pub had been contaminated with a drug that made me sexually incapable. This should not

178

surprise you of course because you already know that dishing out poisons (to dope and kill) was part of Gx1's activities.

Less obvious is how Gx1 knew I had arranged the date with her. There are a number of possibilities. I had a phone in my hospital flat (land line, no mobiles then), did I use it to call her and make the date, with someone listening in, monitoring my phone, to report back to Gx1? We know he was paying close attention to me (to make sure I stayed on the 'ship out' route). We must remember here that Gx1 was able to use police procedures meaning that monitoring phones, getting them tapped, was no problem for him. Or had he been told about an incoming call from DC when he told me about her? There were very few calls in or out on my phone so there wasn't much to monitor anyway.

Then, having found out about the night out, he had someone ready to follow my car from her place to the pub we went to. And it was simply a case of his showing a police badge to the manager with instructions to 'put this in his drink' (having first checked that the manager was 'their man' on his car radio). Another way of doing it (with no radio check) would have been for him to get a drink in the pub and wait for an appropriate time to put the substance/poison in my drink (cause a distraction and drop it in).

How many very good females did Gx1 stop in the 1960s and '70s? I don't like to think about it.

2018

DC and Cardiff Rugby Club in 1966/70

I have no doubt in saying that I would have started to play for Cardiff RFC in 1969 if Gx1 had decided not to stop it (by poisoning me prior to the trial game, etc).

Let's look at DC here. He was about 5' 9" and perhaps three quarters of a stone heavier than me. He was an ideal size for a prop, the position he played in at Llandaff Tech. If I had been playing for Cardiff he would have come to watch the games when Llandaff Tech weren't playing. And he would have been in the clubhouse bar with me after the games. Could he also have played for Cardiff? I think it is very likely. I could have recommended him to the club and the selectors could have given him a game to have a look at him. And perhaps kept him on.

I'll say a bit more on the Cardiff RFC situation. Gerald Davies in the '66/68 years was playing for Cardiff as a centre. It appears to me that the people at Llandaff Tech who had me on course for Cardiff had the idea that I would make an ideal right wing playing alongside him (he'd make the breaks, I had the speed to run in).

Gerald left Cardiff in '69 or '70 and went to London Welsh where he moved from centre to right wing. He played for Wales.

The 1967/68 WT64 and LWR 'Signs'

Does "The Long and Winding Road" mean anything to you? It's the title of a song recorded by the Beatles, a british pop/music group based in Liverpool in the 1960s/70s. It was written in 1968 by Paul McCartney. The first line of the song is, 'the long and winding road that leads to your door'. The title, the first line, was fed in to Paul by Gx1 to give one of his 'signs'.

Gx1 connected this to another sign. Here he gave Paul the title, 'When I'm 64', which the Beatles released in 1967.

I will explain these signs. The "Long and Winding" gives LaW, my father's name backwards (Wal). "Door" gives Dor, my mother's name (Doreen). This sign said, 'Wal there is a long road that leads to your wife'.

"When I'm" gives WT, the T being found in a roman I. The title of the song, the 'sign', said, 'WT (my father) 64'.

Together the two 'signs' said, 'Wal, it will take some time, a few years, for me to get to your wife and you will be 64 when I get there'.

In 1973 my father was covertly knifed by a Gx1 hit man. He was aged 64. This was the first part of the Gx1 plan to murder him, the second part was to be his death using poison, he would then have his wife.

Gx1 had a contact in Liverpool. He obtained the commie sign (Senator McCarthy) from there. He presumably used the same contact to create these Beatles signs.

Gx1 didn't kill my father in 1973. Why? Let's go over a few points. For years he'd been fixing things in my life to ensure that when the time came for shipping me to Australia I'd be easy to ship (no ties). He hadn't done all that just to get me there for a few weeks holiday. It was going to be a permanent move for me. In June 1972 he made sure I bought a one way ticket to Australia, I was going there but not back.

I did however, when I was in Australia, manage to get the money to buy a ticket for a return flight, Sydney to London, in September 1972. And what happened? Fourteen hours or so before I was due to get on the plane I was poisoned in a Sydney hotel. Within three hours I became too ill to travel and so didn't get on the plane. Gx1, having heard I was on my way back to this country, presumably arranged the poisoning with the australian equivalent of MI5/6. The intention being to keep me off the flight and hence lose my airfare. And with no spare money and no insurance I'd have to stay in Australia (return to my brother in Adelaide).

However things went a little wrong for him here in that I did manage four or five days later to get on a plane for this country, without paying any more money.

Gx1 had planned to kill my father in 1973 and part of the plan had me living in Australia when it happened. My return to this country in September '72 wrecked this part of the plan. And, evidently, he had to, decided to, alter the murder plan. He proceeded with the covert knifing of my father but postponed killing him. The false diagnosis he obtained from the covert knifing meant he could kill him at a later date (using poison), with no questions asked.

The Heath and the UHW, 1960/63

A few pages back I told you about the 1960 school baseball game that Gx1 used to hit/dirty me. In this section I will tell you about 'signs' he obtained from the game. These 'signs' 'advertised' the plan to hit my father.

Look at two key words in the game, bowler and backstop. Bowler gives wolbe (my father, his first name is Walby). Backstop gives back stop. When my father was covertly knifed in 1973 it led to him having his back stopped in an operation he had (see "Gx1's Plan to Murder My Father").

The baseball game was played on Heath park, a large parkland and woods area in the suburbs of Cardiff. In 1963 the construction of a new hospital was started on Heath park, it was being built on part of the park (the University Hospital of Wales, also known as the Heath hospital). The baseball pitch was in the area that the hospital was built on. The back stop operation on my father in 1973 was done in the new hospital.

It seems to have been the late fifties when the idea for a new hospital for the Cardiff area came into being. When did Cardiff council say it could be built on Heath park, before the baseball game or after the baseball game? If it was after it means that Gx1 got the new hospital built there to match his baseball 'signs'.

The baseball game illustrates that the Gx1 plan to kill my father was in existence in 1960. And this reinforces the date the spire gives, 1959/60.

The Mortgage Extension

My father told me that Gx1 helped him to obtain the house mortgage from the local council in 1956. He was aged 48 which means he couldn't have got a mortgage with most lenders because of his age. But a 15 year mortgage could be obtained from the local council and this is what he managed to get. In 1967 the loan was increased and extended by two years to buy the freehold (the land), which took the final payment to 1973.

The original finish of the mortgage was going to be in 1971 (15 years on from 1956). The two years extension being decided on in 1967 meant that it was 1967 when Gx1 first knew that the end of mortgage hit was going to be moved from 1971 to 1973. And this shows up in that it was 1967 when Gx1 fed Paul McCartney with "When I'm 64" (my father would be hit when he was 64, in 1973).

Was Gx1's frame of mind clean when he helped my father to obtain the mortgage in 1956, and then, sometime in the next four years (the spire was 1959/60), thought up the plan to kill my father when the mortgage was finished? No. I say this because Gx1 had already been hitting us before 1956. My brother was hit by him in 1952. In other words it is evident that Gx1 in helping my father to obtain the mortgage was continuing the 'hit them' process. He knew that my father would be murdered at the end of it (using 'natural causes'). And he could then obtain the fully paid for house by getting/marrying his wife.

182

In 1975 Gx1 Connects 60, 71 and 75

In September 1971 Gx1 received a shock that was again caused by my rugby. Sudbury Court rugby club had pushed me to the Wasps, I played in their second team and they wanted me to play in their first team. This was against all that Gx1 had done in previous years. He had my life, my rugby, on stop. I was written in for shipping out of the country in mid-1972 and it was easiest to do this if I had no ties (rugby, etc).

So, as stated earlier in this book, Gx1 acted immediately to stop me playing for the Wasps first team (the car theft, moving me out of my accommodation which was near the Wasps ground, etc). In other words in Sept '71 he had to arrange new hits to stop my rugby, which means that this was a busy time for him, and it seems he decided to mark this period with another one of his song 'signs'.

Perhaps you have heard of the song, "Diamonds are Forever", sung by Shirley Bassey in the film of the same name. The song was written toward the end of '71 (the film came out in December '71). Gx1, using his contacts, got the name of the song fed into the song's writer and he wrote the rest of it. Once again you will find this difficult to believe, until, that is, I tell you about Gx1 thinking, as follows.

What happened in May 1960? Gx1 hit me in the school baseball game. The hit was to destroy, at least start to destroy (he had more hits in the pipeline) the reputation I had gained in my first season playing rugby. My physical education teacher thought I was outstanding in rugby and he had big plans for me. So, with the teacher refereeing the baseball game, he covertly hit me, made me look incompetent. With the result that the teacher took me out of the baseball team (which I was due to play in).

The pitch on which a baseball game is played is sometimes called a diamond. Because it's a square standing on a corner. Hence this Gx1 baseball hit can be called the diamond hit.

The song Diamonds are Forever was Gx1 saying, 'once hit always hit', i.e. 'I hit you in the baseball game and I will keep hitting you, putting you down, till you get shipped out'. The 'ship out' plan was of course connected to the plan to murder my father.

There is more I can give you here that reinforces my statement that this song was a Gx1 'sign'. Let's go to Swansea in 1975. At Easter Gx1 got me out of the accommodation I had been in since I started at UCS (Sept '74). And then after Easter he got me into a guest house for about two weeks (the 'marry Miss D' guest house) and then into a room in a dump of a house. I was in this "dump" when Gx1 got the stop Miss K pub poison given to me and when the forged/altered exam papers were given to me at the beginning of June.

Let me take you aside for a couple of minutes. How did Gx1 get me into this "dump of a house"? When I was working as a computer engineer with

ICL in Cardiff in 1973/74 I'd met a person who was about my age. He was based in Swansea looking after some computers in that area. I'll call him Mr U. Well when the pre-Easter '75 UCS accommodation I was in finished I looked him up to ask him if he knew of any place I could stay at. He told me about the nearby guest house and after a short time there I moved into a room in the house he was in, the "dump of a house". What was an ICL computer engineer doing living in a "dump"?

It seems that Mr U was another Gx1 'yes sir, no sir' man. In other words a person acting on Gx1's covert instructions (like Mr E). And he moved into this place on Gx1 instructions ready for my 'looking for accommodation' arrival. Why did Gx1 pick this place? There is only one answer. The address, the street the house was in, 'said' in Group X language, Miss D street (her first name was in the street's name). When I moved in I would be on route for Miss D, i.e. out of UCS, return to Cardiff.

Back to where I was. Whilst staying at this place I met Mr Basey. He was about my age and he lived a few doors away up the street. Mr U introduced me to him. The three of us went for a drink in a pub once.

And here it is. Basey, well, well. Bassey. Any connection? What would you say? The answer is of course there was a connection. It was Gx1 repeating his 1971 statement, he was 'saying', 'diamonds are forever'. Once 'dead' always 'dead'. 'I hit you in the baseball game to put you down and you are staying down'. UCS was 'dead' for me.

Gx1 knew in May '75 that he could get me failed/stopped at UCS before I sat any end of academic year examinations. The forged/altered examination question papers that were given to me at the start of June were just an extra covert arrangement with UCS staff as far as he was concerned. It 'gave out' a 'sign', and he liked to give out 'signs'. The 'sign' said 66 for me, i.e. it was Miss D for me, she lived at a 66. The 'sign' was obtained from section six of the 1913 Forgery Act being breached twice, i.e. two sixes. Both lecturers, one at each of the two examinations, gave me forged documents (documents that were used to deceive and defraud).

Gx1 Breaks the Mast of My Sailing Dinghy in 1976

I've mentioned earlier that in July 1976 (when the academic year at UCC had finished) I went to west Wales for a couple of months. A week or so before I went I bought a second hand sailing dinghy. It was on a trailer and I towed it to west Wales with me. I put it on the side of a river near a boatyard.

Within a day or two of arriving I got the dinghy ready for my first sail in it. It was a dry day with a light breeze. Being near the coast the river was tidal. It was about a half hour before high tide, the best time for sailing on the river.

I got the dinghy onto the water. It was a two man dinghy. I was on my own, which was okay with me because as I've said there wasn't much wind. I sailed up the river with the wind behind me. In a couple of hundred yards I reached a larger expanse of water where another river joined the river I was on. In this area I changed direction and I was sailing across the wind, which means I was sat on the side of the boat to balance the wind force on the sail, when suddenly the mast broke. This caused the dinghy to roll to my side and I was tipped backwards into the water. The dinghy stayed upright.

I was wearing a buoyancy jacket so there was no problem there. I got the dinghy to the river bank, left it overnight, and the next day towed it (using a boat with an outboard motor) back to where the trailer was.

I was very surprised at what had happened. The mast should never have broken. One man in the boat and a light wind meant the mast was nowhere near it's limits.

It occurred to me that it could have been done deliberately by someone acting for Group X to stop me using the dinghy during my stay in west Wales. Was it sawn partly through? I looked closely at the break. No it wasn't partly sawn. So I classed it as an accident, i.e. it just happened to break. The dinghy was about eight years old so perhaps the mast was worn/well used. [It took me ages to obtain a new mast. It was November/December 1977 when I next sailed the dinghy.]

I suspected that it had been done deliberately because I knew that Group X had in the past twelve months been having a go at me. They got me stopped at UCS in September 1975 and there was the taxi poisoning in February 1976. There was also the contaminated petrol and the odd booking that had taken place in the past two months, both of which had presumably been arranged by Group X. [Details on the latter two occurrences are in TCF6 and 9.]

Things are very different now of course. Yes I was right in thinking that Group X (in the form of Gx1) had been hitting me since September 1975 but there were many more times they'd covertly hit me before and after September 1975 that I didn't know about in July 1976. In other words arranging to have me hit was a regular practice for Gx1 and this broken mast was another one of his dirt activities.

This broken mast went something like this. A hit man drilled perhaps four small diameter holes, say an eighth of an inch, into the mast at about four feet from the base of it, the holes being drilled 90 degrees apart around the mast. The holes were then injected with a substance

185

that rotted/weakened the wood. Acid could have been the substance used. And then when a bending force was applied to the mast, when I was sailing, it broke at the weakened point. When I inspected the break I was only looking for saw marks, a straight cut across part of the mast. I did not look for the outlines of small drill holes. The break looked like a natural break, with spiky bits on each part. The acid weakening method would fit this.

A bit more on the mast's "limits". The dinghy's mast would have been designed to cope with the dinghy being sailed in a high wind with a two man crew. The maximum load on the mast would be when the crew were sailing across the wind. In this situation the dinghy would be in about a thirty degree tilt with the two men sitting on the side of it using their weight to keep the dinghy from being blown over by the force of the wind on the sail (together with rudder and sail adjustments). Lets call this situation a 100% bending force load on the mast, i.e. the mast would have been designed (it's diameter) to have no problem handling this 100% load. When I was sailing the dinghy there was a light wind. And with me being on my own in the dinghy there was a load on the mast at the time of the break of no more than 40%. So you see what I mean when I said the mast was "nowhere near it's limits". It certainly should not have broken.

Another angle that says that Gx1 arranged to have it done is that he got at the dinghy again in Nov/Dec 1977 when he had the foot strap cut (see "The Gx1 1977 Cut Strap" section in this book).

I can tell you what Gx1 was thinking when he arranged this mast break. He had managed to get me 'failed' in some of the exams I had recently sat at UCC (when I had passed them) by telling UCC that I had finished with, 'a wonderful church going girl', and stopping my study would push me back to her. UCC were not happy about this but they complied with the request hoping that the block would be removed later and I'd continue at the college. It was perhaps someone at UCC that got me to buy this dinghy with the idea that it would help to keep me involved with the college. In June I'd been sailing with their sailing club.

Gx1 wanted to use the mast break to help to keep me off the UCC course. In September the re-sit exams would be taking place. This was when UCC would be pushing to have me continue the course (by giving me the pass results that I had actually got in the summer exams) and Gx1 would be repeating his 'stop him' argument. When someone with UCC asked, 'how did his sailing go in west Wales?' he could reply with, 'he doesn't have the ability to sail ... for two months he didn't use the dinghy'. He'd say nothing about the broken mast putting the dinghy out of action. In other words Gx1 thought that the mast break would give him a bit of negative stuff, dirt, that he could apply to me when the September re-sits problem arrived.

186

Since I wrote this section I have realised that another occurrence was a Gx1 'sign' and I'm adding it here now (it's 2020) because it indicates that Gx1 broke the mast. As follows.

In 1977 I was living in two rooms and a small conservatory on the ground floor of my parents house. We had converted the rooms into a flat. One day I returned to the house and saw a polished wood table that had been delivered to the flat. It was the sort of table that has flaps, a top that folds down on either side of a central section. My parents told me that it had been given to us by the wife of Gx1 for me to use in the flat.

I already had a table in the flat so I didn't need it. Anyway I found a place for it but didn't use it.

It was some weeks later when I noticed that the legs of the table had many small holes in them (about 3/32" diameter). It was woodworm, but I don't recall seeing any insects so presumably they had been killed off. No mention was made of the woodworm when it was given to us.

This is a typical Gx1 sign. The table was an 'advert' that was meant to say, 'I broke the dinghy mast'. The legs of the table were the mast and the flaps were the sails. He had, as I said earlier, arranged for the dinghy mast to have holes drilled in it which were then filled with acid.

Perhaps the table never had woodworm. He could have picked it up at a second hand furniture place then got someone to drill the holes in the legs, to create his sign.

Gx1 Breaks Mr HC's Leg in 1972

This section connects to "In 1972/73 Gx1 Fixes a Rugby Team and Hits Me Again" earlier in this book.

In Sept 1972 the Cardiff Hospitals rugby team was started up. [In the first game played by the team Gx1 hit a friend of mine, Mr HC. I haven't told you about this before. I will tell you about it now.]

Mr HC, who was about my age, started work in the department I was in at the UHW in Cardiff in August 1969. He wasn't in the electronics section where I was but he was sent with me one day to a hospital near Cardiff just to look at the sort of work we did in the department. We became friends and in about December 1970 we, together with another person who worked in the department, moved into a flat in Cardiff.

In this period, Aug '69 to Dec '70, I was only going out in the evenings with Miss N. In January 1969 DC had started going steady with a female and from that time on we had stopped going out together. I also had college on two evenings a week.

In March 1971 I moved to London when I started work at St Bartholomew's.

In June 1972 I went to Australia. I was there for three months and in Sept '72 returned to the UHW. Within days the Cardiff Hospitals rugby team was started up.

Mr HC had played rugby when he was in university and so he said he would join me in playing for the new rugby team. In other words he was going to be my new rugby mate (replacing DC).

Gx1 was watching me very closely because he had plans to murder my father in 1973 and I was supposed to be in Australia when it happened. My returning to Cardiff presented him with unexpected problems. If my rugby really got going (as he knew it could) he might have to call off the murder. So my rugby again became a target for him. He had to ensure, continue to ensure, that I got nowhere significant in the game (meaning Cardiff RFC).

Gx1 acted quickly. In the first game that the new hospitals rugby team played he hit Mr HC.

The game had not been going for long when it was stopped for an injury to someone. He was laying on the ground and I went over to have a look. It was Mr HC. The lower part of one of his legs was broken. The bone was pushing the skin out.

After a while the game continued. A couple of hours later I went to see him in hospital.

Gx1 done it but it needs a bit of explaining. 'How could he do this?' someone says, 'break a persons leg when he is playing rugby, never'.

During the night before the game Mr HC, when asleep, was 'got at'. Gx1 hit men had access to the flat he was sleeping in, chloroformed him, and then partly cut through the lower part of his left leg using a laser beam. At some frequency a laser beam passes harmlessly through skin but cuts bone. His shin bone was cut about half across. This meant that it still had the strength for him to walk on it the following morning but when it was subjected to greater stress in the rugby game it broke.

The next question to answer is, 'but Gx1 was out to ensure your rugby got nowhere, why didn't he break your leg?' I'll tell you.

It wasn't my playing rugby that Gx1 objected to, from the age of 11 he had let me play the game, it was the playing of rugby at the top level that he didn't want (Cardiff Boys, first teams at Cardiff, Wasps). In top level rugby influential rugby people could form plans for my rugby in this country, and this would block the 'ship him to Australia' plan he had for me, which in turn would stop the plan to murder my father.

Recall here that my brother was a very good rugby player. He played for Cardiff Boys and then when he went to live in Australia in 1959 he played rugby there. The idea that Gx1 had in mind was that when he shipped me to Australia to live at my brother's place I would play rugby there. In other words this is why he hadn't broken my leg in earlier years, i.e. a broken leg would mean a permanent stop on playing the game. Now, at the time of this first hospitals rugby game, he still had ideas on pushing me back to Australia and hence he didn't break my leg in the game.

When I was in Australia I played a game of rugby for my brother's old team, the first team. This helps to verify what I have said in the last paragraph.

'Okay, but why break Mr HC's leg?' Because it would help to keep my rugby down. For Gx1 it was, 'kill off his rugby mate and dirty/smear the team, that should do it'. To dirty the team he, as I told you earlier in this book, got the team's home ground moved from a council's parks pitch to a field in a mental hospital.

I know that some people will still find the details I've given you that explain how the broken leg was done difficult to believe. I understand, it's not the sort of thing you usually see in the press. These people might be interested in looking at this from a different angle, as follows.

We know that Gx1 hit me many times over a period of years to keep my rugby down (he continued to do so in the years that followed this hospitals rugby game). This is a clearly established fact. So, knowing this, is it possible for anyone to think that Mr HC's broken leg, and then the team's move to a ground in a mental hospital, just happened, by pure chance, to support Gx1's long term intentions?

Let me point out that a player breaking his leg in a game of rugby is a very rare occurrence. In all the years I have played rugby this is the only game I have been in where a player has broken a leg. This means that the odds for a broken leg in a game of rugby are say 1,000 to 1 against.

Now look at the team's ground being moved to a mental hospital. The odds against a rugby team establishing a home ground in a mental hospital have to be in the 5,000 to 1 area.

For both of these occurrences to happen to the same rugby team in the space of about two weeks we are looking at odds of at least 80,000 to 1.

So was this an 80,000 to 1 chance that came off for Gx1? Of course not. It was Gx1 with his dirt activities. His plans were my father dead and me in Australia, and he wanted to ensure that the plans stayed on track

The Gx1 1968 False Hospital Diagnosis

I will here give you more details on the hit that Gx1 carried out on me in Sept 1968 to stop me playing as captain for the Llandaff Technical College rugby team.

Gx1 wanted to stop my rugby, not permanently, but for a while, months, preferably a season. And he came up with a 'hairline fracture' plan.

The '68/69 rugby season had just started and it was our second game. About halfway through it I realised that there was something wrong with my left ankle, it was giving me a bit of pain. After the game, in the dressing room, I could see that it was swollen. So I decided to go to the infirmary (CRI) to get it checked.

At the hospital I was shown an x-ray of my ankle that, so the doctor said, showed a hairline fracture. And that meant it would be plaster on my leg for two months. [Weighed down on one side as stated in the Gx1 'sign' he gave out in the weeks before this happened, the 'sign' that 'advertised' what he was going to do, the greyhound joke.]

There was no hairline fracture of my ankle. Gx1 got this false diagnosis issued by using one of the following methods:

(I)   He had one of his 'yes sir, no sir' people in place ready to do the porter job of carrying the x-ray of my ankle from the x-ray department to the doctor and on route he substituted it for an x-ray that showed a hairline fracture of an ankle (or he drew a fine line on the x-ray of my ankle).

(ii)   The genuine x-ray of my ankle was taken to the doctor who had previously been lined up to say, 'you have a hairline fracture', lie to me in other words.

I looked at the x-ray from a distance of about three feet, was there a hairline in it? I just accepted what the doctor said (well what else was I supposed to do?).

I will add that the doctor was Asian and I couldn't understand most of what he said. His english was terrible. [This would fit in with Gx1 activities, he got the rubbish diagnosis given to me by a rubbish doctor.] There was only me and the doctor in the cubicle (partitioned rooms in a hall).

The pain, which wasn't severe, was caused by the rapid swelling of my left foot. When I put my boots on in the changing room prior to the game I did the laces up tightly. The swelling, which took place during the game, was restricted by the tight boot hence the pain.

How did Gx1 get my ankle to swell? No problem for him and his team of experts, you figure out how he did it. As a tip recall the time he got acid put on the laces of my rugby boots when I was in Swansea in 1975 (at UCS).

2019

The 1968 Gx1 Walk in a Graveyard

Mid 1967 - the situation at this time was as follows.

The management at AEI, where I worked, and some staff at Llandaff Tech, where I studied part-time, had decided to get me onto a full time university degree course. A lot that goes on in our society is done quietly, I mean arranged by people in senior positions without telling outsiders about it, and this was the position here. I was happily doing my job with no intentions of leaving it. I knew nothing about the AEI/Llandaff university plan.

AEI/Llandaff knew that I was good at rugby when I was in school and so they decided that when the new academic year started in Oct '67 they would get me to play for the Llandaff Tech rugby team. With the idea that when they got me into university in Sept '68 I could carry on playing there.

Gx1, being part of the 'senior positions' grapevine, had been told about the AEI/Llandaff plans and he didn't like them one bit. And that's putting it mildly. For some years now he had planned to murder my father when he finished paying for his mortgage (in the early 70's) and ship me to Australia. Too much success for me in life could interfere with perhaps block the murder plan and the ship out plan. My going to university was "too much success".

Gx1 decided that the plan to hit my father could proceed untroubled if I wasn't around. And in Sept '67 he tried to kill me, using the 'accident'/'natural causes', method (the LK hit). He almost succeeded. It took place one evening at about 8pm. I made no report to the police about what had happened because I thought it was a natural occurrence, a very odd natural occurrence but nevertheless I did not think that anyone had tried to kill me.

[It was perhaps mid-December '67 when Gx1 placed one of his 'yes sir, no sir' people into the Llandaff Tech rugby team.] **Mr TN, didn't study at the college, he just appeared at a training session one evening and joined in. Soon he was playing in the team. The team comprised mainly of people who were studying at the college (full time or part time) but we had a few players who were not in the college because we were short of players.**

In January '68, when at a dance in Cardiff, Mr TN introduced me to a girl. I stayed with her and at the end of the dance asked her if I could take her out sometime. She said yes. She lived about fifteen miles north of Cardiff.

Some days later I drove to her place at 8pm. I knocked the door and was asked in. Her parents were there and I sat down and talked with them for a few minutes. Then me and Miss VG left the house to drive to a pub for a drink. But before we went to a pub she wanted to go to a nearby church graveyard and walk round it, with me, looking at the graves. And so that's what we did. Being January it was dark but there were street lights near the church.

To use a phrase I have used before, 'let's stop immediately here'. She wanted to walk round a graveyard on our first night out! Again as I've said before, when something odd happens look for Gx1 involvement, look for his 'signs' which, whenever possible, he placed into his arrangements.

And straightaway I see a Gx1 'sign'. She lived in Bedwellty Road. In his mind Bedwellty was Bed, wet, and wt (my father's initials). He was going to get my father knifed at night when in bed asleep and drugged, with the result that his bed would be wet with blood. The walk round the graveyard was to 'say' that he would be in a grave soon after it happened.

A slightly different way of interpreting this Gx1 'sign' is to say that it meant that I was on bed, wet and wt road, and that I would soon be 'in a grave', i.e. the university route would soon be 'dead', because it interfered with, could block, Gx1's plans.

For Gx1 it went something like this. Having selected Bedwellty because it 'illustrated' what was planned, he then used the electoral rolls/lists to find a female who was about my age (19) who lived in a Bedwellty Road (there are three in the area near the town). He found a female who was useable (free), Miss VG. He then used his contacts to bring us together. Presumably he got instructions given to her mother or father, i.e. 'tell her to take him straight to a graveyard'.

I went out with Miss VG a few times. We never got into any sort of steady relationship.

In June '68 I had an interview at Cardiff university, the intention being to start a full time course there in Sept '68. [Soon after the interview Gx1 applied some dirt to me (smeared me). This, it seems, was used to stop me entering university three months later. In other words he put my university course 'in a grave', which is what he 'said' he would do in the January graveyard walk.]

The 1960/61 Gx1 Sheath Knife

It was at the start of January 1959 when I was aged ten that a friend the same age as me, who lived a few doors away, got me to go to a nearby cubs meeting once a week in the evening. After a few weeks I became aged eleven, left the cubs and went to a nearby scouts weekly meeting.

Our scouts had a two week summer camp in west Wales in '59 and '60. I went to both of them.

It would have been the latter part of '60 or early '61, when I'd been in the scouts for a while, that my mother bought me a sheath knife. I was surprised at the knife, I mean it was a big, full size, knife. I had seen one of the scouts wearing a sheath knife on his belt but it was a small knife, about a 4" blade. The knife my mother had bought me had perhaps a 6" blade. Anyway I said nothing and sort of put it to one side. I never used it and as far as I recall I didn't even attach it to my belt when in scouts uniform. Not long after I left the scouts, for no particular reason, I just lost interest.

As usual when something odd happens look for a Gx1sign. If a 'sign' is present it means he arranged it. The 'sign' here is right in front of our eyes. Sheath - heath. Heath hospital, the place where my father would be surgically knifed (using a rusty knife) in an operation that would take place two weeks after Gx1 had got him knifed in a hit made to look like a natural occurrence. The hospital, also known as the UHW, was in it's planning stages (it was built in the 1963/69 years).

How did Gx1 get my mother to buy the knife? He got a woman she worked with to say, 'a scout, you should buy him a sheath knife'. And she told her where she could get one. At the shop the sales person was lined up to sell my mother a standard/big sheath knife.

This 'sign', the sheath knife, is the third Gx1 arrangement in these three years, 1959, '60 and '61, that was used to 'advertise' the plan to murder my father. The first arrangement being the spire and the second the baseball hit.

The 1960 Gx1 'Dead' Cap

Here is a Gx1 arrangement that took place in 1960. The purpose behind this was to 'say' my rugby was 'dead'.

By the time the end of my first rugby season arrived (the 1959/60 season, aged twelve) the school's physical education teacher was very impressed by my rugby. This is clearly illustrated by the end of academic year school report where he wrote that I was "outstanding" in rugby. It seems he was sure I was on course for playing for the welsh boys and he made this known to the 'senior positions' grapevine. I say this because of something that happened in May or June '60.

On this occasion Gx1 got someone to tell a schoolboy what to do.

Schoolboys usually wore caps, it was part of the school uniform. [By the time the 1970s arrived schoolboy caps were rarely seen.] Well on this day it was the school lunch break and I was with two or three other schoolboys on the pavement alongside the cemetery that was near the school. One of the lads caps went over the cemetery wall.

This was the only time in my school career that a cap was thrown into the cemetery when I was present.

When someone played for the welsh boys rugby team he was awarded a welsh boys cap. Gx1 was worried that the plans he had could be blocked by significant success in my rugby. The cap over the cemetery arrangement was to 'say' that my playing for the welsh boys was 'dead'. He would make sure it didn't happen.

As you know, in the 1960 to '62 years Gx1 hit/dirtied me a number of times to 'put down' my rugby, i.e. the baseball hit, the styes on my eyes, the hole in my front teeth, the injection, and he got the physical education teacher moved out of the school.

There's a bit more I can give you here. Do you know who lived in a house that was across the road from where this cap went over the cemetery? Gx1. I'd say he was in the window, watching what was going on, checking that his instructions were carried out correctly. The city hall, where he worked, was two miles or so from his house and he was often home for the lunch break.

More on the Sailing Dinghy

This is the third section in this book on the sailing dinghy. Why separate sections? It's because of the way the investigation process, closely examining what happened, has proceeded.

"The Gx1 1977 Cut Strap'" appears first, in the 2011 chapter (when I wrote it), because it was the dinghy occurrence that I knew was a hit within one day of it taking place. Someone had cut the foot strap to ensure that it capsized when I sailed it. I did not however at the time connect it to Group X because I thought they had finished having a go at me. In later years I realised that Gx1 had got the foot strap cut (who else would do a thing like that?).

"Gx1 Breaks the Mast of My Sailing Dinghy in 1976" appears in the 2018 chapter, because it was 2018 when I became sure that the broken mast was not an accident. Gx1 arranged for one of his hit men to get at it.

In this section I give you some dinghy related details that I haven't gone into before now.

In July 1976 Gx1 put the sailing dinghy out of action by breaking the mast. It was about January 1977 when the insurance company I had the dinghy insured with told me I could have the money for a new aluminium mast and sails (the original mast was wood but aluminium was by this time the material used for dinghy masts). So I presumably straightaway put the orders in, i.e. paid for the new mast and sails. They were to be made at two companies in England. The sails I received by post and I got them within a couple of months of placing the order. The mast however was delayed. It was not until about October 1977 when I collected it from a boat parts place in Cardiff.

Why the long delay in obtaining the mast? I presumably got some reasons given to me but I don't recall what they were. Was it because Gx1 had made arrangements to keep the new mast away from me till the 1977 winter arrived? The answer is yes. The following explains my answer.

First let's look at the question, why would Gx1 want to keep the new mast away from me? It doesn't take much to figure this one out. In June 1977 I would be able to re-sit the end of academic year exams at UCC (as an external candidate), and that meant it would be a chance for UCC to get me back onto the course, which is what they wanted to do knowing that I had in fact passed the exams in the previous year. Gx1 was worried about this, he did not want me to get back into UCC, hence he did not want me to sit the exams.

If I got the new mast in March '77 and fitted it to the dinghy I could have placed the dinghy at the reservoir in Cardiff that I'd sailed on in June '76 with the UCC sailing club. And perhaps got someone who was with the UCC sailing club to be the crew (second man). And this would have been a very favourable factor in support of my getting back on the UCC course. So it now becomes quite obvious as to why Gx1 kept the mast away from me. It was to ensure I did not use the dinghy on the Cardiff reservoir in the spring/summer of '77.

Let's now look at something I haven't considered before now. My purchase of the sailing dinghy. I bought it in June 1976. a week or two after I sailed with the UCC sailing club on the Cardiff reservoir in an eleven foot Mirror dinghy. The dinghy I bought was a sixteen foot dinghy, about eight years old. I used money I had left over from my grant. I don't remember how I came to buy it. I didn't travel far to get it because I'd recall the trip. I believe it's correct to say that I went to see it on the driveway of a house in Cardiff, paid him for it and towed it home (it was on a trailer). Thinking about this recently I can remember roughly where the house was.

It was almost certainly someone in UCC that put me on to the dinghy, got me to buy it. It appears that they thought I would place it at the reservoir and get some new/younger students to sail with me, show them the basics. Yes I was new to sailing but I was, at 28, a few years older than them. And the sixteen foot dinghy offered a faster and more interesting sailing experience than the sailing club's Mirror dinghies (which are a good basic sort of dinghy to start sailing in, I think they also had a few bigger dinghies).

It is quite obvious that Gx1 didn't get me to buy the dinghy knowing he would then have to go to the trouble of putting it out of action. Yes, it was a UCC purchase alright, and Gx1, in line with his 'keep him down' activities, moved in to block it, stop me using it on the Cardiff reservoir.

And the first thing he did was to somehow push me into taking the dinghy to west Wales. This wasn't enough to solve the problem however. Because when I returned to Cardiff some weeks later I could place the dinghy at the reservoir and use it with the UCC sailing club. So to stop this happening he decided to put the dinghy out of action (break the mast) as soon as I got to west Wales.

There is something else I can tell you here. The sailing dinghy was a Hornet. A hornet is a close relative of the wasp. UCC knew I had played rugby at the Wasps. I trained in a Wasps jersey. And what they had seen in the start of season training session meant I was going to be their first team winger and get that position in the UW team. Gx1 however, within a week or two of my starting at UCC, got a hit man to fire an electron/laser beam into me to put a stop to my rugby. UCC didn't know this of course, they thought I had unfortunately got injured (an accident), and they still had big rugby plans for me when I got back into the game. The Hornet sailing dinghy was meant by UCC to keep the ex-Wasps rugby player, me, connected to, in, the college.

In October '76, days after being told I could not continue the UCC course, I recall sitting in the driving seat of a parked taxi at 8am (I was doing a part time taxi driving job, no other work) thinking to myself, 'what am I doing here, this is wrong, it's ridiculous, I passed the UCC exams and Group X have got my study stopped'. I had no UCC/UW rugby and no UCC course. I was very annoyed about it. [I also had no sailing but at this time I did not think it was caused by Group X (I thought the mast break which had put the dinghy out of action some months earlier was an accident).] Group X had smashed my position in life. I also knew that in the previous year they'd got me stopped at UCS. [That was what I knew in Oct '76. What I didn't know (till years later) was that Gx1 had carried out many more vile covert hits, on me and my family, before I ever went to UCS and UCC.]

196

2020

The Knife in the Trunk in 1946

In World War Two my father, who was in the army, was, in 1942/3, sent to India. In 1946 he arrived home from India and left the army. Two months later a large metal trunk that he had filled when in India then posted home arrived. A lot of what was put in it, presents he had bought in the time he was there, were gone, stolen. However a curved indian knife/dagger in a sheath, one of the things he had bought, was still in the trunk.

Now let's take a closer look at Malefant street and the house my parents bought there in 1956. Is it a coincidence that Malefant is close to elephant? An elephant has a trunk, and an elephant is closely associated with India. Was the house meant to 'emphasize' the trunk, and hence the indian dagger? I think it was. Gx1, knowing what the house meant (in Group X language), selected the house and then got my father to buy it using the council mortgage he offered him. He was going to put the knife in, murder my father, when he'd finished paying the fifteen year mortgage.

So it appears that the plan to kill my father originated during the time he was in India. And someone was instructed to go through the metal trunk he had packed and take out, steal, everything apart from the curved indian dagger and clothing. This thieving could have occurred in India or at a postal depot in Cardiff (on the cargo ship is possible but unlikely). I will assume it took place in India soon after he had packed it. I have a reason for saying this, as follows.

During his stay in India my father was sent on his own to deliver something to a town that was some distance from where he was based. The train was his means of transport. He delivered the item but then found that a train back the same day, which he had been told was okay, was not possible. So he slept the night in a stationary train carriage. He got back the next day but soon found he had malaria. The night in the carriage, with no anti-mosquito netting, had obviously been where he had picked it up. He was in hospital for sometime and nearly died (malaria killed many thousands of people). Weeks later he recovered.

I would say that he was sent on the train journey by someone who knew he could not get a train back the same day. Which meant he would have to sleep rough. And that meant malaria, and probably his death. Why did

197

"someone" do this? For the answer let's look at my father, with his wife and three year old son, returning to Cardiff to live in 1940 (having been living in Nottingham since 1934/5. We know from events that took place in later years that Gx1 was keen on, wanted to have sex with, his wife. And in WW2 he was a policeman in Cardiff. I think he had sent out to India in some way the covert instruction to have my father killed (perhaps in army dispatches). There would have been two reasons for his doing this. The first was that my father was a worker, a commie in the minds of Group X type people (a result of covert government directives) and therefore he should be quietly killed on that basis alone. The second was that with my father dead his wife would then be 'available'. And my father being sent on the 'he won't get back the same day' train journey was a Gx1 kill attempt. The attempt failed and later on the trunk was rifled to highlight the Indian dagger, to 'say' that the knife was going in to him at sometime in the future.

The Two Group X Dinner-Dances

I told you in TCF about what happened on these two occasions, here I add some details I haven't given you before.

In October 1972, a month or so after returning from Australia, I got a job for two or three evenings a week working as a wine/drinks waiter at a dinner-dance venue in Cardiff. It was only for the dinner-dance season, about six weeks. I did it to get some extra money.

The first Group X dinner-dance I went to was in November 1973. I was with Miss D, we had been invited to it by her godfather. [Who was in Group X.] It was at the same place as the waiter job I had a year earlier. Soon after arriving Miss D's godfather introduced me to a barrister who was about 20 years older than me. On meeting the first words he said to me were, 'you understand wine I believe?'. Presumably someone had told him that I had worked as a wine/drinks waiter at the place we were now at. I thought it was a bit of an odd thing to say and didn't answer his question, instead I said hello or something like that. The job I had as a waiter was taking drink orders from people who were sat at tables waiting for their meals. When they'd finished eating they stayed at the tables, the dancing started, and they continued to order drinks. It required no understanding of wine at all.

I've known since the 1980s that this was almost certainly the barrister using Group X type 'sign' language to say something. We know that Miss D was into regular covert sex with her brother and that Gx1 knew it. Look at a wine bottle, sex, hard on? He was saying, 'you know about

198

sex, you can do it okay ... and you can do it with Miss D'. I believe he knew about Miss D and her covert sex relationship with her brother, which, being a close friend of Miss D's godfather is what you would expect. Did he make use of, have sex with, Miss D (taking up the turned on rear position)?

The second Group X dinner-dance was in November 1975, I had started at Cardiff university (UCC) two months or so before this took place. [My starting at UCC was completely against Gx1 plans. He had got what he wanted, a 'failed' label attached to me at Swansea university, then by starting at UCC I had smashed it. I had in other words turned the tables on him.]

I was sure that Group X had used their influence to stop me in Swansea but I had nothing to prove it, so I kept quiet about it. It followed that they would try to stop me at UCC but I thought they wouldn't be able to do it this time because I was now on the first year proper of a three year degree course.

At this second dinner-dance Miss D's godfather walked up to me when I was dancing with Miss D (standing apart dancing), touched my nose with his hand, and stood there looking at me. I could not understand it, he had obviously meant to insult me but I didn't think any more of it than that. [It was however in legal terms an assault.] When I'd last seen him (some months earlier) our relations were normal. And nothing untoward had happened recently in my relations with Miss D. Anyway I done nothing about it. It contributed to my reasons for finishing with Miss D some weeks later at the beginning of January 1976.

I have said in TCF that Miss D's godfather was probably put up to it by Gx1 who was annoyed that I had managed to continue my university study and he was 'saying' that it was trouble for me, i.e. Gx1 was now intent on hitting me off the UCC course. Yes that's okay but I would now say that I'm sure her godfather was told to do it by Gx1.

It was an extraordinary thing to do, walks up to me and interrupts our dancing by touching my nose! Why didn't Gx1 tell him to punch me, make it obvious that it was trouble for me? Well quite simply this would not have been the way Gx1 went about things. With witnesses nearby Miss D's godfather could have found himself reported to the police, so that was no good at all. Gx1 didn't want to get Miss D's godfather in trouble, it was me he was after. Getting him to touch my nose was all that was required at this point, it would be a 'sign', and Gx1 seemed to like giving out 'signs', and it 'said' he'd be dishing out trouble for me in the months ahead.

Why did touching my nose 'say' that it was trouble ahead for me? Answer, Gx1 got the idea from two other 'nose' occurrences that had taken place in our family years earlier. And one of them undoubtedly meant trouble ahead. So touching my nose was to 'say', 'you will soon be getting hit'. I tell you about the two earlier nose occurrences in the next section.

My Brother, in School in 1952, is Hit by Gx1 Again

At sometime when my father was in the army in World War Two he had an operation on his nose to improve his breathing. That's all he told me about it. [Seems a bit odd to me, perhaps all he had done was hairs in his nose removed/cut and it was called an operation.]

The second 'nose' occurrence in our family took place in the 1951/2 rugby season. My brother broke his nose and my father took him to the infirmary to have it set. The thinking was that he had done it when playing rugby but hadn't noticed it at the time. [A broken nose that occurred in a rugby game? I have never known it to happen in any rugby game, apart from what supposedly happened to my brother here. Yes "supposedly". Because it was arranged by Gx1. Someone done it at night when he was asleep and kept asleep by chloroform or similar. When he woke up in the morning he noticed it and the assumption that he had done it playing rugby was made.]

On this occasion the 'sign' was a hit in itself, it stopped him playing rugby for a few weeks. But the 'sign' meant more than that to Gx1. He was going to stop his life at Cathays High School, the school he was at. He was the top schoolboy in his year in sport and academically. This year, 1951/2, was his 'O' level year and the teachers would certainly want him to continue on to 'A' levels (then perhaps university). In the mind of Gx1 he was the son of a worker/commie and his continued success was not on. He got him out of the school weeks before he sat the 'O' level exams. That was it, no more school, no Cardiff Boys rugby, and no excellent 'O' level results. Exactly what he wanted, he had put down a very bright son of a worker/commie.

I say "again" in the title of this section because earlier in this rugby season Gx1 had arranged to have my brother poisoned, to make him ill, to stop him playing in the welsh boys trial game (see page 174).

Gx1 used my brother's nose to 'say' he was going to be hit because it connected to my father's army nose operation which in turn connected to the knife in the trunk. The knife that 'said' it was going in to my father at sometime in the future. Breaking my brother's nose and the early school exit was part of putting the knife in to my father.

Now back to the touch on my nose at the Group X dinner-dance. It 'said', in Gx1's mind, 'what happened to your brother is going to happen to you'. And what happened to me? At the end of my year at UCC he got me stopped (using illicit methods). No degree for me, and

200

no top job to go with it. And no playing for the University of Wales rugby team either.

Most people will know what I mean when I say 'putting the knife in', but I will define it here anyway for those that don't. It means to quietly, surreptitiously, hit or dirty someone ('put the poison in' is much the same). Gx1, who was very adept in this area, would, if he couldn't get his way using his position (using open requests that were to be kept quiet, if you see what I mean) used, for example, a planned accident, or poison, or a laser/electron gun hit man to 'put the knife in'.

The Covert Sex Opinion, Formed in 1974

This is an important part of what happened in my relationship with Miss D. I've given you an adequate description of it in TCF6 and 9. I will improve on it here by giving you additional details and a number of my comments.

In April 1973, toward the end of the '72/3 rugby season, Gx1 used an electron gun man to hit me when playing rugby. The hit stopped me going from Cardiff Hospitals RFC, the club I was with, to Cardiff RFC.

If Gx1 had decided not to hit me here and let me go to Cardiff RFC a decent female would have been found for me by the respectable parts of Group X (meaning Mr Q, he could still have been on the fringes of Group X). The decent female being a 'stay in this country' female. But, by hitting me here, Gx1 had again got me placed on a 'ship out' route. And any female placed in front of me in the coming months would also be okay for shipping out.

Miss D was evidently okay for shipping out because in May '73 Gx1 got Mr E to try to get me going out with her. But I just wasn't interested, and I made no attempt to start going out with her. [Details in TCF.]

[In September '73 Gx1 renewed his efforts to get me to Miss D by getting her mother to push her toward me.] In the lunchtime Miss D, once or twice, came into my part of the department to talk to me for a while. And a woman aged about 40 who worked in the same room as her, just the two of them, typing, told me that she liked me, went to church regularly and lived with her parents, that sort of thing. Miss D was aged seventeen.

I was doubtful about the innocent church girl image that apparently had been accepted by some of the staff in the department. I mean in my mind she didn't fit it. This means that when I asked her out, a day or two after talking to her typist friend, I was actually thinking to myself, 'let me get a closer look at you, I think you're a fake'. When she replied to my invitation by saying yes, I said, in a light hearted way, 'I suppose you're a virgin'. And she replied with 'yes I am'. This was the only time I'd ever said

201

anything like that to a girl I was asking out, it was, as I say, caused by the fact that I didn't believe the innocent church girl story I'd been given.

A month or two later, with my having told her she was conning me about the virgin stuff, she accepted that she'd mislead me, lied to me, yes she had sex with someone else before I came along. So in this early stage of our relationship I had established that my original thoughts on her, a fake, were getting confirmed. [That however was as far as it went at this time. It was not till March 1974, six months after first going out with her, that I formed the opinion that she was in a covert sexual relationship with her brother. So how did I form this opinion?]

In March '74 I met her brother for the first time. [I said April in TCF but it's more likely to have been March.] He was married with three children. I had a reason to go to his house a couple of times (to buy something from him) and I had a drink with him for twenty minutes or so in his local pub. He was in his early thirties and sort of okay but he was a bit of a wide boy. Put him alongside Miss D when she was wearing a dress that was 'up to her behind' and it seemed obvious to me what would happen.

When she had told me, some months earlier, that she'd had sex with someone else before I came along, she didn't say who the "someone" was but she did say that he lived nearby. Well now, March '74, it had become apparent to me that her brother was the "someone". He lived nearby (about three hundred yards away).

When forming an opinion of a person (or two people as is the case here) there are often small indicators taken into account. I must have noticed some of these and hence formed my opinion but I don't recall the details. I can however remind you of the very odd "Brotherly Love" book incident that had taken place about three months before I formed my opinion. I referred to the book and she froze. A week or two later I saw that the book was no longer there, it had been hidden away somewhere. At the time I was mildly surprised at these two events, the freeze then the book's disappearance, but I didn't connect them to anything. All I knew was that the book had some sort of meaning to her, and her hiding it meant that she didn't want me to refer to it again. Well in March '74 I knew that what happened with the book could be explained, or perhaps I should say was explained, by the opinion I had formed. For her the book, the words "brother" and "love", meant sex with her brother. And it was a secret.

I can also tell you about something else that occurred in the first six months of the relationship that in a small way probably served to verify my opinion. I haven't told you about this before.

I had left the hospital job and was was working with ICL in Cardiff. I arranged to meet her in town one lunchtime. I wanted to go to a photographic shop to buy a roll of film for my 35mm camera and I met her to go there with her. [Perhaps also go for a drink afterward.] In the shop she said, 'I've been here before'. I said, 'what for?' She answered saying she was with her brother and they had bought a cine projector for his kids. I found the answer odd but said nothing. Didn't her brother go shopping with his wife when they wanted something for their kids?

Well in March '74 I knew that what she said in the shop could be explained by the opinion I had formed. Was the projector bought so the two of them could put porn films on when together? For use in their covert sex relationship. With the kids angle just being a front for the projector being in his house. It was more than likely that the answer was yes. [I will add, because some people might not think of this, that there were no computers/internet in the 1970s. The only way to see porn movies was from cine projectors, usually on 8mm wide reels, with the films purchased from some sort of surreptitious source.]

Later events, in the summer of 1974 and in January 1976 (the door not answered, and the rear sex name), confirmed that the opinion I'd formed was correct.

And then of course from 1980 on, when I started to become aware of Group X sign language, I got more confirmation that I was right, i.e. Gx1 and her mother knew all along that Miss D and her brother were in a covert sexual relationship with each other. They probably got it started in the first place. Perhaps her mother bought her the Brotherly Love book as a 'sign' to 'say' she was going that way (sex with her brother).

I think that every person has the ability built into them, inherited from previous generations, to form an opinion of another person. It starts by looking at the individual. The person's face tells you something and his/her general appearance tells you more. However with most people the ability goes no further than that. Meaning that the ability of most people to judge an individual's character correctly, when having only limited information on them, is minimal. This is partly because they don't notice, don't look for, the small indicators that people unknowingly give out. It appears to me that I am a very good judge of character, based first on their looks yes but I also pick up the indicators. I can say this because my success rate is high, i.e. 'I was correct in my opinion of him/her'. I have however made a notable error in this area therefore I don't rate as excellent. I did not, before 1978, think that Gx1 was a doubtful/bad individual, I thought he was okay. Which as we now know was a very incorrect opinion to have. It's not surprising that I got it wrong with him because my parents thought he was okay and so I just followed their ideas on him. I actually had very little to do with him, only brief sentences were exchanged between us when we met.

[Back to March '74, when I first knew about Miss D's secret and I intended to finish with her.] I should make it clear that my thoughts on finishing were not just because of the covert sex with her brother. When I first asked her out I had my doubts about her and what I'd seen in close up since then had not improved the position. So I was already heading along the 'finish it' lines before I formed my "opinion". The opinion was something that just made me certain I should finish with her.

After forming my opinion it took only minutes of thought to realise that the thing to do was a quiet, slow, say nothing, departure, for the following reasons.

Finishing with such a female, a young girl with an excellent public image, was not going to be easy. Finish with a girl like that giving no reason for finishing to the public/friends could see me in trouble. Comments like, 'what a terrible thing to do, finishing with a young living at home, church going, piano playing girl who must have been a virgin when he started to go out with her', would be given out. And I'd get hit (arranged by her mother or her Group X godfather, etc). Find myself out of a job or something like that, or get physically hit by a hit man. So it is not difficult to understand why I thought the best way to finish it was to say nothing and quietly leave her. No problems for me, no problems for her. If I did manage to get out of it quietly that is, which I assumed I would.

Now a person reading this might say, 'you could have told her you believed she was having covert sex with her brother, she could have said she'd stop it'. But surely you can see a whole host of problems taking this route. Would she have admitted it? Would she have denied it? If she admitted it and said she'd stop it how could I believe her when she had lied to me before? And there again would she have gone straight to her mother with it? As far as I was concerned there was no point in making an accusation and receive answers that would be full of problems. So you have to agree that going for a say nothing and slowly out method was the best thing to do.

As for going public with it. Finishing with her, saying nothing to her about the covert sex, and then telling friends that, 'I finished with her because she and her brother are having covert sex together'. Well I'd say that would have been an obvious route to trouble (it would get back to Miss D and her mother), I'd definitely be hit for dirtying a young church going piano playing girl.

Miss N, who I went out with from mid 1969 to Sept 1971, was a female who I didn't want to stay with, I didn't think was my type for marriage. And this relationship had finished by the slowly leave her method (my staying in London at weekends when she was in Cardiff) and there had been no problems at all. Well I felt that my moving to Swansea in Sept '74 would do the same for Miss D (I usually stayed in Swansea at weekends and she was in Cardiff). I assumed she would be going out with other blokes and she would finish with me having found someone else, which is what I wanted to happen (a finish like that would see me in the clear, I wouldn't get hit because I didn't finish it). Miss D and I, as was the case with Miss N, never at any time had an 'only me only you' agreement in place.

Let me give you a bit extra here on "indicators". I said above, "when forming an opinion of a person there are often small indicators taken into account". Here is an example of an indicator that I saw today. A girl aged about twenty and her boyfriend walk into a library. She is walking in front and so she gets to a long desk first and pulls a chair out. For her to sit on you would think. But no, having done this she then sits on the next chair and her boyfriend sits on the chair she pulled out. Now I would say that what the girl has done is an indicator that tells me about her character. She is thoughtful and helpful. This is just one small indicator. To judge a person's character, without even talking to him/her, a few indicators would be useful.

[Some other person, commenting on what I have said in this section, could say, 'sex between a brother and sister is a criminal offence, incest, so you could have reported it to the police'.] I knew that what she was doing was criminal but I did not think reporting it to the police was the route to take. The first thing they would say to me is, 'what evidence do you have?' In March '74, when I formed the opinion, I had no usable evidence. 'I believe they are at it, based on my intuition', would not be usable evidence. So they would tell me to go away and close the report. Another possibility is that they would have interviewed Miss D and her brother about my accusation. Well all Miss D and her brother had to do was deny it, then it would be no further action, case closed. My relationship with her would finish at this point but then at a later date I'd probably be covertly hit, by her mother or their Group X friend, for dirtying Miss D.

Yes in the summer of '74 I got more evidence, evidence as far as I was concerned that is, when 'the not opened front door' took place (the long delay). But again this was not what I considered to have been usable evidence. I mean I didn't actually see them at it. They could simply say, 'he is wrong to think that'.

And then in Jan '76 I got yet more evidence that I was correct when 'the rear sex name' took place. [Would the police have made anything of this? Probably not.] Days later I stopped the relationship. I done it over the phone saying, 'we don't get on with each other' (nothing else, i.e. nothing about her covert sex with her brother). Our not getting on with each other was very evident as far as I was concerned, only weeks earlier she had given me an absurd reaction to what her godfather had done at the dinner-dance. [The assault.] And during this period I recall sitting in a pub with her one night, that was in her area, when she had almost nothing to say, about anything. It made me think, 'what am I doing here with this thicky, we just don't get on?'

I realised that my finishing the relationship would set me up for being hit but I just had to take that chance. The finish was long overdue, it couldn't go on any longer.

And what happened in the months that followed? Gx1, who had already, three months earlier in Oct '75, tried but failed to get me stopped at UCC, now used my finishing with Miss D to support his 'stop him' request. He told UCC, 'he has finished with a wonderful church going girl', 'stop his study it will push him back to her'. He also carried out more 'stop him' activities (detailed elsewhere). At the end of the academic year, June '76, UCC stopped my study (I had passed the exams).

The 1973 Pickup at the Church Hall

Since I wrote about this in TCF6 (p 248) I've given it more thought. I here repeat some of it with a correction and I add some details.

The overcast daylight was fading and I'd say that by 8pm it would have been dark, which would place it in Oct '73, a month or so after starting with Miss D.

One day Miss D told me she wanted me to pick her up a couple of days later from a church hall at about 7pm on a weekday night. She would be in a choir there with an audience present. The hall was eight miles or so north of where she lived. I said okay.

When I arrived I saw that the building was a large wooden hall in a side street just off the main road. The area was full of parked cars and I parked on the street about eighty yards away from the hall. I walked to the hall, went in through the main entrance and found myself at the side of a seated audience of about two hundred. The choir of about forty singers was on a stage at the end of the hall to my right. [In TCF I said I sat down but I got this bit wrong. The place was full so to get a seat I would have had to walk to the back of the audience, to my left, to find a vacant seat and I definitely didn't do that.] I just stood there looking for ten seconds or so and went back out. I'd seen Miss D in the choir, she was wearing a white hat, the only one in the choir with a hat on. I returned to my car to sit in it and wait for her.

I was in my car for perhaps five minutes when I could see that the meeting had finished. I was parked facing the hall. Most people walked away from the place but many of them stopped to talk outside the hall. A lad aged about seventeen who was walking along the pavement on his own stopped by my car to talk to me. He said he was Miss D's boyfriend before I came along. I just said, 'oh yes, hullo'. He said no more and left. He was a nice, naive, church going type of young lad. A few minutes later Miss D arrived at the car and got in. I told her about the lad and asked her if she had sent him over to me. She said no. I found the answer odd, well who had sent him over to me? I asked her but she didn't know. I thought she was probably lying for some silly reason but I didn't pursue the subject and left it at that.

It was obvious to me that the lad had been sent to me to push the 'Miss D is a nice church girl' angle at me, i.e. the sort of people Miss D goes round with are nice and innocent (the lad) and therefore she is also nice and innocent.

[I now give you some details that didn't occur to me when I was writing TCF.] My car was a four year old MGB which I had bought in the summer of 1973. [With a Gx1 'u to Australia sign' attached to it.] My father had the Cortina that we had bought in 1969. Well on this church hall pick up night I was in the Cortina. I borrowed it from my father for the night because I thought there might be more than one person to pick up (the MGB was a two seat sports car, the Cortina a four seat saloon). [Well only Miss D would have recognised the Cortina. The lad, if he'd seen me before somewhere, would have seen me with the MGB, i.e. he would not, on the night, have picked me out in the Cortina. So someone told him to go to the Cortina where he would find me inside and introduce himself. The "someone" had to be Miss D because no one else would have recognised the Cortina. So Miss D lied to me. Why?]

Miss D had almost certainly been told by her mother to introduce the lad to me and she knew that the purpose behind it was a con job ('show him your nice innocent ex-boyfriend, it will put you in the same bracket'). And by telling me she didn't send him over to me she was avoiding having to admit that she was involved in a con job.

Miss D's mother probably thought that when the singing finished I'd be standing outside the hall waiting for Miss D, and the ex-boyfriend introduction could easily be done. When Miss D saw I wasn't standing outside the hall she was at a bit of a loss for what to do. She looked for my car, knowing I'd be sitting in it and decided to send him to me.

This church hall pickup night was thought up by Gx1. It was part of his 'push the innocent church going girl' line, the idea being that it would help to make me like her. It could be that it was Miss D's mother who added the, 'introduce him to your ex-boyfriend' bit.

Gx1 got the idea for this pickup night from a photograph he had seen. The photograph was of Cardiff Boys rugby team with my brother standing at one end of the back row of three or four rows of players. Each row set higher than the one in front to show the faces. The choir at the church hall had the same sort of row formation. My mother had of course shown the photograph to my father's sister and she had shown it to Gx1. This church hall pickup was Gx1 'saying' it was Australia for me with Miss D. He had me written in for marrying her then shipping the two of us to Australia.

A mention here of the 'killing me softly with his song' 'sign' that appeared some months later when Gx1 got Miss D to sing it to me. This was the 'sign' that said he was planning to kill my father and me. With regards to me it could have meant he was killing me metaphorically by shipping me to Australia, or, that he intended to use Miss D to literally kill me (by making sure I found out about her secret sex life, catching them at it perhaps, and got hit). My saying this should not surprise you because he had already twice tried to kill me in 1967/68 (by 'accident').

The Church Piano

[I haven't told you about this before.] It took place in about June 1974 (three months or so before I moved to Swansea). I drove to Miss D's place. It was a Sunday. I was told by her mother that she was at the local church playing the piano and I could go round there and see her. [Presumably I'd told Miss D I'd be calling, she'd said nothing about being out.] Her mother told me where the church was, a few streets away, and I went there.

I went through the open outer doors of the church and found myself in a small hallway. Double doors to the main part of the church were in front of me and they were closed. I decided not to open them and went back to my car. I didn't wait for her to come out. I left and went somewhere else. [This must have been the time I went to look at a second hand car that was for sale about eight miles east of where she lived.]

I believe I had the impression that she was playing the piano in a church service. This would explain why I didn't open the inner doors. I didn't want to join a service. Which would place this at about 6-30 pm when most churches have a service on a Sunday. But I don't actually recall the time and it could have been in the afternoon, if it was it would mean she could have been playing the piano with no service on.

I suppose I thought I was being given more of the, 'she's an innocent church girl' line.

Two Snacks

[This is in TCF6. I will here add a few more details.] It was on one of these two snack occasions, when I was in the kitchen on my own, that I decided to look in an eye level cupboard to see what they had in it. It had double doors and was obviously the main food cupboard. There was about four small tins together at the front of it. They were made by Goblin. Nothing else was near them, the cupboard was nearly empty, a few things were at the back of it.

I wasn't impressed. Goblin was a cheap make that was only seen in small corner shops.

From about 1980, when I first realised that covert sign language was standard Group X practice, I made a bit more of these two snacks. In TCF I explained how her mother's Jaffa Cakes gave the 'sign' that said 'rear sex with my daughter', I will here add my thoughts on the Goblin tins. Did Miss D's mother buy them because they didn't have much money or because the word goblin was closely related to her way of thinking?

[I'll put something in here that I found very odd at the time.] One day I was with Miss D (before I went to UCS) when I brought up the subject of going for a bike ride, the two of us. She replied by saying she couldn't ride a bike. I was quite astonished, I had never met anyone who said they couldn't ride a bike. She added that her parents wouldn't let her ride one when she was young. [Did her parents keep her off a bike for safety reasons or did her mother have another reason for it?]

The Boat Parts Place

This connects to the "More on the Sailing Dinghy" section earlier in this book.

The boat place in Cardiff where the new aluminium dinghy mast was sent to and where I picked it up from in October 1977 was called Parkwood Marine. [In terms of what Gx1 done to my father in 1973 the words Parkwood Marine were/are very, very, relevant. So much so that I will say that Gx1 named the company.]

The Heath hospital, where Gx1 had my father surgically knifed in '73, was built in the 1960s on about 30% of Heath park. The hospital building itself was built on a part of the park known as Heath park woods (mainly small trees and dense undergrowth). Accommodation for staff and students (tower blocks and some low level buildings) were built next to the hospital, on the field where I was playing in a school baseball game in 1960 when Gx1 hit me (in which he included the 'sign' that said, 'I am going to knife your father here').

209

The word Parkwood in the mind of Gx1 was a synonym for the main building of the Heath hospital (i.e. it was built on park wood).

Now the word Marine. Take the first part, Mari, it gives the name of DC's wife, Mary, who was a nurse on the ward my father was in during the days after his '73 operation at the hospital. I would not say, with Gx1 around and running things, that this placement was a coincidence.

For Gx1 the two words, Parkwood Marine, meant, equated to, hitting my father at the Heath hospital in 1973.

Perhaps Gx1 was connecting the plan to murder my father to the sailing dinghy, i.e. using the dinghy would help to get me back into UCC and if that happened it would make it more difficult for him to complete the plan. So he made sure the dinghy stayed out of action for the summer of 1977.

With Gx1 having got the boat parts company to use Parkwood Marine as a trading name it follows that he had no problem getting the manager to hold on to the new aluminium mast, stop me from receiving it, for perhaps seven months (assuming they received it from the manufacturer in March '77). This would have been the easiest way for him to arrange the delay, easier than getting the manufacturer to hold onto the mast, or postpone making it, for nine/ten months from the date the order was placed (in January '77).

Gx1 Breaks Mr Rowlands' Leg in 1966

When Gx1 arranged for the cap to be thrown over the cemetery wall in 1960 ("The 1960 Gx1 'Dead' Cap" section earlier in this book) he made sure that one of my teachers was nearby to see it happen. His name was Mr Rowlands. He reported what had taken place to the headmaster and because I was involved in it the headmaster caned me (hit me a few times on the hand with a cane).

We already know that Gx1 was at this time working on countering/ destroying the physical education teacher's, 'he is outstanding at rugby'. We know this because the Gx1 baseball hit, which was meant to help destroy it, had taken place perhaps a couple of weeks before this cap went over the cemetery. Well it looks like the cap over the cemetery was, as well as giving the 'dead' cap 'sign', also meant to dirty me, i.e. get me seen by a teacher and reported to the headmaster as a bad lad (it would help to flatten the physical education teacher's opinion).

In December 1966, I was with DC watching Cardiff RFC play on the Arms Park when Keith Rowlands, one of the Cardiff forwards, was carried off on a stretcher. Later we were told by the local press that he had broken a leg.

I've said earlier on that a player breaking a leg when playing rugby is a very rare occurrence, I was talking about Mr HC. And I said that the odds for it happening in a game are in the 1000 to 1 area, i.e. you would expect to watch 1000 games of rugby before seeing a game in which a player broke a leg. And the odds could be a lot more than that.

Gx1 broke Mr HC's leg, there is no doubt about that. Gx1 arranged the 'dead' rugby cap with Mr Rowlands present, there is no doubt about that. And here we have a Rowlands broken leg. It has to have been arranged by Gx1 (laser beam, see Mr HC section).

Look at the odds if you want. 1000 to 1 against me watching a game where a broken leg occurs. 20,000 to 1 against me watching a game where a player with a surname that has a particular relevance to me breaks his leg. The name Rowlands is exactly that. So was this a 20,000 to 1 chance that happened to occur on this day at the Arms Park? With Gx1 around the answer is no, he was into covert dirt activities in a big way and Keith Rowlands broken leg was one of his arrangements.

Gx1 knew I watched Cardiff RFC at every home game, and he saw a Rowlands in the Cardiff team (from the local press, he never went to rugby games). The only question that matters here is why did he do it, what 'sign' was he giving out? Perhaps the 'sign' said, 'I broke your leg (meta-phorically), stopped you going on to play for Cardiff Boys, when I got the cap thrown over the cemetery wall and had you reported for it'.

What happened to Keith Rowlands on the Arms Park takes me to what happened to my brother's rugby in the early 1960s. See the next section.

Gx1 Breaks My Brother's Leg in 1960/61

In 1953 my brother was conscripted into the armed forces. After a while they sent him to Australia and he spent the rest of his time there. In 1957 he left the armed forces, returned to Cardiff for two weeks, then went back to Australia to marry a girl who lived there. And he stayed there. He and my father wrote to each other regularly (my mother wasn't a letter writer). And we posted to him every week in the rugby season the Football Echo. This was a newspaper printed in Cardiff once a week on a Saturday afternoon. It contained sports results from across Britain paying particular attention to results and reports from games in south east Wales (no general news stories in the paper, only sports). It was in broadsheet form (large pages), printed on pink paper and contained six or eight pages. Usually it was me that folded it into a small package and posted it. I also sometimes wrote to my brother and received replies.

It was 1960 or '61 when my father received the news, in a letter from my brother, that he had broken a leg. He was either in a trial game for the Australia team or he was expected to soon be in the

211

Australia team. I recall my father telling me about it when we were in the living room of our house.

When he went to Australia my brother had continued his rugby playing there. He played for a club in Adelaide and for the South Australia team. So we knew he was doing well in the game. To hear that the next step, into the Australia team, had been stopped by a broken leg was very bad news for us. He never played rugby again.

Can you see what I am going to tell you next? Gx1 arranged to have his leg broken. Using the method I have told you about in the Mr HC section. Laser beam research had been going on for many years before 1960, evidently by 1960/61 it was known that a beam could cut through bone leaving the surrounding soft tissue (skin) unharmed. Why did he do it?

Gx1 had got him shipped to Australia on the government's covert 'keep down the bright sons of workers' policy. Shipped one way. Now what would have happened if he had played for Australia? It no doubt would have made it into the sports press in Cardiff ('an ex-Cardiff Boys player is playing for Australia') and that could have meant the main rugby clubs in South Wales, Cardiff RFC for example, saying, 'let's get him to play for us, it'll be a big draw'. And that, getting him back to Cardiff, was exactly what Gx1, who had gone to a lot of trouble to get him there in the first place, didn't want. So, in his warped mind, it was stop his rugby, break his leg.

Another thought that would have got into the mind of Gx1 is that if he played for Australia he could arrive back in this country playing for them. So of course the answer was the same, break his leg before he gets into the team.

A temporary stop on his rugby (using poison to lay him up in bed for a week or two) would not have been enough, because when he started playing again the problem would repeat itself in the months after and the following seasons. So it had to be a broken leg, a permanent stop.

In the last section I said, 'why did Gx1 break Keith Rowlands leg?' And I gave a possible answer. Another answer could be that he was connecting it to my brother's broken leg. My brother played on the Arms Park when he played for Cardiff Boys, so he could have been giving a 'sign' that said he had broken my brother's leg.

[There is a 'sign' Gx1 gave out in 1965 that supports my saying that he broke my brother's leg. I'll tell you about it. We already know that Gx1 sometimes gave song 'signs' ("When I'm 64" etc), well this is another one of them.] In 1958 when my brother returned to Australia he travelled by ship. In a letter to us he said that Rolf Harris, an entertainer, was on the ship. [This bit of information got to Gx1. Quite simply my mother often met his wife (my father's sister) and they talked about bits of news etc. His wife would then have given the news to him. And here is the Gx1

212

'sign'.] **Rolf Harris produced a song in 1965 called, "Jake the Peg".** [The initials JTP are Gx1's initials backwards (i.e. he was PTJ then his surname, he had two middle names). Jake, the name of the man in the song, said he had an extra leg, the peg being the extra leg, a crutch in other words. When does a man need a crutch? When he has broken (or seriously injured) a leg. Gx1 was covertly saying in this Rolf Harris song that he was the crutch man, the man who arranged to have my brother's leg broken.]

[I have another bit of evidence that fits in here.] **My brother sent us a programme (small booklet) for a game he was due to play in.** [Months before he broke his leg.] **He was playing for South Australia, I think it was against the New Zealand Maoris. In the programme there was a short summary on each player. For my brother it said, "Hails from Wales".** [An ordinary comment it would seem. But look at it in Group X language and we see 'Jails from Wales', which we know is very relevant. My brother was a Gx1 covert prisoner. His 'crime' was to be the very bright son of an original white british worker (a commie in Group X warped minds). And that meant he was to be kept down and shipped to Australia. And when his success at rugby in Australia was threatening to upset his 'keep him down' policy he broke his leg. Gx1 did the same sort of thing to me and my rugby in later years (the false fracture diagnosis, poisoned before the Cardiff trial game, etc).]

A Musician Poisoned by Gx1 in 1964

We know that "heath" was a big word in the vocabulary of Gx1 in the 1960s. In this period he gave out 'sign's which 'said' my father would be knifed at the Heath hospital, i.e. the scouts sheath knife, the baseball hit on Heath park and Heathway (the road).

There is another heath in Cardiff in the 1960s. The british bandleader Ted Heath had a concert with his band in Cardiff in 1964. At the event he suffered a brain thrombosis and collapsed. He was taken to a local hospital and then transferred to his home in London to be looked after by nurses on a 24 hour basis.

He was never the same again. He had become irritable, his thought process had changed and he didn't return to leading the band. The band stayed together but without his presence they did less touring. He died in 1969 aged 67.

It appears to me that Gx1 arranged to have him poisoned. I will remind you here that he murdered the carpenter's son in 1969/70 perhaps using the same poison. He died of a brain haemorrhage, probably started by a thrombosis (blood clot). And in 1977 he used what could again have been the same poison on me. It was a death by brain haemorrhage poison and it very nearly done it's job. As it was I came through it unharmed.

213

When Gx1 hit my brother (more than once) in the 1951/2 years (age 15) one of the hits was stopping his saxophone playing. He had played once or twice in a dance band. He 'put the knife into him' in other words. Well in the '60s Gx1 knew the knife was going in to my father at the Heath hospital, and seeing Ted Heath as a bandleader he perhaps thought that poisoning him would give a 'sign' that connected what he was going to have done to my father to what he/they had done to my brother.

Gx1, in 1966, Inserts Another Ship Out 'Sign'

It was about August 1966 when a lad my age started work in our drawing office. He had been a trainee draughtsman with another company and for some reason he left there and moved to us. [His starting is significant. Why? His initials were/are CRP. My brother's initials are CRT which are easily seen in CRP. Gx1, with the plan to ship me out in mind, got him moved to our company. He wanted him working near me to 'say' it was CRT, Australia, for me. Why did he get him moved to our office at this time?]

I said earlier in this book that management at AEI together with some staff at Llandaff Tech decided in April/May 1967 to put me on route for a full time university course (without telling me). But the date may be wrong. They could have decided it earlier than that, and it could be as early as mid-1966.

I will here assume/say that the date AEI/Llandaff decided to put me on route for a full time university course was mid-1966. On this basis I will answer the question I asked at the end of the last but one paragraph. Gx1 had for years had me written in for shipping out, and he was annoyed that AEI and Llandaff Tech had come up with a plan to get me on a university course, but he couldn't say this to the clean people at AEI/Llandaff Tech, he had to keep his warped thinking to himself. So he said to himself, 'he is not going to university, and I will make sure he doesn't go there'. And he decided that another 'you to Australia' 'sign' was called for. And the new 'sign' was the arrival of CRP next to me.

If the date AEI/Llandaff formed the plan to get me to university was in 1967 and not 1966 well it just means that CRP was a 'sign' Gx1 placed before the AEI/Llandaff university plan was formed. Either way it doesn't alter the fact that CRP was a ship out 'sign', there is no doubt about that.

In the winter of 1966/7 I was going out with with Miss C which meant I went out with her one or two nights a week and I saw very little of DC (I was also in college two evenings a week). But when we finished in April '67 me and DC started to go out again in the evenings. And BK sometimes came out with us. CRP had introduced him to me, he was his cousin. CRP never came out with us in the nights because he was going steady with a female.

When the summer came along me and DC played tennis, as we had done in previous summers, and this year BK joined us. The three of us were up to a good standard in the game.

It was at about this time when BK's parents moved to Waterston Road in Cardiff. In the road there is, easily seen, WAT, my father's initials, and ers, hearse, a vehicle for carrying a coffin. Gx1 got BK's parents moved to Waterston Road to 'say' my father was on hearse road. And he connected himself to BK, as follows.

There was a place in the suburbs of Cardiff called the K rooms. It was a small/medium sized hall on the first floor of a building and it was sometimes used for dances or meetings. I have used "K" here in preference to giving the full word because the K was the same as BK's surname (I usually don't give the complete names of people I refer to). Well at sometime in the 1968-72 years Gx1's son opened an office on the ground floor of a house that was across the road from the K rooms. He had a small one man business. Gx1 worked there part time.

The house was a small terraced property, not the sort of place you would expect to find an office in. I'd say that Gx1 moved his son into the house because it was across the road from the K rooms.

And there's another point here. I can't tell you exactly how Gx1 done this but he connected BK to the Long and Winding Road song that he fed into the Beatles at this time. The song that 'said', Wal (my father), there is a long road that leads to your wife (Dor). So with BK 'giving' my father and hearse, and then the K rooms being across the road from Gx1, we have Gx1 'saying' that he was the one who had my father on hearse road. He was planning to have my father murdered to make his wife available.

The 1964 Gx1 'Leve Land' 'Sign'

Here is another 'sign' produced by Gx1 in the 1960s to 'say' he had me covertly routed for shipping out of the country (my life in our 'free' country).

At the end of my full time year at Llandaff Tech (when I did 'O' levels) in the summer of 1964, aged sixteen, I went to a few job interviews. One of them was at a company called Firth Cleveland Fastenings about eight miles north of Cardiff. At the interview there was a very odd occurrence, as follows.

I was sat on a chair in front of a long table that had five or six people sitting behind it. They were asking me questions and I was answering them, things were going fine. Until, having answered a question, there was a blank spot, a pause in the questioning. I sat

215

there looking at them waiting for the next question and, as the silence went on, for perhaps ten or fifteen seconds, it became an odd situation. Then one of them broke the silence by saying something, apparently someone had asked a question and I hadn't answered it. But I hadn't heard the question. I don't mean that it was a, 'could you say that again please, I didn't catch it', situation. I mean that I had finished answering a question and then there was complete silence for ten/fifteen seconds. Presumably the question was repeated and we continued to the end.

Yes very odd. And I again remind you that when something odd occurs the first thing to do is look for Gx1 'signs'. The 'sign' is easily seen here because we know what the thinking was with regards to my life. It was, 'ship him out', i.e. in a few years time Gx1 was going to ship me to Australia (for a permanent stay). The 'sign' was in the name of the company. Cleveland, leve land, it was leave land for me. My just being there was enough to create the 'sign' but he added this extra bit of bright boy stuff, the odd silent period, to highlight the 'sign'.

How was this done? Had the interview panel all decided, prior to my appearance in front of them, to have this odd silence placed in the middle of the interview? I don't think so, the company can't have had five/six idiots on their interview panel. I think it went like this. One of them, the Gx1 contact man (the hit man), as he was about to ask a question, pressed a button on a device he was holding that he had pointed at me, the device blanked out my hearing (made me deaf) for as long as he had the button pressed. When he finished his question he released the button.

You would like to have details on this "device". Well let's just say that it was along the lines of the electron/laser beam devices/guns that were used at other times by Gx1 to hit me. Perhaps the device fired a beam of white noise at me that blanked out all other sounds. Maybe there was a low level hum in my ears that I didn't notice.

I will now make an obvious connection. This 1964 'leve land' hit is very similar to the October 1980 government hit at Swansea Town Hall (the false evidence plant) in that both of the hits were aimed at my hearing. In the Oct '80 hit the device used created a loud high pitched noise in my hearing system to make me incapable of hearing what was being said. Was the 1964 Cleveland hit, where I was again deafened but in a different way, also meant to dirty me, to ensure I didn't get the job? Perhaps but I think the main reason for doing it on this occasion was simply to emphasise the 'sign', it was leve land for me.

Gx1 had already hit me and placed 'signs' a number of times before this 'leve land' hit took place. The fact that I was hit in a similar way in the Oct 1980 town hall false evidence plant indicates that he was involved in that hit as well. Which as I have said before is quite possible. Because it was not till

1982/3 that 'clean officials' found out more about what had been going on over the years, realised he was dirt in other words, and stopped him using his influence.

Gx1 and His Thinking

My father had two sisters, born in the 1910 area. The first name of one of them was Queenie, she married Gx1 in the 1930s. Her name, given to her by her parents, tells us that my father's family, ordinary decent people, were happy with the way this country was run, i.e. naming one of their daughters Queenie is a clear indication of this (the country being a monarchy with the king/queen being the monarch).

What Gx1 did for a living before World War Two I don't know. But I do know that in the war he was in the police force in Cardiff. I'd say that influential official people in Cardiff in the 1930s had him lined up for a high level job. And they put him on to, and then got him married to, Queenie, because in their minds it 'said/advertised' that he was going to be one of the people who run this country, i.e. he was married to, having sex with, Queenie, meaning 'I love the Queen'. The next thing they did was to ensure he stayed alive in the war, and they did this by getting him a job in the police for it's duration.

It was in these years that the thinking of the ptrtc (people that ran this country) changed. From, in the 1910 area, the acceptance/belief that british people were decent people, to, from 1919 on, that british people were dirty/enemies, or at least suspects.

Why did this change take place? Well quite obviously it was because of what had happened in Russia in 1917/18. First of all russian people had taken over the government using force of arms. Then later the russian ex-monarch and his family, friends/relatives of the british monarch (the british king and the russian king/tsar were cousins), were killed by the government. From this point on the ptrtc made sure that the russian people, who used to be 'decent people', were labelled 'dirty/enemies'. And in Britain the british people found their position changed (by the ptrtc) from being 'decent people' to being labelled 'dirty/enemies/suspects'. The ptrtc done this because they thought that british people could do the same as the people in Russia, i.e. rise up against them and get them out of their positions (or kill them). Hence the ptrtc made sure from 1919 on that british people were kept down.

However the ptrtc realised that it was overdoing it a bit to label all british people as being 'dirty/enemies/suspects' and they thought it would be better to place the label on british people who were workers, meaning the manual workers. Because it would be an easy way to decide who got the label (non workers could be added if necessary).

217

Therefore Gx1 in his covert policing job (latter part of the 1940s on) was, in his office everyday, looking for british workers to keep down, and, when they appeared to be doing too well in the society, hit them (poison, smear, etc).

In about 1950 the job of Gx1, and people like him, changed a bit. From, keeping down british workers, to, keeping down british workers who were white. I will explain this.

British people before 1950 were white skinned because Britain is not a particularly sunny country (together with Scandinavia and northern France for example where a thousand years back some invaders came from, many of whom stayed here).

The 1950 on immigrants however had a dark brown skin because they came from hot/sunny countries.

Obviously Group X type people were not to 'keep down' the immigrants because they had been brought in to help the ptrtc break up worker communities (most of the immigrants stayed unemployed for many years, their living expenses being paid by the government). So, as I said, from about 1950 Gx1 was told to keep down workers who were white. In other words he was to keep down the original white british workers.

The 1969 Lake Road East 'Accident'

I am writing this section in 2019. I have known what I tell you here since perhaps 1980. I have made notes about it in the past but this is the first time I've written it in complete form.

I started work at the Cardiff Royal Infirmary in September 1968. [On crutches, hit by Gx1 to stop my rugby.] I worked on the first floor of a small building at the rear of the hospital with two other electronics technicians and one graduate technician. The ground floor was used as a work space by three mechanical engineering technicians.

In Jan/Feb '69 a ground floor room in our building started to be used as a base for servicing kidney dialysis machines. Apparently a technician who worked in the kidney dialysis department which was in the main part of the hospital would sometimes come to our building to work on a machine. Up to this point our department had nothing to do with the kidney dialysis department.

One day the chief technician told me I could use my car to take the dialysis technician to addresses where dialysis machines were located (he was a young technician without a car) The dialysis technician would repair/service the machine and then we'd drive back. I would of course be paid petrol money for it. I said okay I would do it. The first time I did this the following happened.

I had driven with the dialysis technician to a place about fifteen miles north of Cardiff, where a dialysis machine was located at a patients home. He had done his job and we were returning to the infirmary. It was about 5pm and getting dark. I drove round a roundabout in Cardiff (in a 30mph area) at the north end of Lake Road East and proceeded south. Three hundred yards or so along the road the car in front of me stopped hard, I mean the driver just hit the brake pedal and brought the car to an emergency straight line stop. I immediately braked but couldn't stop my car before it hit the back of his car. I was probably travelling at about 10mph when I hit him.

Sometime later my car insurance broker told me that my insurance company was to pay for repairing the damage to the cars, even though I had not caused the accident. It was caused, so I was told at the time of the accident, by a taxi driver travelling in the opposite direction. He had driven across our line of traffic in front of the car two cars in front of me, to park on our side of the road (his taxi was not hit by the car he drove in front of). And the driver in the car two cars in front of me had jammed his brakes on and come to a halt. And so the driver of the car in front of me did the same.

The insurance broker also told me that the driver of the car I hit had claimed damages for an injury to himself. It seems he had hit his knee on his dashboard or something when his car was pushed forward by my car into the car that was in front of him. And because he had difficulty walking he took some time off work. I found this odd. When the accident had occurred the drivers involved, myself, the driver of the car in front of me, the driver of the car in front of him, and the taxi driver, were all walking around with no problems at all.

I went to see a solicitor about the accident. I remember him saying to me, "you skidded on leaves". I remembered this because I considered it to be an odd thing to say. I had said nothing about skidding on leaves. It was Jan/Feb, there were no leaves on the road.

Now I will look at this in detail, a sort of investigation process if you like. There are a number of odd occurrences in what happened, as follows.

(i)   The driver of the car two cars in front of me. A touch on the brakes and perhaps a slight swerve and continuing on his way would have dealt with the problem. But no. He stayed on a straight course applied the brakes hard and quickly stopped. The taxi had parked by the kerb. A complete stop when the taxi had cleared his way was a ridiculous piece of driving, explained by saying that he was acting on Gx1 instructions.

(ii)   The driver of the car in front of me. Making an insurance claim for physical injury when there was nothing wrong with him. This was no doubt his pay off for doing the job, i.e. Gx1 had told him to get money for it by making a claim from my insurance company. Perhaps he split the money three ways, himself, the driver in front of him and the taxi driver.

(iii)   Lake Road East, LRE, can give in Group X language lbj (the b is found in the R and the j in the E). A few months later I was told about, started to go out with, a girl with the initials LBJ (Miss N). And it was around this time when I was coaxed into buying a painting/print for my bedroom wall. It was by Le Ba Dang, which gives LBJ. Well, well, an LBJ accident followed by two more LBJs in the space of six months. The painting and Miss N's appearance in August '69 tells us that the Lake Road East accident was no accident. It was arranged by Gx1 to 'say' that it was Miss N for me.

(iv)   The solicitor's use of "leaves". He was 'saying', following Gx1 instructions, that it was 'leave' for me, I was going to leave Britain, get shipped to Australia.

(v)   It looks like Gx1 arranged all of this from the very beginning. The kidney dialysis department in the hospital had, as I said, nothing to do with us. They had their own staff to operate, service and repair the dialysis machines (they probably called the manufacturer in for all but the easiest of repairs). Then in Jan/Feb '69 a dialysis machine appears in a room in our building and a technician who worked in the dialysis department would sometimes work in the room. Why move a dialysis machine to a room in our building when the work on the machines was getting done satisfactorily in their own department? The answer that makes sense is that Gx1 arranged it knowing he could use the home service/repair visits to get me into a car crash on Lake Road East.

Having established the dialysis machine service room in our building, Gx1 then told my chief technician to offer me, tell me, about the petrol money I would get if I drove the dialysis technician to places where the machines were installed. When he knew I'd do it he arranged a home service visit and the crash that would go with it. Needless to say the crash drive was the last time I drove the dialysis technician anywhere.

How did Gx1 arrange the crash? I'll give you a few details. The two cars in front of me were parked near the roundabout, as I drove from the roundabout, at about 10/15 mph, they pulled out in front of me. The taxi driver was parked four hundred yards or so down the road and he was in radio contact with one of the two cars in front of me. Having been told they were in place, driving along in front of me, he pulled out and drove toward us. When he saw the car that was two cars in front of me (that was easily recognisable in some way or other) he pulled across it to create the 'accident'.

It appears to me that Gx1's plans in early 1969, six months or so before I started to go out with Miss N, were to ship me to Australia with her if we got on with each other and got married. If I didn't get on with her I'd get shipped out on my own. Her father (Mr Q), who became a member of Group X at this time, had presumably said to the other members of the group that he wouldn't mind if his daughter went to live in Australia. This would be because the family seemed to have overseas ideas, his son, Mr Y, had spent some time working in Canada.

Gx1 when he hit me at the start of the 1968/69 rugby season had done so to keep me away from top level rugby (which was where I was heading). And he intended to keep it like that till I left the country (got shipped out). When I was living in Australia however he would leave off, meaning he would let me play there without blocking/hitting me. Miss N would fit the bill for the pre ship out period, she'd fill the vacancy for a female position, and, if we stayed together, she might see me play in top level rugby in Australia. Gx1 had told Mr Q that I was good at rugby which was probably the reason I got lined up for his daughter in the first place, i.e. he was a rugby man.

So with Gx1 having lined me up for Miss N an obvious question presents itself. Why did he let Miss H appear on the scene two months before I got to Miss N? I have given you details of what happened on my first night out with Miss H in the "The Speedometer and the 1969 Engine Overheat Drive" earlier in this book. Near the end of it I give two possible answers for why Gx1 arranged the hit. Now, having told you about the Lake Road East 'accident', I have a bit more to add to the two answers.

Mr Q knew about the block that Gx1 had placed on my rugby in this country and he wanted it overturned, i.e. wanted me to play in top level rugby in this country and stay in this country. And he felt that Miss H, who was not a ship out female, would be an ideal partner for me, he thought in other words that I was more suited to Miss H than to his daughter. And he managed to get it passed at Group X level, meaning that it was decided that I should meet her and see how we got on. And if we stayed together he would get what he wanted.

Gx1, who for years had me written in for shipping out, was quite obviously against Mr Q getting what he wanted. So how was he going to stop her? Well however he went about it he wasn't going to tell Mr Q what he was doing. He picked on my car as a way of stopping the relationship starting. He arranged to have the engine fixed an hour or so before I used it to take her out in. He expected the engine to seize and ruin my first night out with her. The engine didn't seize but my night out was ruined and the car put off the road for weeks. Which meant he got what he wanted, I hadn't started with Miss H and I was still on course for Miss N, with top level rugby blocked, and a one way ticket to Australia.

This reason for Gx1 arranging the engine overheat night, to stop what Mr Q wanted, is supported by the fact that Miss H started a job in London in

221

November '71 when I was working there. It seems that Mr Q had jumped up again with renewed vigour when he knew what Gx1 had recently done, blocked my playing for the 1st/2nd teams at the Wasps. And he again tried to get it overturned by placing Miss H in front of me. If I started with her he perhaps could get the block removed. And here again Gx1, without telling Mr Q, moved in to ensure he didn't succeed. He arranged to have my first night out with her in London ruined. And our relationship ceased. [Details in "The Gx1 'Stop Sex' Poison in 1971" section earlier in this book.]

In my entire life there is a total of two car accidents that I have been involved in. The 'accident' on Caerphilly Road in 1972, and this Lake Road East 'accident'. There is also the fact that once in my life I have had my car stolen (in 1971). All three occurrences were arranged by Gx1. He seemed to have a special liking for cars and what he could use them for.

Gx1 and His Ship Out Timing

Gx1 knew that for me to stay in Australia permanently I had to move in with my brother and his family. I'd have very little money to spare and certainly no money for hotel accommodation. But in the latter part of the 1960s my brother was living in a small flat with his wife and one child. This meant they had no room for me. So Gx1 couldn't ship me out in these years. What he had to do was wait till my brother got into accommodation that was suited to my arrival. And he did more than wait, he used his position to make sure he got into suitable accommodation before 1973 (from 1967 on he knew my father was going to be hit in 1973 and he wanted me out of the way, living in Australia, before then).

My brother was looking for ways of improving his accommodation. And as his job income increased he could see the possibilities. He formed the idea that he would move into a newly built house.

Let me take you aside for a minute to explain something. The way people in Australia move into a newly built house is different to the way people in this country do it. In Australia a large area of building land is divided into building plots and a member of the public comes along and buys a plot. Then sometime later, it could be years later, he gets a mortgage and pays a builder to put a house up for him (it's more often than not a bungalow because land is cheaper there, i.e. instead of building up they build out).

To move into a new house the first thing for my brother to do was buy a plot of land. And he did this in 1969 or thereabouts. [Gx1 then made sure that he could get a mortgage in the latter part of 1971. Soon after this the house started to be built.]

222

In April/May 1972 the house was finished and my brother and his family moved into it. [This was what Gx1 wanted. Living in a new house he would have ample room for me. I would be impressed by the place and pleased to stay there till I got some sort of worthwhile job. Gx1 shipped me to his house in early June '72.]

I'd say Gx1 made a mistake here. He appears not to have taken into account the fact that DC was getting married in September and I was the best man. This of course meant that as far as I was concerned it was a three month stay at my brother's house then back to Britain. If he had shipped me out after DC got married I would not have had a reason for returning to this country after three months. It could be that he was worried that if I stayed in London any longer and got to the start of the new rugby season in September he would have rugby problems again. I would be at pre-season training with the Wasps from August on and perhaps I'd try to return to living at my friends place which was near the Wasps ground. So in his mind getting me shipped out before the new rugby season came along made sense.

It is also possible that he thought I lacked interest in being at DC's wedding. As I've said earlier when DC started, in Jan '69, to go out with the female who was to be his wife, we stopped going out together in the nights. And, some months earlier in Sept '68, we had stopped playing rugby together (when Gx1 hit me, put me on crutches). So Gx1 by 1972 considered him to be an ex-mate and so wouldn't be a problem, meaning I'd lost interest in him and his wedding. But he got it wrong here. In the years before Jan '69 DC and I were very good mates, watching rugby together then playing the game together made us very good mates. And even though this period had finished a while back I had not forgotten it. And so it was important for me to be at his wedding. And, with some difficulty, I got there on time.

There's something else that's of interest here. DC's wife's best friend when they were both working as nurses in Cardiff was Miss L. Soon after I moved to the job in London in March 1971 Miss L also started working in London, and as I've previously told you, we began to go out with each other on a 'good friends' basis. Then near the end of '71 we became closer. This was when Gx1 moved in to stop it. As you know he didn't want me to form a relationship with a female when in London because he intended to ship me out in 1972. And in January '72, four weeks or so after she'd started work as an air hostess, he stopped the relationship. But I didn't know this. At the end of a night out we were on very good terms (as usual) when we said goodnight. It turned out to be the last time we met. The fact that she didn't phone me after this night out was, I thought, because she was out of the country.

In the 1980s, when I was aware of Gx1 activities in earlier years, I realised that he stopped this relationship and he'd probably used the 'dirty

223

him' routine to do it, i.e. got some dirt applied to me and had it fed it to her.

At DC's wedding I expected to see Miss L. I was looking forward to meeting her because we had got on with each other very well. Perhaps the relationship or at least our friendship could be continued. But she was not at the wedding. DC's wife said she was supposed to be there but hadn't arrived. I phoned the number I had for Miss L and she answered. She said she hadn't come to the wedding because she was on standby for the airline. [Did Gx1, knowing I'd appeared back in this country three days before the wedding, tell her management to tell her she had to be on standby for a few days?]

[There's one other thing to give you here.] I got the job at Bart's in London in March 1971 because the head of the department I was in at the UHW in Cardiff had told me about it. [He was presumably put up to this by Gx1 who was working on shipping me to Australia and he looked on London as a step in that direction.] Well when it came to my last day or two in the UHW job the head of the department told me that if I returned to Cardiff at sometime in the future he would give me a job. [What he said here was his own thinking. I mean Gx1 would obviously not have told him to tell me this.] What this means is that when I was in Australia it was another reason I had for returning to this country. The main reason I had was of course DC's wedding, but knowing I would have a job as soon as I got back and seeing Miss L at his wedding were significant small reasons for returning that were also present in my mind. If I hadn't been given the job offer before I left the UHW I would have returned anyway. And looked for a job.

If things had been allowed to proceed naturally in my life, I mean by that with no Gx1 hits to block, dirty and fix me, I could have gone to Australia to see my brother and his family anyway at sometime or other (if I had the money). I had a high regard for him which was mainly derived from my parents. This was because I was aged five when he was conscripted in 1953 and the first real memory I had of him was when he came home for a week or so in 1955 and helped me to learn to ride a bike. Then in 1958 he was home for two weeks, took me to an old boys rugby game (the school he was at), then returned to Australia. So the idea of going to see him in Australia would have been quite a natural thing to occur in my mind. But natural occurrences was something Gx1 didn't know much about, for him it was 'fix this', 'fix that', 'make sure things go the way I want them to go'. From about 1945 he was out to knife my father, because he was a commie in his warped mind, and by the middle of the '50s he had formed a plan to murder him and make his wife 'available' with a fully paid for house to her name. And he labelled his sons commies. For Gx1 it was 'keep them

224

down', 'hit them' if necessary. And for me, when I was getting a bit of a handful for him, doing too well, he added, in 1967, 'kill him'.

The 1974/75 Rugby Season

There is something I haven't gone into before now. Why was I selected for the first team at UCC (Cardiff university) almost as soon as the college rugby season started and not selected for the first or even the second teams at UCS (Swansea university) until the end of the season? Very odd.

It was September 1974 when I first went to UCS to attend an interview with a lecturer in the electrical engineering department. Gx1 knew I was applying to start a degree course and via the college administration staff he got the lecturer to offer me a four year degree course and only a four year degree course, meaning I had to do an extra year at the front of the usual three year course. If I said no to the extra year I couldn't start at the college. I said okay, I would do the extra year, even though it seemed odd to me (with a HNC I should have been able to go straight into a three year course).

Gx1 was going to use my study at UCS to stick a 'fail' label on me, to 'put me down'. And he'd arranged 'one year and out' with the administration staff. It was they that probably said it would be best to use an 'unimportant' place on a preliminary year to do it rather than a place on the first of a three years course.

Gx1 knew that my rugby would be a problem for his 'one year and out' hit plan. I'd play for the UCS first team and that would help to keep me in the college. So he made plans to block my rugby.

Before I tell you about the rugby block I'll give you details of a 'sign' that Gx1 got applied to me within days of my starting at UCS.

On my first day at UCS (a week or two after the interview) I went to the college accommodation office to see what they had to offer. They told me about a bed and breakfast place near the college that I could stay at for a couple of days and then return to them to see what they had in terms of long term accommodation. Perhaps three days later I went to see them again and they told me about a place a mile or so from the college. It was a room in a house with a shared kitchen, two other students had rooms in the house, the owner and his wife lived on the ground floor.

It seems that Gx1 selected the street I was to stay in and he told the accommodation office to find me a place in the street. He selected the street because it gave a 'sign' that he wanted attached to me. The name of the street the house was in was the same as the first name of the head of the department I was in at St Bartholomew's hospital. He knew the name of the Bart's man because he had told him to get me into the on call job that he

225

used to stop my two evenings a week rugby training at the Wasps. And the Bart's job was itself an on route to Australia job, on route via London.

So the house I moved into when at UCS gave, in Gx1's mind, a 'sign' that said two things:

(i)   I was again on route to Australia.

(ii)   My rugby was blocked.

It was going to be one year and out, failed, back to Cardiff where I would grasp/marry Miss D and get shipped to Australia.

Mr Q had presumably not been told about the plan Gx1 had for me at UCS. As far as he was concerned my starting at UCS was a chance for him to correct things for me on the rugby front. He got me introduced to the daughter of the secretary of the Welsh Rugby Union thinking that if I began a relationship with her it would lead to my playing for Swansea rugby club. But, as we know, Gx1 stopped this happening by using his covert dirt activities.

Exactly how Gx1 arranged to have my UCS rugby blocked is difficult for me to tell you about because of the methods used. But nevertheless I can tell you a bit about it. The administration office put him on to one of their 'fix it' people (a college employee). In TCF I identified him as SV. He fixed it to ensure that I was not selected for the first or second rugby teams.

The first team played every week but the second team often did not play at all. And training was only done on a tennis court area, a hard surface, where players abilities can't be seen (because there's no tackling, etc). So once SV had 'put the poison in' with one or two of the lads that ran the rugby, which he done soon after I appeared at the college, I found myself not selected for even the second team when it played and therefore didn't have a chance to show what I could do (exactly what Gx1 wanted).

It was perhaps January 1975, halfway through the season, that Gx1 got the acid put on my rugby boots laces. To give a 'sign' that said, 'your rugby is going nowhere because you are on route for Miss D', and that meant out of UCS in five/eight months time. I said (in TCF 6 and 9) that the acid was put on the laces by SV (or, less likely, by the landlord where I was living using bleach instead of acid).

I think SV was also involved in the forged documents activities at the start of June. Gx1 had to tell someone on the UCS staff what to do and it's probable that he told him. SV then told SJ and, a few days later, SF, what to do. I know that the forged documents were used, given to me, by SJ and SF. Who made the forged documents? SV, or SJ, or someone else? The South Wales Police and the DPP should have the answer to this question.

Gx1 succeeded in blocking my rugby at the start of my year at UCS because he had time to make the necessary arrangements before I ever put my rugby boots on there. My leaving Swansea in September 1975 and then within days getting accepted at UCC was a shock for him, which means he had no time to make arrangements to have my rugby blocked at UCC before I appeared in their start of season trial game. Hence I was selected for their first team. But within a week or so he had made arrangements to stop my rugby. In the first game I played for the first team he got me hit by an electron gun man (out of rugby till January '76).

2021

1975, Another Gx1 'Sign'

There is something I have looked for recently that I thought I mentioned in TCF6 but no, it seems I didn't. I will tell you about it here.

Straight after I was told at Swansea university (UCS) in September 1975 that I could not continue there I returned to Cardiff. [And within hours Gx1 got the words, "the best thing since sliced bread", said to me. In the mind of Gx1 these words meant that his getting me stopped at UCS was the best thing he had done since he put the knife into me at Llandaff Technical College in the 1960s.]

The person who said the words was told to use the phrase. He was using it in a context that had nothing to do with UCS. He had no idea of what it meant in Group X language. I will now explain how Gx1 connected "sliced bread" to Llandaff Tech.

At the school I started at in 1959 age 11 the leaving age was 15 (four years in school). In the final year there were exams organised by the local council. More advanced exams, 'O' levels, were done in schools that were called grammar or high schools when the pupils were aged 16 (five years in school). Well at the end of my final year in school, having got the best exam results in the school, one or two teachers thought I should go on to do 'O' levels. And for this purpose I went to Llandaff Tech, a mile and a half from the school, to sit an entry exam to see if I could get on their one year full time 'O' level course. The result was I got accepted onto the Llandaff Tech one year course.

I started by doing five subjects but soon dropped one and concentrated on four subjects.

There was only four students of my age on the course (including me). All the others were aged 17 or over, they had sat 'O' levels in school, left school, and were now doing the course to re-sit subjects they had failed when in school. There was about thirty eight students on the course.

At some point in the academic year, perhaps January, a lad on the course who had a car, he was aged about 19, offered to take us 15/16 year olds, the four of us, on a drive the next day to the Sugar Loaf mountain at Abergavenny. It would take about four hours there and back. It wouldn't cost us anything. We said okay.

This was unusual for me. I mean I never took time off when I had a class to attend. This applied not only to Llandaff Tech but also the school I was at. My attendance record at my 11 to 15 school was excellent, not even one day off for illness. But anyway somehow he encouraged us to go on the drive and we said okay.

We parked at the base of the Sugar Loaf mountain, and walked up to the top. From the car park it is just a hill ascending a couple of hundred feet

This, the name of the destination, is where Gx1 got the "bread" from. Loaf being synonymous with bread.

So how did Gx1 know about this drive to the Sugar Loaf mountain? The obvious answer, or certainly by far the most likely answer, is that it was he that fed the drive idea to the 19 year old lad together with the instruction to get us to go on the drive with him. By "fed" I mean he could for example have told the lad's father what to do and he gave the instructions to his son. Perhaps the lad's father was a policeman.

So why did Gx1 get us 15/16 year olds onto the drive? Answer, because he wanted to get me away from the college for the afternoon for some reason. And I can tell you what the reason could have been.

There was at this time a weekly quiz programme on the south Wales and the west country region of BBC television with teams from colleges in the region competing with each other. Two teams per programme and the winning team got through to the next round. Llandaff Tech had entered the competition.

I'm not sure if the team comprised of three or four people, anyway it was a student aged 16/18 then the others were each a year older than one another. Our college had small quiz competitions to pick the students who would represent our college.

The quiz programme's questions were all about what was in the news. This was my area. I mean I always read the local evening newspaper (my mother bought it when she'd finished work) and I bought a Sunday paper (such as the Telegraph, Express, Observer, Times). And from our small Llandaff Tech competition for the 16/18 place it looked I'd get it.

As I have said elsewhere we have a sort of senior positions covert grapevine in our society and this information had reached Gx1. He, as we know very well, was out to keep me down, ship me down under (Australia) and in general terms keep me down. Which means he would not have wanted me to be in this tv programme ('a bright tv star', me, would be no good for his plans). So on the day when the final selection of the 16/18 representative was to take place he arranged for me to be away from the college.

When the lad with the car invited us to go on the drive I knew nothing of a meeting the next day that was connected to the tv programme. My being away from the college for the afternoon meant that another student was chosen for the 16/18 place, and I was made first reserve.

You might say but what if I had said no to the offer of the free half day drive? Well the offer, being made one day in advance, means that if I said no Gx1 had time to get a poison given to me that would make me ill by the following morning, and hence a day in bed away from the college. Maybe the 19 year old lad, having been told to make the offer of the drive, had been given a substance to put in a drink I had if I said no to the offer.

I recall the trip to a BBC studio in Bristol for the quiz programme. The college hired a coach. The programme was recorded in the day for transmission in the evening. Our team lost so it didn't continue to the next round.

I can also add here that Gx1 would not have liked the idea of my starting the 'O' level course in the first place. But he evidently had to accept the pressure from my school to get me on the course. Presumably he was thinking that a few 'O' levels wouldn't affect his plans (shipping me, one way, to Australia and murdering my father). But when, in 1967/8, Llandaff Tech and AEI made plans to get me onto a full time university degree course in September '68 it created a different reaction in him. A degree was far too much for him to take. And his solution was to murder me, by accident.

Gx1 was up in numerous dirt procedures/routines. He was an ex-policeman who from the late forties on was occupying a high level covert policing job. For him it was, 'fix the workers because they are commies'.

Gx1 put the knife into me three times at Llandaff Tech. Yes he stopped me being in the tv quiz team and he stopped the Llandaff Tech (and AEI) me to university plan, he also stopped me playing for, captaining, the Llandaff Tech rugby team in 1968. And there is the fact that he hit me, put the knife in, a number of times in the years between Llandaff Tech and UCS, 1969-74. And these were very good hits in his mind because they were successful (he got what he wanted in nearly all of them, and he went unnoticed). Presumably in Sept 1975 the only reason he referred to his Llandaff Tech hits was because they gave him an obvious sliced bread, knife in, connection. Not because he actually thought these hits were any better than his 1969-74 hits.

Conclusion (2)

What happened in the 1940s, 50s, 60s, 70s and 1980 can be likened to a jigsaw puzzle, when you only have one piece it doesn't make any sense, but if you have a lot of it's pieces and you manage to fit them together you see the picture. Before 1975 I was only looking at a single odd occurrence at any one time and I did not think that any of them had been deliberately caused by someone. In 1975, when I was stopped at Swansea university, I realised for the first time that some people in the Cardiff area, Group X, were using their influence to hit me, they were ensuring that I wasn't too successful in life. From this point on I started to fit the pieces together.

In the late 1977 to the early 80s period I realised that a number of odd occurrences that had taken place before I went to university were pieces in the jigsaw, they fitted in with the university pieces. The partly completed picture showed that Group X had covertly hit us (me and my family) many times.

It was about 1980 when I found out that it was Group X member number one, that I refer to as Gx1, who had been using his government position to hit us.

Since starting a book on this in 1997, looking closely at what had taken place over the years, I have fitted more pieces in. I now know, for example, that in 1967/68 Gx1 tried twice to kill me using the planned accident method. He wanted me dead because I was becoming too successful for his liking. I was interfering with his plans, one of which was a plan to murder my father. He also made it plain that bright sons of manual workers were not meant to go to university (a covert official directive).

After he failed to kill me in 1967/68 he concentrated on shipping me to Australia, one way. And until the time came for shipping me out he proceeded to hit me a number of times, to keep me down, to ensure I stayed free from ties (making it easier for him to ship me out when the time was right). "Free from ties" means making sure I wasn't too successful in education, rugby and work, and ensuring I didn't get married. It would be quite accurate to say that Gx1 shipped me to Australia, on a one way ticket, in 1972. I managed however to return to this country after a stay of three months.

In 1973 my father was covertly hit by Gx1 using the planned

accident/natural causes routine. This was the first part of a two part plan to murder him.

In September 1974 I left my job and started a full time degree course at Swansea university. At the end of one year I was failed in an examination that had been improperly conducted. The 'fail' meant I couldn't continue at the university. I was sure Group X arranged to have me stopped but I had nothing to prove it so I kept quiet.

I managed however to continue my university study at Cardiff university in September 1975. Within a week or so I was told by a lecturer that someone had tried to get me off the course, but the request had been denied. At the end of the academic year I was stopped, three 'fail' examination results were used to do this. I was sure I had passed the examinations and that Group X had again arranged to have me stopped.

Gx1 was not happy though, yes he'd managed to stop my university study (twice in recent years) but I was apparently still causing him problems. Some staff at Cardiff university, knowing I'd been unfairly stopped, wanted me back on a course. Gx1 did not want this to happen. And in May 1977 he got me poisoned on a cross country walk. I was supposed to end up flat on my back, dead, somewhere in the countryside.

I came through the poisoning alive and without any long term injury. Before the year was up Gx1 arranged another hit that was perhaps meant to kill me.

In 1978/79 I was making headway with the false examination results that had been given to me at Cardiff university in 1976.

At this point two occurrences took place that I did not understand. I talk about these later in this conclusion.

My statement that I'd been given false results at Cardiff university went into the civil court in 1981 (under the UW heading) as a claim for damages. The negligence at Swansea university was included in the claim. The court however cancelled the claim at an early stage.

I looked more closely at what had happened at Swansea in 1975. Was it negligence, a mistake? I made enquiries and found out more. It was not a mistake, it was the criminal act of forgery. In the improperly conducted end of academic year examination I was given question papers that had been altered, the other candidates received the correct question papers. The question papers I had been given were forged documents (documents used to deceive and defraud).

In 1983 I sent the police evidence that substantiated my accusation of forgery and I expected a prosecution to start. The prosecution should have involved:

    (i)   My accusation of forgery at UCS (Swansea university).

    (ii)   The cover up of the forgery that was started by UCS lecturers in 1975 and repeated by UCS administration staff in 1981-83 when, apparently, they gave false statements to the police.

The question of whether or not to include my accusation of fraud (false results) at Cardiff university (UCC) in this prosecution should also have been looked at.

Gx1 should have been in the dock, with others, for planning/arranging the forgery at UCS. And from this it would have been obvious that his activities had got me stopped at UCC.

But, as we know, a prosecution was not started because, it seemed at the time, the police believed the UCS version of events (a cover up story) and chose to ignore the evidence I had given them that substantiated the accusation of forgery.

I had kept all my university papers and in 1985 I gave the question papers I had been given at UCS in the 1975 examination to the police.

In 1987 the police confirmed that forgery had taken place at UCS in 1975 when they accepted (in writing) that they had forged documents (the question papers I'd given them). I again expected a prosecution to start.

But no, a prosecution was not started. So I made extensive efforts to get the situation corrected. The media however would not publish a word on it. It was obvious that the government had censored the affair.

In 1990 I stopped trying to get the affair into the open and decided to write a book about it, hoping of course that when the book was written the censorship would be removed, and then perhaps I'd receive explanations for the many odd responses I'd got in the 1983-90 years.

In 1994 it became apparent to me that the two odd occurrences that had taken place in 1979/80, referred to earlier in this conclusion, were government hits.

In the first one I was poisoned (made ill) and was directed to the roof of a five storey hotel. I stayed on the roof for a couple of minutes then went back down to my room.

In the second hit a government official fired a covert beam at me when I was standing up and expected to say something at a seated public meeting. I could call the beam a 'bullet'. It made me collapse onto a seat. The result was that I lost the UCC dispute.

The government wanted me to lose the UCC dispute because they knew that a hearing into what had happened at UCC would see UCC saying that I was right and that they had been pressurised and deceived into giving me the false results by Gx1, who wanted me stopped.

Gx1 was a covert policeman, in MI5, and the government wanted his involvement to stay in the dark. And a way of doing this was to silence the people in UCC who wanted me to be shown to be correct. And making me look stupid, 'he collapses when under pressure', ensured that I lost the support of UCC.

It was therefore apparent to me in 1994 that the 1983/90 censorship was in place because the government prosecutor (the DPP) decided not to proceed with a prosecution that would be a corrupt prosecution. "Corrupt" because it would use the October 1980 false evidence as genuine evidence. So to ensure the government didn't have to answer any awkward questions in the media, e.g. 'why no prosecution when there is evidence of forgery that can start a prosecution?', the affair was censored.

The government prosecutor, in the 1980s, could have come clean on the situation by having a prosecution and stating at the outset that the 1980 town hall evidence was false and that it had been created by government officials to ensure I lost the support of UCC. But evidently he was not allowed to do this.

In 1998 I had written the book. It was censored. In the years that followed I produced new books/editions on the affair, each one containing more details. Most of these details are on the vile activities of Gx1 that had taken place over a period of many years. The censorship of my books is still in place at the time of my sending the digital file of this book to the printers.

Many times in this book I have said that Gx1 was warped, yes there is no doubt that he deserves that label. But I have also called him 'dirt', and I hear someone say, 'isn't that overdoing it a bit?' Well his fixing it so I could or could not get a job is one thing, stopping my advance in education is another, but crippling me (putting me on crutches for two months) to stop my rugby, and then in the following years stopping my rugby by poisoning me, getting electron/laser guns fired at me, etc, has to place him in the dirt/perverted category. Add what he did to my father, my brother, the carpenter's son, Mr HC, Keith Rowlands, Ted Heath, and his attempts to murder me, and you have confirmation of this.

The way Gx1 thought was formed by anti-worker/commie government propaganda that had been fed into his mind for most of his life, and he was told to apply it.

What you see in this book is one of the worst series of reports of corrupt/warped/criminal use of covert official influence/directives that has ever been presented to the public.